Disenchantment

RELIGION, THEOLOGY, AND THE HOLOCAUST

Other titles in Religion, Theology, and the Holocaust

Absence/Presence: Critical Essays on the Artistic Memory of the Holocaust
Stephen C. Feinstein, ed.

Emil L. Fackenheim: A Jewish Philosopher's Response to the Holocaust
David Patterson

Fiorello's Sister: Gemma La Guardia Gluck's Story
Gemma La Guardia Gluck; Rochelle G. Saidel, ed.

Four Letters to the Witnesses of My Childhood
Helena Ganor

Harry Haft: Survivor of Auschwitz, Challenger of Rocky Marciano
Alan Scott Haft

Murder Without Hatred: Estonians and the Holocaust
Anton Weiss-Wendt

Nitzotz: The Spark of Resistance in Kovno Ghetto and Dachau-Kaufering Concentration Camp
Laura Weinrib, ed.; Estee Shafir Weinrib, trans.

Obliged by Memory: Literature, Religion, Ethics
Steven T. Katz and Alan Rosen, eds.

The Warriors: My Life as a Jewish Soviet Partisan
Harold Zissman

When the Danube Ran Red
Zsuzsanna Ozsváth

Disenchantment

George Steiner and the Meaning of Western Civilization after Auschwitz

Catherine D. Chatterley

SYRACUSE UNIVERSITY PRESS

Syracuse, New York 13244-5290

First Edition 2011
11 12 13 14 15 16 6 5 4 3 2 1

∞ The paper used in this publication meets the minimum requirements of the American National Standard for Information Sciences—Permanence of Paper for Printed Library Materials, ANSI Z39.48-1992.

For a listing of books published and distributed by Syracuse University Press, visit our Web site at SyracuseUniversityPress.syr.edu.

ISBN: 978-0-8156-0960-5

Library of Congress Cataloging-in-Publication Data

Chatterley, Catherine D. (Catherine Dawn), 1969–
Disenchantment : George Steiner and the meaning of western civilization after Auschwitz / Catherine D. Chatterley. — 1st ed.
p. cm. — (Religion, theology, and the holocaust)
Includes bibliographical references and index.
ISBN 978-0-8156-0960-5 (cloth : alk. paper)
1. Steiner, George, 1929—Criticism and interpretation. 2. Civilization, Modern—20th century—Philosophy. I. Title.
PR6069.T417Z56 2011
809—dc22 2011004144

Manufactured in the United States of America

With great respect and humility, this book is dedicated
to the victims and survivors of the Shoah.

Catherine D. Chatterley is Founding Director of the Canadian Institute for the Study of Antisemitism (CISA), based in Winnipeg. A specialist in the history of antisemitism and the Holocaust, Dr. Chatterley trained as an intellectual historian at The University of Chicago in the fields of modern European and Jewish history. Today, she teaches history at the University of Manitoba, where she is currently writing a second book entitled *A History of the Antisemitic Imagination*. Until May 2011, she is a Social Sciences and Humanities Research Council (SSHRC) Postdoctoral Fellow. Dr. Chatterley can be reached through the Institute website: http://www.can-isa.com.

Contents

Acknowledgments

This book began as a doctoral dissertation, written for the History Department at The University of Chicago. So it is with deep respect and gratitude that I acknowledge Moishe Postone, Lionel Steiman, and Michael Geyer for their careful supervision and reading of this work. Mark Krupnick also made a valuable and generous contribution to my work on George Steiner before illness made his further participation impossible. For introducing me to the work of George Steiner many years ago, and for encouraging my application to The University of Chicago, I would also like to thank my dear mentor and friend Frederick Krantz.

Steven T. Katz and Ellen Goodman deserve special thanks for their early and consistent support of this publication. I am grateful to the staff of Syracuse University Press for their talent and professionalism.

Most important, I would like to acknowledge the many years of support I have received from my family, particularly from my beloved mother, Barbara Chatterley. I would also like to thank my dear friends and colleagues for their ongoing support and encouragement: Jayne Kadynuik, Lara McRitchie, Kim Green, Lionel Steiman, Deborah and Mendel Schnitzer, Steven Katz, Alvin Rosenfeld, David Hirsh, and Charles Small.

I am indebted, above all, to Joan Ste-Marie for her unwavering commitment to me and to this project, and it is to her that I also dedicate this book.

Thank you all from the bottom of my heart.

Chronological Guide to the Life of George Steiner

1929	Born in Paris on 23 April
1940	Leaves Paris for New York (via Genoa) with his mother and sister in January
1947	*Bachelier-és-lettres,* University of Paris, Sorbonne
1948	BA, The University of Chicago
1950	MA, Harvard University
	Rhodes Scholar, University of Oxford
1952–56	Editorial Staff, *The Economist,* London
1955	D. Phil., English Literature, University of Oxford
	Marries Zara Alice Shakow, an American historian of British diplomacy
1957–59	Member, Institute for Advanced Study, Princeton University
1959	Publishes "The Hollow Miracle"
1961	Founding Fellow, Churchill College, Cambridge
1964	Publishes *Anno Domini: Three Stories of the War*
1967	Publishes *Language & Silence: Essays on Language, Literature and the Inhuman*
1967–97	Succeeds Edmund Wilson as Principal Literary Critic at the *New Yorker*
1969	Extraordinary Fellow, Churchill College, Cambridge
1971	Publishes *In Bluebeard's Castle: Some Notes Towards the Redefinition of Culture* after delivering the T. S. Eliot Memorial Lectures at the University of Kent at Canterbury; Publishes *Extraterritorial: Papers on Literature and the Language Revolution*

1974–94 Professor of English and Chair of Comparative Literature, University of Geneva

1981 Publishes *The Portage to San Cristóbal of A.H.*

1987 Publishes "The Long Life of Metaphor: An Approach to the Shoah"

1989 Delivers the Remembrance Day Address, "Remembering the Future," at King's College Chapel, Cambridge

1990 Delivers the Gifford Lectures at the University of Glasgow (published as *Grammars of Creation* in 2001)

1991 Delivers "Through That Glass Darkly," in honor of Raul Hilberg at a symposium held in his name at the University of Vermont

1992 Visiting Professor, Collège du France

1994 First Occupant of the Lord Weidenfeld Chair of Comparative Literature, University of Oxford; Professor of English Literature, University of Siena; *Reading George Steiner* is published by Nathan Scott Jr. and Ronald Sharp

1997 Publishes his memoir, *Errata: An Examined Life*

1998 Fellow, The British Academy

2000 Portrait placed in The National Portrait Gallery, London

2001 Charles Eliot Norton Professor of Poetry, Harvard University; *Commandeur dans l'Ordre des Arts et des Lettres,* France; Prince of Asturias Award for Communications and Humanities, Spain

2003 Jan Patocka Lecturer, *Institut für die Wissenschaften vom Menschen,* Vienna; Ludwig Börne Prize, Frankfurt

2005 Delivers the Schiller Anniversary Address at the *Schiller-Nationalmuseum,* Marbach

2008 Publishes *My Unwritten Books*

A complete list of Steiner's works appears on pp. 167–70.

Disenchantment

Introduction

Recognized internationally as a leading critic of Western culture, George Steiner is respected for his uniquely penetrating gaze and supreme talent for wordcraft.[1] Since the fifties Steiner has engaged in a continuous commentary on the nature and meaning of Western culture from a variety of cities: Cambridge, Paris, Geneva, New York, and Siena. From these centers he has executed a powerful critique of Western culture in which he scales the summits of the Western mind and, from there, peers into the violent abyss of the twentieth century, thereby evaluating both the accomplishments and failures of Western civilization.

Through his wide-ranging scholarship, Steiner has established a reputation as one of the foremost representatives and guardian expositors of the Western cultural tradition. Steiner's fluency in German, French, English, Italian, and Spanish, as well as Greek and Latin, combined with his voracious appetite for reading, has allowed him the unique opportunity to master the literary, philosophic, and aesthetic canons of Western civilization. This deep level of polyglot learning is Steiner's most obvious strength and one that sets him apart from his readers and from most contemporary critics. As a comparatist of literature and culture he is thought to have few living rivals. *L'explication de texte* is his specialty and his virtuosity as a teacher is well known. Steiner's renowned pedagogical ability is displayed in hundreds of book review essays published over the last forty years in the *New Yorker*, the *Times (London) Literary Supplement (TLS)*, and the *Guardian*. Indeed, one could argue that these reviews first introduced English-speaking readers in North America and Great Britain to the major works of prominent continental writers and thinkers.[2]

Steiner sees himself not simply as a pedagogue but as a translator of texts and ideas, a messenger carrying knowledge across the tightly patrolled borders of language, nationality, and academic specialization. He has published twenty-six books, including a memoir, five essay collections, three collections of short fiction, two books of verse translation, a novel, and a book of poetry, as well as several interviews, symposia, and book introductions.[3] This great range in genre is matched only by the variety of subjects Steiner has pursued over the years. He is perhaps best known for his "Hitler novel," *The Portage to San Cristóbal of A.H.*, but is also recognized for his masterwork on the subject of translation, entitled *After Babel,* and for producing an excellent introduction to the work of Martin Heidegger. His work on tragedy, especially *The Death of Tragedy,* is today required reading in many literature courses, and scholars of both literature and religion have embraced the debate found in *Real Presences,* his discussion of post-Derridean hermeneutics.

Perhaps less noticed, but equally powerful, is Steiner's writing on the nature and meaning of the Holocaust as a product of Western culture. Having escaped the Nazi onslaught as a child, Steiner vowed as a young intellectual to become a *remembrancer*. For the last fifty years, he has argued relentlessly that *we come after* the Holocaust, and, as such, are morally obligated to work toward an understanding of this tragedy at the heart of Western culture. There can be no doubt that Steiner's experience as a European Jew during the twentieth century has determined his dominant intellectual concerns, particularly his interest in the effects of the Holocaust upon language and culture, the nature and meaning of the humanities, and the relations between Jews and Gentiles in Western culture.

George Steiner tells us that intellectual passions are personal. Indeed, my work attempts to demonstrate how his intellectual concerns and critical style evolve directly out of his own experience in the world. As we shall see, Steiner's powerful persona as a leading European intellectual rooted in the classical humanities is indelibly fused with his childhood experience of leaving France for New York in 1940, an experience that made him a "kind of survivor." This is a man who as a Jew and a European feels he has lived the two conflicting tendencies of Western culture: classical humanism and brutal inhumanity. Steiner acknowledges the burden this paradox places on his life and work:

> The background to this question is, of course, that of my own life. Even before I began writing, let alone teaching or publishing, it seemed to me

> that the problem of the relations between culture and politics, between humane literacy and the politics of torture and mass-murder, was such as to put in question every aspect of the life of the mind. Educated in the classical framework of "the humanities", feeling myself utterly drawn to the life of intellectual argument and the arts, of philosophy and poetics, I was confronted by an overwhelming, brutal paradox. The edifice of total warfare and of the death-camps, of totalitarian torture and "the big lie", had its base, had its contemporary triumphs, in the heart-lands of western culture. The spheres of Auschwitz-Birkenau and of the Beethoven recital, of the torture-cellar and the great library, were contiguous in space and time. Men could come home from their day's butchery and falsehood to weep over Rilke or play Schubert. The Jeffersonian, the Arnoldian promise that the spread of education, together with the cultivation of the arts and sciences, would humanize man, would bring with them a civilization of politics had proved illusory. How could this be?[4]

The relationship between humane literacy and political terror in Western culture has haunted Steiner throughout his career and it remains the underlying concern of his critical enterprise.

One image in particular, which reflects this collusion of humanism and barbarism, obsesses Steiner: the polished Nazi officer who operates a death camp during the day and in the evening reads Rilke and listens to Beethoven. There is no question that this image of the cultured Nazi death camp commandant forces the allegedly opposed worlds of culture and barbarism together in a shockingly unexpected manner. Clearly the Holocaust violates cherished European assumptions about the humanistic nature of Western culture, the importance of "good breeding," and the progressive and humanizing tendencies of education. But for European Jews like George Steiner the revelation of the Holocaust is a disorienting tragedy of immense proportions owing to the enormous personal investment these people made in European culture. These "Jews beyond Judaism"[5] placed a deep faith not in the religion of their ancestors or in narrow nationalistic ideologies but in the universal humanism of European high culture.

For Steiner, the crisis precipitated by the Holocaust is both intellectual and existential. It does not however lead him to reject Western culture categorically, but instead precipitates a deep and abiding ambivalence toward it.[6] Steiner's devotion to European culture remains reverential but, at the same time, his persona (his cultural standards, terms of reference, and intellectual passions) is grounded in a culture he holds responsible for the murder of six million Jews. This violent betrayal, which leaves Steiner outraged, reverberates through his scholarship. Some observers recognize this personal dynamic in Steiner's work, as one of Steiner's former students recalls: "he belongs to that generation of Jewish immigrants who were raised in the Germanic system of values, and had to fight their way to thinking there were any values left, and to reinvesting in those that had let them down."[7] The historian Peter Gay, another European Jew who fled Hitler, acknowledges the role played by trauma in the intellectual preoccupations of scholars: "There are times of upheaval and calamities—the twentieth century was only too rich in them—when a historian cannot shake off early experiences; we have all met refugees from totalitarianism, at once horrified and fascinated by their travail, who have spent their career desperate to understand, to explain, perhaps compulsively to reenact, the traumas of their youth."[8]

George Steiner sees himself as a surviving son of the central European Jews who made vital contributions to modern European culture before being annihilated by Nazism. He was fortunate to have a prescient and well-connected father who could ask the French prime minister to allow his family to join him on business in New York City in January 1940. Steiner's extended family, schoolmates, and friends were not so lucky. The Holocaust, a personal tragedy for the Steiner family, stands at the epicenter of Steiner's analysis of Western culture and from there casts its shadow. There are many cultural critics who have had no interest in the Holocaust and who continue to celebrate Western culture without the distraction of Auschwitz. George Steiner has spent his entire career railing against these critics, arguing that "those who found this question irrelevant to their spiritual and pedagogic pursuits, those who dissociated the practice and study of the humanities from the facts of the age, seemed to me profoundly irresponsible. . . . How can scholarship and criticism be divorced from the crisis of the humane without, by this very divorcement, being reduced to academic trivia? I cannot think of any serious work which I have done, as writer of fiction, as critic, as scholar and teacher, in which this has not been the cardinal issue."[9]

At the heart of Steiner's cultural criticism lies a paradox that defines his oeuvre. He is a cultural critic who firmly believes that European culture is morally and intellectually superior as Matthew Arnold's embodiment of "the best that has been thought and said in the world."[10] Yet this same advanced culture, according to Steiner, is riddled with hatred for Jews and in the twentieth century actually attempts to annihilate them. This paradox, the nexus between barbarism and humanism in Western culture, is the pivot upon which Steiner's thought turns.

It is important to realize that George Steiner is not a literary critic in the traditional English sense of the term. Although characterized by some literary scholars as a "historical critic" because of his "conviction that no literary work can be approached as though it were complete in itself . . . [but] must be studied with reference to its dossier, that is, the entire body of information pertinent to it,"[11] Steiner's criticism is not strictly literary or restricted to the study of literature in one language but is interested in culture and is comparative and historical by nature. As John Carroll, one of Steiner's former students, argues, Steiner is a *Geisteswissenschaftler,* who is "interested in taking literature as one particular manifestation of cultural expression, and extracting from it clues to the large historical movements of human values, repressions, ideals, and currents of feeling. . . . This is criticism in the urgent, immediate sense of exploring and evaluating the past in order to illustrate the present."[12] This style of criticism reflects the central European milieu with which Steiner identifies as a European Jewish intellectual.

Steiner's cultural criticism, I suggest, has evolved within an important temporal context, in relationship to the aftermath of the Holocaust, an event that has come to influence many historians and force some to reconceptualize Western culture, especially the study of the twentieth century.[13] As a result, the contour and concerns of Steinerian cultural criticism are largely determined by the disorienting tragedy of the Shoah, in terms of both Steiner's personal experience and his *post-factum* attempt to wrestle with the Holocaust and its significance. My analysis reads Steiner's work as a career-long response to the Holocaust by one of the most prominent postwar critics of Western culture, and locates his response within the larger ongoing historical process of uncovering and integrating, that is, attempting to understand, the Holocaust.

The purpose of this book, then, is to describe and explain the trajectory of Steinerian thought on the Holocaust and its relationship to Western culture. In general, studies of George Steiner's work are partial and tend to focus on specific subjects found within his criticism instead of its broader themes and general intellectual concerns. Against this background, my work attempts to provide a more comprehensive analysis of Steiner's multidisciplinary critique of Western culture after Auschwitz by connecting Steiner's evolving conception of the Holocaust and his theoretical understanding of antisemitism to his larger analysis of Western culture. To execute this task I trace the evolution of Steiner's ideas, through his many written works and published interviews, in relation to the larger cultural and intellectual developments of the post-Holocaust period. Through this process, I hope to demonstrate, first, the centrality of the Holocaust to Steinerian cultural criticism, and, second, the larger historical significance of Steiner's post-Holocaust analysis of Western humanistic culture. As we shall see, the trajectory of Steinerian criticism is also a trajectory of the development of Holocaust consciousness in postwar Western culture; therefore, studying the work of George Steiner provides valuable insight into this complex, multifaceted historical process.

The book begins with Steiner's biography, which demonstrates the profound influence of his father on the development of his Jewish identity and intellectual formation. Subsequent chapters trace the subjects of the Holocaust and antisemitism throughout Steinerian criticism as it evolves from the 1950s to the present. It soon becomes apparent that Steiner's understanding of the Holocaust changes over time, in relation to larger cultural and intellectual developments in Western culture, and as part of his ongoing reflection on his personal experience of childhood exile and post-Holocaust survival. Between 1964 and 1969 there is a permanent shift in Steiner's Holocaust thought. Instead of continuing to view the Nazi murder of European Jewry as another example of general human cruelty, he argues that the Holocaust must be seen in its own unique specificity if it is to be understood at all. This new focus on specificity leads Steiner to begin an investigation into the phenomenon of antisemitism. According to Steiner, the tension and animosity created by *the blackmail of transcendence,* the imposition of Jewish ethics upon human beings who are unable to meet such severe standards of behavior, creates instability deep inside Western culture. While this primary conflict plagues the Jewish-Gentile relationship throughout Western history, it is compounded by a second problem: the Christian obsession with the so-called Jewish rejection and murder of Jesus. Steiner believes that these two dynamics, the Jewish invention and destruction of God, combine to create a perennial hatred of the Jewish people in Western culture. And it is this anti-Jewish hostility at the center of the Western religious imagination that eventually animates the Holocaust.

Why this occurs in the middle of the twentieth century is related to the secularization of Western culture, the "long summer of 1815–1915," and the destruction unleashed by World War I. The one hundred years between The Congress of Vienna and the First World War was a period in which human hopes were embodied by the rational and progressive humanism of the Enlightenment, and in which bourgeois high culture hit its zenith of humane literacy. However, alongside these optimistic hopes for the European future, argues Steiner, there existed a frustrated feeling of stasis resulting from the failure of revolutionary change, and this reservoir of frustration eventually resulted in a unanimous thirst for war and destruction. Steiner believes that both world wars, and the barbarism of the Holocaust, create a general crisis of confidence in Western culture, which further erodes both ethics and aesthetics, and has the potential to actually destroy the humanistic foundations of Western culture. These foundations rely on a future-oriented idealism, on the confident hope that things will improve for humanity. This core dynamic, which has until recently propelled Western culture, has suffered a debilitating lethargy as a result of the failure of a variety of Western movements for human emancipation and the barbarism unleashed by world war and genocide.

Steiner's study of language, which he believes both conditions and is conditioned by the surrounding culture and its history, becomes increasingly important to his study of this crisis in Western culture. Just as the future of Western humanistic culture is dependent upon the dynamics of optimism and idealism, these dynamics are themselves dependent upon human language. The future tense allows human beings to imagine and therefore to create what is yet to be, and it is this uniquely human capability that allows for our idealism and optimism. As a whole, then, Steinerian cultural criticism can be interpreted as an attempt to resist the destruction of humanistic culture by defending its philosophic, religious, linguistic, and aesthetic foundations, and by preserving an orientation toward a humanistic future.

To begin to fully appreciate the meaning and significance of Steinerian cultural criticism, we must first understand Steiner's conception of "Central European Judaism," which is the product of his family and his heritage, his early education and general intellectual formation. To these foundational subjects, we shall now turn.

1

Exile and Edification

All things excellent are as difficult as they are rare [Steiner family maxim].
—Baruch Spinoza, *The Ethics*

Those familiar with the work of George Steiner know that his intellectual passions are personal. Nonnegotiable, these passions arise from within and are the result of his unique perception of the world. Born in France, naturalized an American citizen in 1944, and a resident of Great Britain since the sixties, it may seem strange for George Steiner to insist that he is central European. Nevertheless, Steiner has actively cultivated a central European Jewish identity based upon that of his parents, Frederick and Else Steiner, who developed a highly assimilated, culturally sophisticated, central European Jewish identity as the foundation for their family. This chapter demonstrates how Steiner's conceptions of Judaism, antisemitism, and Western culture germinate in this fertile family soil.

Vienna, Paris, New York

The first and most powerful influence on George Steiner's intellectual formation is his father, Dr. Frederick George Steiner. Steiner recalls his father teaching him to read Homeric Greek at the age of almost six years old. Father and son sat closely, sounding out the strange new syllables and tracing Greek letters with Papa's treasured Waterman pen. This intimately described winter evening evokes the sense of wonder and awe George felt for his accomplished father as a young child. As we shall see, this powerful pedagogical relationship between father and son, which continued until Frederick Steiner's death in 1968, determined important aspects of Steiner's life, including his education, ideas, attitudes, and academic career.

Frederick Steiner was born in 1890 and moved to Vienna with his family from a northern Bohemian village when he was just a child. He studied law and economics at the University of Vienna and later published studies of the nineteenth-century Austrian banking crises and the economics of Saint Simon. At the age of twenty-four, Frederick Steiner began work as a lawyer for the Austrian Central Bank, and in 1921 he married Else Franzos, the daughter of an affluent Jewish Viennese family.[1] Their first child, Ruth Lilian, was born in Vienna the following year. Germany and Austria suffered extreme financial crises in the early 1920s, especially the catastrophic inflation of 1923 and the collapse of the Austrian stock market in 1924. This desperate economic situation fueled traditional resentment against the Jews, who were perceived by many Austrians to be a controlling force in the national financial institutions centered in Vienna. Frederick Steiner, who worked for Austria's largest financial institution, was well aware of the risks posed to Jews by a prolonged period of economic recession. Now responsible for a wife and child, Frederick became concerned about the rising tide of antisemitism in the Austrian capital. Preparing to leave the city in 1924, the Steiners considered England for a time but, because of Frederick's rheumatic fevers, settled on France in 1925 as the more temperate climate. Starting from scratch in France, Frederick wrote articles on economics for the *Manchester Guardian* before acquiring a position as an investment banker with the Dillon Reed Corporation, a large American firm based in Paris. George Francis Steiner was born four years later, in April 1929, in the posh sixteenth arrondissement of Paris.

Steiner's mother, Else, came of age in an affluent, multilingual Viennese environment and she maintained this kind of home for her young family in France. She spoke English, French, and Italian, in addition to her native German, often using them interchangeably in conversation. Many accents were heard throughout the Steiner household: from the "Potsdam" German of George's nanny, the Hungarian spoken by the kitchen staff, to the English of the "diminutive Scottish lady" charged with teaching George the works of William Shakespeare.[2] Steiner tells us he has been trilingual since birth, adding Italian and Spanish in later years. Given this polyglot existence, it is easy to understand Steiner's passionate interest in language and his inability to isolate just one as his "mother tongue." In his recollections of the past,

Steiner briefly mentions his mother and only once mentions his sister, who is seven years his senior. It is possible that George had as much or perhaps more contact with his governess than he did with his own mother, which is not an uncommon experience for children of the European upper bourgeoisie. When mentioned, Else appears as a rather frivolous and emotional Viennese woman, who is most definitely secondary in importance to his intellectually demanding and talented father. As the foremost influence on his son's life, Frederick Steiner provided both a living example of what Steiner would later characterize as "Central European Judaism" and the basic content of Steinerian interpretations of Western culture and antisemitism.

Frederick was deeply involved in determining the course of his son's edification, both at home and at school. He first registered George at the American School of Paris, where the language of instruction was English, before transferring him to the Lycée Jeanson de Sailly. Several nights a week father and son would read together, one book at a time, proceeding only after George had completed a précis. The Steiner family, who combined the confident humanistic values of enlightened Europe with a proud secular Jewish identity, taught their children that these two cultural traditions were complementary by nature and were theirs by birth. Like all assimilated European Jews of the upper bourgeoisie, young George was taught to *revere* the humanistic high culture of European society, especially its literature and poetry, art, music, and philosophy. In this world, *Shabbes* was enjoyed in museums and bookshops and the Talmud was a careful selection of texts from the European philosophic and poetic canon.[3] In the secondhand bookshops along the Seine and in the museums of Paris, and later in New York City, Steiner's father schooled his son in the "worship of the classic."[4] At home, the family library was crowded with the philosophic works of Kant, Schopenhauer, and Nietzsche; the ancient and German literary classics, including first editions of Heine; and, the histories of Ranke, Mommsen, and Gregorovius.[5]

While Frederick was challenged by certain aspects of his work in finance, his real passion was intellectual history, particularly that of biology, music, and the study of language (he was acquiring Russian at the time of his death).[6] The entire family loved music, especially Mozart, Beethoven, Schubert, and Mahler, and hosted concerts for German and Austrian refugee musicians during the 1930s. Steiner fondly recalls his father refusing to abandon his love of Wagner, owing to the composer's antisemitism, by playing his recordings in French.[7] Frederick taught his son that intellectual and aesthetic cultivation, understood in terms of the German concept of *Bildung*,[8] was the most meaningful pursuit of human existence, and that these humane spheres were set apart from, and at odds with, the more common aspects of life: the dim and dirty human spaces of politics and finance. This paternal division between aesthetics and politics is reflected in Steinerian scholarship, which demonstrates a definitive preference for aesthetics and ideas over economics and politics.

According to his son, Frederick Steiner's Judaism perpetuated in a secular European form the traditional rabbinic exaltation of scholarship: "I accepted, with unquestioning zest, the idea that study and hunger for understanding were the most natural, the determinant ideals. Consciously or not, the sceptical ironist had set out for his son a secular Talmud. I was to learn how to read, how to internalise word and commentary in the hope, however chancy, that I might one day add to that commentary, to the survival of the text, a further hint of light. My childhood was made a demanding festival."[9] As George matured, he began to see his father as the very embodiment of liberal humanism and European sophistication. At the same time, these fine characteristics defined the "proud Judaism" of his father, which Steiner compares to that of "an Einstein or a Freud, one of messianic agnosticism. It breathed rationality, the promise of the Enlightenment and tolerance. It owed as much to Voltaire as it did to Spinoza."[10] The Steiners were not observant Jews and George did not receive a Jewish education. He began studying Hebrew to prepare for his Bar Mitzvah but Latin and Greek soon displaced it. Steiner tells us that his parents gave him *time* as the source of his Jewish identity and thereby provided him with a connection to the history, suffering, and fate of the Jewish people.[11] For example, the "High holidays, notably the Day of Atonement, were observed not for prescriptive or theological motives, but as a yearly summons to identity, to a homeland in millennial time."[12]

Steiner's father consciously groomed his son from childhood to become a scholar, the vocation he had chosen for himself until the needs of his own parents, aggravated by the First World War, forced him into finance.

Frederick's goal for George to become a teacher and scholar became a sacred pact between them.[13] Steiner interprets his father's wish as an investment in love and hope "during years of private and public torment, when the bitter need to find some future for [his family] as Nazism drew near, left him emotionally and physically worn out."[14]

To understand George Steiner is to understand the history of his family, especially their experience of European antisemitism and the Holocaust, and how it shapes their values and assumptions. Living the conflicts unique to modern European Jewry, Frederick Steiner instilled in his son both a profound love for European culture and an awareness of its contempt for Jews. As a young student in Vienna, Frederick Steiner recognized "a systematic, doctrinal Jew-hatred [seething] below the glittering liberalities of Viennese culture."[15] Steiner tells us that his father perceived the rise of Hitlerism after World War I, recognizing a new vulnerability in the cultural and financial foundations of the former Dual Monarchy. With the economic crises of the 1920s, the threat to Jews was growing in his estimation, and the fear of conflict "would engender violent upheavals where the scapegoats were already determined."[16] For this reason he left a promising career at the Austrian Central Bank and uprooted his distraught Viennese wife from her family and friends to start over again in France. His son, many decades later, would see this perception as the result of surreal intuition, stating, "With grim clairvoyance, my father perceived the nearing disaster . . . the world of Freud, of Mahler, of Wittgenstein was also that of Mayor Lueger, Hitler's exemplar."[17]

Steiner's father faced other forms of antisemitism in France and in the United States too. Frederick "never felt at home among what he judged to be the arrogant chauvinism, the frivolities, the myopia of French politics, finance, and society. He would mutter under his breath (unjustly) that all nationalities would sell you their mothers, but the French delivered."[18] The American patricians Frederick encountered on Wall Street during the 1930s and 1940s were also hostile toward Jews, perhaps not to the same degree as in Europe but hostile nonetheless.

When the family listened to Hitler's speeches on the radio, throughout the 1930s, Steiner remembers his father assuring them that this man would do exactly as he promised. A marginal opinion at the time, Frederick Steiner endured ridicule for his views. In his 1997 memoir, *Errata: An Examined*

Life, Steiner conveys the frustration and fear his father suffered during this period before the war:

> Over and over, even prior to 1933, my father laboured to warn, to alert, to awaken to refuge not only those whom he and my mother had left behind in Prague or in Vienna, but the French political-military establishment with which his international dealings had brought him into contact. His "pessimism", his "alarmist prognostications" elicited only officious dismissal or hostility. Family and friends refused to move. One could come to reasonable terms with Herr Hitler. The unpleasantness would soon pass. The age of pogroms was over. In diplomatic and ministerial circles, my father was regarded as a tedious Cassandra, prone to well-known traits of Jewish hysteria. Papa lived those rancid 1930s like a man trapped in cobwebs, lashing out and sick at heart.[19]

Frederick taught his son about the dangers of antisemitism during this menacing period; however, he also introduced him to the Jewish strategy of survival, which results in a uniquely spectacular kind of creativity: "[My father] thought deeply about politics, and saw Nazism [as] an Austrian, not a German phenomenon—he could smell it in the air. He thought Jews were endangered guests wherever they went, and wanted to equip his children—my elder sister and myself—with languages to earn a living, the ability to pack a suitcase rather than a steamer trunk, and take joy in the adventure. If he transmitted one thing to me, it was how lucky I am to be under pressure."[20] Frederick Steiner believed that Jews should always be prepared to leave a place and flourish elsewhere by adopting new languages and adapting to new cultures. This pressurized existence on the periphery of other national cultures made Jews uniquely creative, spontaneous, and adaptable. This was the bounty for a life lived in exile. No doubt, the Steinerian philosophy—have your bags packed, and teach your children foreign languages so they will survive in new environments when the need arises[21]—and well-known creed, "whereas trees have roots, men have legs and are each other's guests,"[22] are products of this paternal teaching.[23]

Steiner assures us that this paternal survival strategy mollified the fear produced by antisemitism: "I'd like to stress that this, far from introducing any particular sense of instability and schizophrenia, helped enormously—it took away a lot of fear."[24] Frederick presented antisemitism to his son within a cultural and historical context, rather than simply neglecting the problem altogether or internalizing it as fear or self-hatred. In the winter of 1934 a financial scandal known as the Stavisky Affair broke out in France, and because a Jewish politician was involved, French antisemitic groups like the Croix de Feu, the Camelots du Roi, and the Franquista began marching in the streets. Steiner remembers being taken home early at the age of five by his governess as a result of these demonstrations, in which people were smashing windows and shouting, "Death to the Jews." At home, his mother immediately closed the blinds to avoid the spectacle, but when his father arrived, he said, "'Up with those shades!' and [took him] by the hand to look outside." Steiner recalls, "I was fascinated, of course; any child would be. And [my father said,] 'You must never be frightened; what you are looking at is called history.' I think that sentence may have formed my whole life."[25]

Still, Steiner remembers well his feelings of anxiety as war approached. In 1939, business brought the Steiners back to Paris from a holiday in Saint Nazaire. Prime Minister Paul Reynaud asked Frederick Steiner to direct a mission to the United States negotiating the purchase of Grumman fighter planes for France. While at lunch with the French delegation in Manhattan, Frederick met a former German colleague who was now bearing a swastika on his lapel. Meeting in the bathroom, the German banker informed Steiner's father that the Nazis would be coming into France shortly and he should get his family out at any price. Frederick immediately called the prime minister and asked if his wife and children could join him in New York for a few weeks because of protracted negotiations. Upon receiving the news, Else was reluctant to leave France and begin yet again in the United States. Her family was doing very well in Paris, now living in a luxurious apartment in the seventh arrondissement with a stunning view of Le Pont Alexandre III. Frederick Steiner's request, however, was approved, and Else left Europe, via Genoa, with her children in January 1940 on one of the last American ships.[26]

Else took time to adjust to living in the United States; Frederick, however, "saw this second exile the same way he saw the first: it belonged to history and came as no surprise. Despite the difficulties, he considered it an enriching experience."[27] In New York, George attended the Horace Mann School for two years and then returned to the French system at the Manhattan Lycée, which was administered by Vichy until mid-1944. Steiner's early adolescence was spent in this contentious environment where the "sons and daughters of diplomats, colonial servants and military personnel loyal to the Vichy regime mingled with the children of exiles, of Jewish refugees and of European families variously stranded in the New World."[28] These were years of desperation for refugee scholars but also of spectacular luck for young students like George who attended lectures by Simone de Beauvoir, Claude Lévi Strauss, Jacques Maritain, and Alexis Saint Léger (better known as the poet Saint John Perse).[29] During this time, Frederick Steiner worked for the Arnholt Family Syndicate as their chief American representative and served as board director of ten other international companies.[30] Lilian was now studying Romance languages at Radcliffe College after graduating from the Manhattan Lycée with the highest marks of any student in attendence.[31]

George received his Bachelier-és-Lettres in 1947 from the Sorbonne, and his dream was to attend L'École Normale Supérieure in Paris, through which he would enter the French mandarinate. George returned to Paris with his mother that year to see the few friends and relatives who survived the war, to retrieve their buried library, and to investigate the Lycée Louis le Grand. Steiner soon discovered that he was one of only two Jewish children to have survived the war out of his entire class. They also learned that George's young cousins had died in the camps.[32] Frederick allowed the trip back to France but forbade his son to stay, forcing him to return to the United States and begin studies at Yale University. The Steiners decided to live in New York and not return to France as they had expected earlier in 1940.[33] It is reasonable to assume that, given a choice between living in New York City or one of the European capitals struggling to rebuild after the war, Frederick chose to remain in the United States. Not to mention the obvious fact that Europe was now a graveyard, where the Jewish people, including the Steiners' family and friends, had been hunted like prey. Moreover, Steiner's father felt strongly that English would become the dominant language of the future and felt that attending an American university would be in his son's best interest. This disagreement was the first major conflict between father and son, and Steiner still keeps the decisive letter from his father stating, "I assume the grave responsibility for taking the French Academy from you."[34]

Yale, Chicago, Harvard, Oxford

George Steiner arrived at Yale for freshman orientation in September 1947 and found an environment where Jews were "consigned to a ghetto of pinched politeness."[35] Soon bored and frustrated, Steiner began to pressure his father about returning to Paris. By chance, Steiner came across a story in *Time* magazine about Robert Maynard Hutchins, the new chancellor of The University of Chicago. Hutchins was an advocate of comprehensive testing that allowed gifted students to take final exams upon arrival. Steiner wrote to Hutchins about his predicament and was subsequently admitted to the university. He arrived in Chicago and passed ten of the fourteen final exams required for the BA, failing mathematics, physics, chemistry, and biology. He was given a dispensation for all courses except the last four and completed his BA in one year.

After studying physics with Enrico Fermi and chemistry with Harold Urey, both Nobel laureates involved in the Manhattan Project,[36] Steiner decided on a future in the exact sciences and applied for entrance to the graduate program at Chicago. His application was rejected based on the results of his final exams. Instead, he was offered entrance to the study of biology, as it did not require the same level of mathematical ability. This rejection was a devastating blow to a young man so confident of his intellectual superiority and primed so early for academic success.[37]

Steiner began graduate work at Chicago in literature and philosophy, unable to choose between them. Among his professors were the Southern poet Allan Tate, Aristotelian philosopher Richard McKeon, social anthropologist Robert Redfield, and conservative political philosopher Leo Strauss. It was in Strauss's class on Plato that Steiner first heard of the philosopher Martin Heidegger. Entering the classroom, Strauss announced that he refused to discuss the work of this particular philosopher, piquing his student's interest. After class, Steiner went to the library and found a copy of *Sein und Zeit,* inaugurating his fascination with Heideggerian philosophy.[38]

A second discovery occurred that year at Chicago during exam period. Several students in Steiner's dormitory asked if he could help them understand Henry James's *The Golden Bowl* and Joyce's story "The Dead": "Not long after, a group came to my room. They crowded the upper and lower bunks and the floor. . . . I found myself conducting an unauthorised seminar into the long night, reading with and just ahead of these concentrated listeners. I glimpsed them taking notes, underlining and filling the margins in their text. . . . I knew now that I could invite others into meaning. It was a fateful discovery. From that night on, the Sirens of teaching and interpretation sang for me."[39] The University of Chicago holds a special place in Steiner's memory. It was the first time he was on his own, away from the demanding and highly structured environment of his family, and was "one of the happiest, most passionate periods of [his] life."[40] The city of Chicago introduced him to jazz, American politics, and football. He learned to play poker with Hugh Hefner and shared a room with a worldly ex-paratrooper and veteran of World War II named Alfie, who introduced Steiner to the opposite sex. Perhaps most important, though, the university was a place where "no one had to apologize for intellectual passions" or feel embarrassed by excellence.[41] In addition, Chancellor Hutchins welcomed Jewish scholars and students to The University of Chicago, and this uplifting attitude provided Steiner with a new feeling of confidence and optimism: "The full news of the Holocaust wouldn't impinge until some years later. It looked as if Hitler had been well and truly beaten, and as if American horizons for Jews were unlimited—as they were. All the doors were opening. So I met something I hadn't met in the tragic European situation—a *confident* intellectual Judaism. [This] was a great discovery."[42] Many years later, in a review of Harry S. Ashmore's biography of Robert Maynard Hutchins, *Unseasonable Truths*, Steiner revealed his continued admiration for the university and attributed much of his own intellectual development to its influence. He admits, "What very probably decided my life and work was the sheer genius of intellectual exhilaration, the passionate electricity of spirit, that had made the University of Chicago under Hutchins the best there was."[43]

In 1949, Harvard University offered Steiner a bursary and he transferred there to study literature with Archibald MacLeish. Drawn by the prestigious Harvard name, several weeks later Steiner regretted his decision to leave

Chicago. However, he completed his MA in English Literature at Harvard the following year and won the Bell Prize in American Literature.

Still wishing to return to Europe, Steiner decided to apply for the Rhodes Scholarship to the University of Oxford. He wrote to Hutchins at Chicago requesting his support and received one of the university's two annual nominations.[44] Steiner emerged victorious from the exhausting seventy-two-hour exam competition, known as "the house party," after answering a final question on the difference between "a split-T, a T, and a single-wing formation" in American football.[45] He arrived in England in October 1950. Unlike the United States, Great Britain was still recovering from the war, still rationing food, and many homes lacked adequate heating. Steiner, however, fell in love with postwar England. He remembers "such a climate of solidarity, one that I have never encountered anywhere else, there was a pride and decency that reigned back then. I fell in love with England profoundly."[46]

The Polish-born British historian Sir Lewis Namier was a close friend of Steiner's father.[47] Namier had attended Balliol College at Oxford in 1908 and insisted that George do the same. Peter Scott, former editor in chief of the *Times Higher Education Supplement,* has suggested that this intervention by Namier was a mistake and had negative ramifications for Steiner's experience at Oxford. As a graduate student in literature, Scott suggests, Steiner should have attended a college like Merton: "[Steiner's] Oxford experience was not happy. No one had told him how to set about writing a thesis and . . . his viva [oral examination] verged on a show trial. His use of references from 'paperbacked' books was ridiculed; he was savagely criticized for not knowing the difference between *belles lettres* and literary criticism."[48] Steiner's doctoral thesis, published in 1961 as *The Death of Tragedy,*[49] was indeed rejected for its impressionistic and comparative nature. At this time, the field of comparative literature did not exist at Oxford. It was perceived to be a questionable German American invention and was to be resisted. Also, during this time, the English literary establishment had little respect for doctoral-level research in literature, and some held the PhD in contempt as a German invention.[50] Steiner left Oxford after producing two publications, a book of poetry called *The Fantasy Poets*[51] and an essay entitled *Malice,*[52] which won the Chancellor's Essay Prize in 1952, but without his doctorate.

The *Economist*, Princeton, Cambridge

Penniless, but wanting to stay in England, Steiner applied for an entry-level position in the editorial department of Geoffrey Crowther's *Economist.* After writing summaries of three economic texts by Ricardo, Keynes, and Marshall, he was hired without a salary. Steiner worked at a table in the hallway and was paid only for the articles accepted by the editor. Several months and many articles later he was offered an editorial position. From 1952 to 1956 Steiner covered Europe, American politics, and science for the *Economist,* writing on a range of subjects from NATO to the Atomic Energy Commission.

Humphry House, the literary critic and respected scholar of Charles Dickens, was a professor at Wadham College and had taught Steiner at Oxford. One day he walked into the offices of the *Economist* and asked Steiner whether he would like to rewrite his doctoral thesis. It appeared that there were other students at Oxford from America who were now having similar trouble, and House felt it was unethical to accept these students and not teach them how to write an Oxford English dissertation. Steiner recalls, "He asked if it was true that my thesis had received no proper supervision. It was. Did I wish to be taught seriously, thus making up for my own derelictions and what House knew to be the ways of too many of his colleagues? What little I know of textual scholarship, of bibliographic competence, of the use of primary sources and recensions, I owe to the hours House accorded me in Jermyn Street in London and at his private residence in Cambridge."[53] In 1955 Steiner was awarded a D.Phil. in English Literature for his thesis on the anti-tragic thrust of English romanticism after the French Revolution. In July of that same year, he married an American woman named Zara Shakow, who was a historian of British diplomacy working at the Foreign Office.[54] While Steiner travelled through Europe as a correspondent for the *Economist,* he also hosted a weekly BBC broadcast called "*Bonjour la France.*"

As part of a story he was writing on the Atomic Energy Commission, Steiner travelled to Princeton in 1956 to interview Dr. J. Robert Oppenheimer,[55] the director of the Institute for Advanced Study. After a brief and unpleasant interview, Oppenheimer invited Steiner to have lunch without him at the university cafeteria.[56] There he met several prominent members of the Institute: George Kennan,[57] professor of historical studies, the art historian Erwin Panofsky, Renaissance historian Ernst Kantorowicz, and renowned Plato scholar Harold Cherniss. Founded in 1930, the Institute was described by Oppenheimer as an "intellectual hotel." It was "to be a new kind of research center. It would have no students, no teachers, and no classes. The world's greatest scientists would gather there to do research, but they would have no laboratories, no machines, no apparatus for doing experiments. . . . From the start, the Institute for Advanced Study was to be a hotbed of pure theory . . . a refuge to which scholars could repair for any length of time and have their worldly needs taken care of by others."[58]

After lunch Steiner had a second exchange with Oppenheimer, this time in front of Cherniss, which ended in Steiner being offered a fellowship to the Institute.[59] Steiner was awestruck by Dr. Oppenheimer, who was a master of many languages, including Sanskrit, a scholar of literature, poetry, and philosophy, in addition to being a brilliant physicist, and by the Institute itself as the creation of von Neumann and the intellectual shelter of Einstein. At the time Steiner was writing his first book, *Tolstoy or Dostoevsky: An Essay in the Old Criticism*,[60] and the *Economist* gave him time to work on it around the corner at the London Library. Oppenheimer, however, dismissed Steiner's attempt at trying to write seriously while working as a journalist by characterizing his effort as "19th century British amateurism."[61] Steiner recalls, "Oppenheimer told me one can't do good books part-time, which cut through me like a knife. Is it true? I don't know to this day. But his words cut through me at that time: the authority of that man, the charisma, the apodictic contempt in that statement. So I accepted."[62]

Steiner left the *Economist* and moved with his new wife to New Jersey. The Princeton years were very rich, with Steiner publishing *Tolstoy or Dostoevsky* and a new draft of his failed Oxford thesis. During these years, Zara gave birth to their children: a son David and a daughter Deborah.[63] George Steiner was a fellow at the Institute for Advanced Study until 1960, when R. P. Blackmur invited him to give the Gauss Seminar in Criticism at Princeton University. Productive though these years were, Steiner missed Europe and found it difficult to adjust to living in the United States. When Robert Oppenheimer asked Steiner if he was interested in returning to Europe, the answer was an unequivocal yes. In 1961, Steiner began directing English

Studies for Churchill College at Cambridge, where he remains Extraordinary Fellow today.

Since the seventies Europe has been George Steiner's base of operation, teaching during the academic year in Geneva (from 1974 to 1994) and returning to his family in Cambridge during the summer. This again is due to his father's influence.[64] In the late sixties two American universities offered Steiner posts in comparative literature and he discussed the positions with his father: "I asked him what he thought . . . he said 'How sad that Hitler has won.' What he meant by that was that Hitler had sworn Europe would be *Judenrein,* that there'd be no Steiners there."[65] This comment devastated Steiner and he promptly refused the positions. He remembers telling his wife that "nothing was strong enough in me to bear the immense world of sad disdain in that remark. I knew he was right. He had given his life to saving us, to trying to save others, and his son was not going to be driven out by any circumstance."[66]

This biographical discussion of George Steiner places several aspects of his life into perspective. We know that Steiner is not actually a Holocaust survivor. This fact requires emphasis because of the incorrect assumptions readers and critics alike make about him and the impression his writing sometimes leaves with those same readers. Born in Paris, Steiner escaped the Holocaust by leaving France with his family at the age of eleven. A young adolescent during the war years, he lived with his family on Fifth Avenue in Manhattan and eventually attended the finest educational institutions in the United States. This privileged existence, led by the Steiner family during World War II, will later produce feelings of guilt in Steiner as he begins to confront the Holocaust in his writing.

The first half of his education is French, and focused on literature and philosophy, while his university years are spent in American and English environments rather than in the European schools many assume he attended. Although this is the case, Steiner's intellectual and linguistic sensibilities are more the result of his European Jewish upbringing, especially the influence of his father, and his French classical education than of any Anglo-American training he received at university. As Mark Krupnick argues, even Steiner's American experiences are characteristically European:

> However much Steiner may sound at times like an old New York intellectual fretting about mass culture or like a Yale professor of literature mourning the passing of a text-centred public, he is not one of us. True, he studied in the United States and has written fondly of his undergraduate career at the University of Chicago under Robert Hutchins . . . Moreover, he wrote his first book, *Tolstoy and Dostoevsky,* at the Institute for Advanced Study in Princeton. But very little of what we think of as characteristically American rubbed off. On the contrary, it may be argued that Hutchins's University of Chicago and R. P. Blackmur's circle at Princeton were two of the most singular, uncharacteristic American institutions of their time.[67]

The English environment, in which Steiner found himself both directly after the war as a doctoral student and again later in the 1960s, did not provide him with similar European enclaves in which to retreat. Instead, it demanded that Steiner conform to the norms of English academic life and assimilate its traditions and sensibilities, especially in his chosen field of English literature. Steiner was unwilling to do so and, as we shall see, suffered ostracism for his status as a continental outsider.[68] This hostile context, however, provided an environment against which George Steiner further refined his central European Jewish identity.

Steiner's father, Frederick, is the prototype for his son's image of the central European Jew: a brilliant cosmopolitan intellectual who is at once ethical, wise, cultivated, and accomplished. Steiner sees his father, whom he compares to Siegmund Warburg, Gershom Scholem, and Sigmund Freud, as a member of the spectacularly gifted Jewish intelligentsia emanating out of central Europe during the early years of the twentieth century. He considers himself a legatee to this glorious tradition, destroyed by the Holocaust, and later dedicates himself as a teacher and scholar to its memorialization.

Frederick Steiner has an enormous, even determinative, influence upon the ideas, interests, and attitudes of his only son. One can see how Steiner's love of culture, particularly language, literature, philosophy, and music, is first nurtured within a family environment that valued the cultivation of aesthetics and intellect above all else. Steiner's preference for aesthetics over economics and politics, as well as his suspicion of direct political action, are the product of his father's attitudes toward these subjects and Frederick's "uncompromising resolve that his son should know next to nothing of his . . . profession. . . . [not even] the difference between a bond and a share."[69] Also, Frederick's clear-sighted focus on the problem of European antisemitism, and his lessons in the methods of Jewish survival, have a direct impact on the development and content of his son's thought and identity.

Long after his father's death, George Steiner acknowledges Frederick to be "the indispensable friend, the exigent partner in dialogue."[70] Although Steiner dismisses Freud's "Oedipal Complex" as "irresponsible melodrama," he does admit that "there may be a mustard-seed of truth in the psychoanalytic conjecture that an overthrow, a psychically homicidal erasure of one's father-figure is necessary to independence; that there can be, without such rebellion, neither sufficient originality nor will to power."[71] In his 1997 memoir, Steiner candidly admits that perhaps "too much of my father's 'library', of his 'syllabus' of the supreme and caustic certitude that in the face of a Homer, of a Goethe, of a Beethoven or a Rembrandt, the second-rate is precisely that, conditions and confines me still."[72] Steiner believes that his wholesale acceptance of his father's canonical scale of value has weakened his sensitivity to contemporary culture and, as a result, partly disabled his critical antennae. Perhaps his "hypertrophied reverence for the classics" has distracted his attention from the more "ephemeral, . . . fragmentary, . . . derisive, [and] self-ironising . . . modes of modernity" and he wonders whether he could have contributed more to our knowledge of the interactions between high and popular culture.[73]

The only area in which Steiner and his father appear to diverge is on the subject of Jewish nationalism. Since 1967, George Steiner has been an outspoken critic of both Zionism and the State of Israel. Frederick, like his friend Lewis Namier, was a dedicated Zionist, whose bookplate displayed "a bark, a seven-branched candelabrum at its bow, approaching Jersualem."[74] Steiner's father died the year following the Six-Day War so it is impossible to gauge how he would have evaluated the ongoing conflict between the Israelis and the Palestinians, and whether or not this problem would have affected his view of Zionism, as it has that of his son.[75]

This chapter introduces the personal connection that George Steiner and his family have with the Holocaust. The Shoah displaces the Steiners from their beloved Europe to the shores of North America, transforming their lives and changing the future of each member of the family. Steiner's exile from Europe deprives him of the French academic career that he had coveted as a child, as well as the living heritage of Central European Judaism of which he would have been an active member. The task of the following chapters is to trace the evolution of Steiner's thought on the Holocaust and to explain how it impacts his cultural criticism in general. We shall see how Steiner's project on the Holocaust and Western culture develops during the long period of discovery, reflection, and aftermath in which the Holocaust becomes the historical event we know today.

2

Early Writings, 1952–1961

This chapter examines the early writings of George Steiner, which he composed during the years between his doctoral studies at Oxford, through his tenure at Princeton, to his arrival at Cambridge in 1961. The purpose of this examination is to demonstrate what too few scholars of Steiner acknowledge: his multidisciplinary cultural criticism revolves around several key interests that determine the nature and tone of his criticism, all of which are either stimulated, or affected, by the Holocaust. These early writings are also important as they clearly illustrate the fact that Steiner's understanding of the Holocaust changes over time, evolving in relationship to broader intellectual and cultural developments. The four essays and two books discussed here establish Steiner's interest in the following interrelated subjects as early as the 1950s: the nature of evil and the relationship between humanism and barbarism; the meaning and purpose of literary criticism; theories of language; the effects of the Holocaust on language and Western culture; the challenges inherent in Holocaust representation; the nature of the relationship between Athens and Jerusalem in the formation of Western culture; and the condition of ethics and aesthetics in the secular world.

The Holocaust, sometimes a spectral presence and other times addressed explicitly, is very obviously on George Steiner's mind in these early writings. During the 1950s little was published in English on the Nazi murder of Europe's Jews, so people had very little knowledge about the details of the Jewish experience under Nazism or the workings of the Nazi killing process. Steiner, however, was in a unique position: his fluency in French, German, and Italian allowed him access to the earliest work on the subject by scholars like Theodor Adorno, Hannah Arendt, Léon Poliakov, Viktor Frankl, and Bruno Bettelheim, as well as to the poetry and memoirs of

Holocaust survivors like Paul Celan, Elie Wiesel, and Primo Levi (many of whom Steiner came to know personally and professionally).[1] As a young man in his twenties, George Steiner was like many Jews, trying to understand what had happened during the war and how *six million Jews* could be murdered *en masse*. As an eleven-year-old Jewish boy who left France in 1940 and who lost cousins and friends in the Nazi camps, Steiner was personally haunted by this catastrophe. As a European, he was shocked by the fact that this outbreak of barbarism erupted in his beloved heartland. These, then, are the two legs, one Jewish, the other European, that have carried Steiner on his journey through the aftermath of the Holocaust. Walking has not always been easy.

Malice (1952)

The first reference to the Holocaust in Steiner's work is found in his first publication, an Oxford English essay entitled *Malice* for which he won the Chancellor's Essay Prize in 1952. This paper on the origins of human evil offers a fascinating look at how Steiner first perceived the Nazi murder of European Jewry in the early fifties, long before many considered the Holocaust to be the defining event of the twentieth century. The essay, already Steinerian with its rich polyglot style, demonstrates the continuity of ideas and assumptions that comprise Steiner's oeuvre and connect his work on the Holocaust to his criticism of Western culture in general.

The epigraph on the title page strikes one as perhaps too optimistic for the author we know today as it confidently asserts, *Nihil humani alienum*.[2] Within the context of Steiner's future attempts to comprehend Nazism and antisemitism, this rational and optimistic sentiment seems somehow out of place. *Malice* was written when Steiner was just twenty-two years old and it showcases his multilingual talents, vivid imagination, and extensive French classical learning. The first five pages tell the tale of one night in the life of the demon Malice, who flies from Italy to London, via France, and on to New England, striking humanity with a great range of cruelties. The following twenty pages are a quintessential Steinerian mix of history, theology, and philosophy cast as literary essay. He describes how our significant thinkers, artists, priests, and scientists have, over the centuries, understood the demon Malice.

Though, it is in modern times, "alas, [that] Malice has taken on forms more refined and horrible. . . . On the listing of the Titanic men gambled for the remaining life-belts with marked cards, and in concentration camps violinists were compelled to play the Kreutzer Sonata whilst their wives and children were being hurled into the ovens."[3] Here we have, in the same sentence, a description of wealthy passengers trying to survive a sinking ship by cheating at cards and violinists (no mention of Jews) forced to act as musical accompaniment to the murder of their families. This is one comparison or association, I would argue, few scholars of the Holocaust would make today. It does demonstrate, however, that in 1952 Steiner viewed the events in Europe during World War II as another dismal chapter, perhaps one "more refined and horrible," in the long story of human evil and therefore comparable to other acts of malice. The evil he discusses in this short story is universal; it may have "myriad configurations" but it is also of an "ever-recurrent sameness."[4] There is no sacralizing or privileging of the Holocaust experience here.

What is striking is that this first description of the Holocaust turns on the humanism barbarism nexus (Beethoven becomes the soundtrack for the German crematorium), which will eventually become the center of Steiner's critique of post-Holocaust culture. The image of violinists forced to accompany their families to their deaths is explicitly related to the Holocaust iconography most closely associated with George Steiner, that of the highly cultured death camp commandant who reads Goethe and Rilke, and listens to Bach and Schubert in the evening, before waking up to operate Auschwitz in the morning. These images illustrate the shocking fact that high culture coexisted comfortably with Nazi barbarism. Apparently, the most sublime poetry and music provide succor to those who commit the most heinous crimes against humanity. And, against Steiner's previous assumptions and those of his father, it appears that humanistic art and learning have little effect on the morality of their audience. The wealthy Titanic passengers and Nazi-created death camp orchestras force Steiner to admit that education and refinement do not stop people from participating in acts of evil, but actually have a role to play in its execution.

"But these are outward manifestations of Malice. What is it per se?" asks Steiner. "Neither the historians nor the painters have replied adequately;

perhaps we should look to literature for guidance and Ariadne's thread."[5] Here is one of Steiner's persistent arguments: historians have not provided an adequate explanation for Nazi behavior, so we must look to the poets instead. Steiner firmly believes that literature is the best method human beings have for self-understanding. In this essay, however, even modern literature "with its pride in psychological insight"[6] fails to identify the source of malice. For an explanation, Steiner turns to a Flemish proverb that finds malice rooted in familiarity: "Malice is created by low garden fences, or in narrow streets, where men unceasingly rub shoulders, and this man's orchard casts a blighting shade over that man's vineyard. It is an elixir brewed by close contact, by noses stuck through a neighbour's shutter and ears flowering on the wall. *Indifference yields no malice,* and vessels gliding past one another in the night exchange neither shot nor salutation"(italics mine).[7] Here, indifference is a benign state of bliss. However, in subsequent years, the concept of indifference becomes central to Steiner's understanding of the Holocaust. He comes to believe that without the massive indifference toward the fate of the Jews on the part of Europeans in general, Hitler's regime could not have killed six million of them. Steiner reverses his original suggestion and argues instead that "*men are accomplices to that which leaves them indifferent.*"[8] Indifference toward Jewish suffering is viewed as a kind of silent, passive antisemitism, which is indispensable to the physical destruction of European Jewry.

At this point in Steiner's intellectual journey, however, Malice grows out of envy, which produces a lingering hatred, "a cancer of the feelings and infects both will and reason."[9] What will cure this cancer that "flourishes where truth is bent out of shape?"[10] Steiner argues that we must keep our hearts pliant and awake: "Nothing is more essential than the power to admire unstintedly what is truly noble and of lasting fineness. The success of one's contemporaries is difficult to bear, and there is a secret pain in the witness brought to the brilliance of a friend. Yet the worm must be trodden down and the heart kept from shrivelling into loneliness . . . What will ultimately drive Malice from the heart is charity in the widest sense, a giving of oneself to admiration, to breadth of sympathy and insistence on truth."[11]

Instead of appreciating the talents of others in a spirit of generosity, human beings tend to focus on their own inadequacies in relation to other people, and this focus breeds resentment and envy, which fuels malice.[12] According to Steiner, "Malice springs from invidious comparison and self-matching against our betters. It grows like a slow cancer out of admiration unrequited and lingers in dark corners after hatred has died down."[13]

Malice begins its conclusion with the confident assertion that "the demon of Malice has been pitched into the gaping jaws of Hell by Good Counsel,"[14] and the participants of the morality play make their way home feeling secure and satisfied: "But lo! What figure is that, gliding from roof to roof and casting the shadow of its plumes into Orion? There it is, disappearing behind the chimneys with a soft laugh! *Sound precepts have never wrought much transformation in the world*—and a boon it is for essay writers! The demon of Malice has emerged once more, and will steal on its nocturnal rounds, aforethought and thousand-tongued, until time itself is but a memory!" (italics mine).[15] Here Steiner ends on a pessimistic high note chastising our naïve hope in human reason and our recalcitrant human nature. We have fooled ourselves once more by overestimating our human capacity for rationality and ethical behavior. This despairing view of human nature is an undercurrent in the work of George Steiner and in his broad assessment of the Western condition at the end of the twentieth century.

This Oxford essay projects many of the themes and presuppositions fundamental to later Steinerian thought, with one major distinction. George Steiner's labyrinthine oeuvre has it own Ariadne's thread composed of several key intellectual concerns: the relationship of humanism to barbarism; the roots of malice in the soil of envy, resentment, and feelings of inadequacy; and the inability of historical analysis to plumb the depths of human existence and help decipher the "big questions." However, the murder of European Jewry, while mentioned, is not the focus of this essay on evil. At this early stage in Steinerian thought, just seven years after World War II, the Nazi crimes are subsumed within a general human category of malice. As we shall see, Steiner only begins to focus on the Holocaust as a unique event in the history of Western culture during the late 1960s. During this early period, Steiner's interest in language and literary criticism leads him to attempt to establish his own position within these fields of study and their contemporary debates.

"Marxism and the Literary Critic" and "Lukács's Devil's Pact" (1958–1960)

Written at Princeton and in Austria, respectively, these two essays assert Steiner's interest in the work and critical style of Georg Lukács and several other Marxist critics. Steiner's first scholarly article, "Marxism and the Literary Critic" (1958), discusses the conflict between two schools of Marxist literary criticism: the orthodox and the para-Marxist (Steiner employs Michel Crouzet's term). Members of the first group follow Lenin's view of literature as *Tendenzpoesie,* in which writing is a political act that explicitly communicates the programmatic goals of social democracy. The para-Marxists follow Engels, who argued that the progressive intentions of the author were more effective if they were implicit in the story itself. Steiner discusses the work of Georg Lukács as an attempt to reconcile "Engels' defense of the poet's uncommitted integrity with Lenin's demand for total partisanship and aesthetic discipline."[16] Steiner believes Lukács to be one of the master critics of the age, whose philosophic literary criticism demonstrates that Marxism can generate "a poetics and a metaphysic of the highest order."[17] Although dedicated to communism, Lukács refused to deal with Soviet literature and focused instead on the German, French, and Russian literary traditions, writing on Schiller, Goethe, Balzac, Pushkin, and Tolstoy. This focus made him vulnerable to the charge of harboring counterrevolutionary, or bourgeois, tendencies in his placement of "'pure' and 'formalistic' literary canons above Party and class interests."[18]

Steiner's goal in this essay is to demonstrate the unique and important contribution made by Marxist critics to the resources of literary criticism in general. Like Steiner, although a generation ahead of him, many of these critics are central European Jews engaged in the difficult process of trying to understand the Holocaust and its implications for the future of Western culture. In the essay, Steiner briefly discusses this prominent group of so-called para-Marxists, critics like Lucien Goldmann, Theodor Adorno, Walter Benjamin, Edmund Wilson, and Jean Paul Sartre, who share in common:

> the belief that literature is centrally conditioned by historical, social, and economic forces; the conviction that ideological content and the articulate

> worldview of a writer are crucially engaged in the act of literary judgement; a suspicion of any aesthetic doctrine which places major stress on the irrational elements in poetic creation and on the demands of "pure form." Finally, they share a bias toward dialectical proceedings in argument. But however committed they may be to dialectical materialism, para-Marxists approach a work of art with respect for its integrity and for the vital center of its being.[19]

According to Steiner, Marxist criticism has developed our sense of time and place by focusing our attention on the specific historical, cultural, and sociological foundations of literature. Most important, for Steiner, is the fact that, unlike many of their colleagues in the West, Marxist critics *take literature seriously.* Steiner argues that in the West, literary criticism is perceived by some to be a frivolous enterprise, merely an academic pursuit in America, and a wholly provincial affair in England. In the Communist world, however, "the poet is regarded as a figure central to the health of the body politic. Such regard is cruelly manifest in the very urgency with which the heretical artist is silenced or hounded to destruction. This constant preoccupation with the life of the mind would alone serve to distinguish Marxist autocracy from other species of totalitarianism. To shoot a man because one disagrees with his interpretation of Darwin or Hegel is a sinister tribute to the supremacy of ideas in human affairs—but a tribute nonetheless."[20]

While Steiner does not endorse Marxism per se, he does respect what he sees as the protection of culture in Marxist societies, where he believes people are more sensitive to the condition of language and seem more concerned about maintaining traditional standards of literacy. On this subject, Steiner echoes the Marxist critique of Western consumer capitalism:

> The dread gravity of the Marxist view of literature should remind us of certain truths which few Western critics, with the exception of Ezra Pound and Dr. Leavis, seem willing to affirm. The health of language *is* essential to the preservation of a living society. It is in literature that language is most truly challenged and guarded. A vital critical tradition, vital even in its polemics, is not a luxury but a rigorous need. The abandonment of values under the pressures of commercialism, the failure of the journalistic-critic to discriminate between art and *kitsch*, does contribute to a larger decay.[21]

This same seriousness is what Steiner respects in Lukács, who perceives literary criticism as a central force in the shaping of human lives. "Georg Lukács and his Devil's Pact" (1960) is a short essay on the literary criticism of Lukács, with whose style Steiner clearly identifies. Steiner defines Lukács's critical perspective as "rigorously Marxist" but his choice of themes as "central-European and conservative."[22] While Steiner refers to Lukács's masterpiece, *History and Class Consciousness,* he feels "his pre-eminence lies elsewhere": in his studies of Goethe; Russian and German Realism; Balzac, Stendhal, and Zola; Hegel; and his book *The Historical Novel.*[23]

What appeals to Steiner about Lukács is his style of criticism, his "close study of a literary text in the light of far-reaching philosophic and political questions. The writer or particular work is the point of departure. From it Lukács' argument moves outward traversing complex ground. But the central idea or theme is kept constantly in view."[24] Steiner consciously models his own critical style upon this type of philosophical approach to literature and upon Lukács's "largeness of vision," based upon his mastery of a wide range of literatures. The so-called para-Marxist critics influence Steiner's approach to literature in general: he also takes literature and literary criticism seriously, he seeks to understand art with reference to its social and historical context, and he values art as a uniquely effective medium of social critique. Eventually, Steiner will be associated with this style of criticism, for better or worse depending on the cultural context of his readership. As we shall see in the following chapter, when he decides to establish an academic career in England (already referred to here as "deliberately provincial"[25]), his Lukácsian approach to literature will mark him as a continental outsider.

These essays reveal, for the first time, another major trope in Steinerian cultural criticism: his concern for the contemporary condition of language, as it is revealed primarily in literature and the print media. Like a kind of national pulse, Steiner believes that the state of language reflects the larger condition of the surrounding culture. And it is the responsibility of literary critics to both reveal and protect the state of language in society. In subsequent years, Steiner will address the problematic state of English in Great Britain and the United States,[26] but his first attempt at revealing the contemporary condition of language converges with his interest in the Holocaust.

"The Hollow Miracle" (1959)

Written in 1959, while Steiner was a Fulbright scholar at the University of Innsbruck in Austria, "The Hollow Miracle" is his first publication to deal specifically with Germany. The essay unleashed a storm of controversy among German readers at the time, and again in 1966 at a meeting of German writers in the United States, and as Steiner remembers, "understandably . . . caused much hurt and anger."[27] The title refers to the emptiness Steiner saw at the center of Germany's postwar recovery. The country was growing economically and Germans were actively engaged in building a better future, but they were also committed to burying the past without first confronting it. According to Steiner, the message Germans received after the war was: "Forget the past. Work. Get prosperous. The new Germany belongs to the future."[28] Steiner worried that this message guaranteed that "'let us forget' [would become] the litany of the new German age."[29]

Of lasting significance here is George Steiner's theory of language. He diagnoses the crisis in postwar German society through his own evaluation of the contemporary condition of the German language: "The thing that has gone dead is the German language. Open the daily papers, the magazines, the flood of popular and learned books pouring off the new printing presses; go to hear a new German play, listen to the language as it is spoken over the radio or in the Bundestag. It is no longer the language of Goethe, Heine, and Nietzsche. It is not even that of Thomas Mann. Something immensely destructive has happened to it. It makes noise. It even communicates, but it creates no sense of communion."[30]

Language is central to Steiner's understanding of culture and humanity. He believes that it is our linguistic capability that makes us uniquely human, and through our creative use of language we relate humanity to that which is humane. According to Steiner, "languages are living organisms. Infinitely complex, but organisms nonetheless. They have in them a certain life-force, and certain powers of absorption and growth. But they can decay and they can die."[31]

Steiner believes the corrosion of German begins with national unification in 1871. Nationalism and the imposition of Prussian authority, represented by militant historians, philologists, and "incomprehensible metaphysicians," "produced that fearful composite of grammatical ingenuity and humorlessness which made the word 'Germanic' an equivalent for dead weight."[32] Those writers who carried the poetic genius of German were those who wrote either before unification or outside the new nation: Luther, Goethe, Schiller, Kleist, Heine, Nietzsche, Kafka, and Rilke.[33] In Steiner's estimation, there is a dialectical relationship between language and culture wherein social and historical pressures affect language, which in turn conditions the habits of a culture. For Germany, Steiner argues, this relationship had profound consequences:

> For to the academicism and ponderousness of German as it was written by the pillars of learning and society between 1870 and the First World War, the imperial regime added its own gifts of pomp and mystification. The "Potsdam style" practiced in the chancelleries and bureaucracy of the new empire was a mixture of grossness ("the honest speech of soldiers") and high flights of romantic grandeur (the Wagnerian note). Thus university, officialdom, army, and court combined to drill into the German language habits no less dangerous than those they drilled into the German people: a terrible weakness for slogans and pompous clichés (*Lebensraum,* "the yellow peril," "the Nordic virtues"); an automatic reverence before the long word or the loud voice; a fatal taste for saccharine pathos *(Gemütlichkeit)* beneath which to conceal any amount of rawness or deception.[34]

Myths and lies are communicated through the vehicle of language. In Germany, they begin to take on a deadly importance after 1918, especially the infamous "stab in the back" mythology used to explain Germany's defeat in World War I.[35] Before the rise of Hitler, there was a window of opportunity for German literature. Unfortunately, the "brilliant, mutinous period" of 1920–30, host to Bertold Brecht, Thomas Mann, Rilke, Kafka, and Robert Musil, was but "a brief noontime" after which Adolf Hitler turned language into one of the most powerful political weapons in history.[36]

Under Nazism, the German language was used to transform human beings into vermin; to secretly orchestrate the destruction of the Jewish people; to chronicle the humiliation, torture, and murder of Germany's "enemies"; and to deceive foreign governments and the domestic population about any number of issues. Referring to the "Horst Wessel Lied," the "fight song" of the S.A. (Stormtroopers), Steiner asks, "how should the word *'spritzen'* recover a sane meaning after having signified to millions the 'spurting' of Jewish blood from knife points?"[37] The point of Steiner's essay is to demonstrate that languages, like institutions and cultural traditions, can be permanently scarred when they are used to facilitate crimes against humanity.[38] Like human beings, languages are resilient but there is a point at which they break:

> Use a language to conceive, organize, and justify Belsen; use it to make out specifications for gas ovens; use it to dehumanize man during twelve years of calculated bestiality. Something will happen to it. Make of words what Hitler and Goebbels and the hundred thousand *Untersturmführer* made: conveyers of terror and falsehood. Something will happen to the words. Something of the lies and sadism will settle in the marrow of the language. Imperceptibly at first, like the poisons of radiation sifting silently into the bone. But the cancer will begin, and the deep-set destruction. The language will no longer grow and freshen. It will no longer perform, quite as well as it used to, its two principle functions: the conveyance of humane order which we call law, and the communication of the quick of the human spirit which we call grace.[39]

The essay concludes with Steiner's frustration over the return of mythology and lies to the German language in a postwar period characterized by "dissimulation and deliberate forgetting."[40] Steiner states categorically that the only way to rehabilitate the German language is for Germans to begin speaking the truth about Nazism.[41] At the same time, Steiner's statement acknowledges the very possibility of rehabilitation (even in the extreme case of Nazified German), the resiliency of human beings and language, and the centrality of literature and criticism to this recuperative process. He continues to develop his argument on the importance of literary criticism to the preservation of language and culture in his first book, also published in 1959.

Tolstoy or Dostoevsky (1959)

Steiner's *Tolstoy or Dostoevsky: An Essay in Contrast* was written at Princeton University while he was a Fellow at the Institute for Advanced Study.[42] Against the New Criticism,[43] Steiner argues that literary criticism should "arise out of a debt of love" and be unapologetic in its praise of books that enrich our consciousness.[44] What Steiner terms the Old Criticism is philosophic in range and temper and is aware of the importance of historical political context to our understanding of literature. As first cousin to history, the novel, for example, documents our sense of the world and its past. The Old Criticism admires the moral purpose of both literary creation and criticism. Steiner connects the waning of this perspective to the "wars and bestialities of the 20th century," which have created a "sense of disorder and vertigo" and made us question the value and meaning of Western culture.[45] Optimistically, Steiner argues that "criticism should recall us to the remembrance of our great lineage," thereby defending Western civilization from the new dark ages.[46]

Steiner begins his analysis with the assertion that there are three "principle moments of triumph" in Western literature: Athenian drama and the works of Plato, the Age of Shakespeare, and the nineteenth-century Russian novel. Steiner argues that his chosen subjects, Tolstoy and Dostoevsky, are out of tune with the rational skepticism of the New Criticism, and that its scholars marginalize the Russian masters in favor of James, Conrad, Joyce, Proust, Kafka, and Lawrence. Tolstoy and Dostoevsky break with the secular rationalism of these modern writers, with the "realistic portrayal of ordinary experience" by writers such as Balzac, Dickens, and Flaubert.[47] Steiner admires the Russian novelists for their exploration of important philosophical and religious questions: the meaning of life and the state of humanity, the existence of God, and the possibility of faith and redemption in a world of war and suffering. Steiner's interest in transcendence is central to his later works of criticism, and is apparent here in his argument that the great poets of the world are "compelled either to acquiescence or rebellion by the mystery of God," and that there are "magnitudes of intent and poetic force to which secular art cannot attain, or, at least, has not as yet attained."[48]

Steiner's book compares what he terms "the opposed theologies" of Tolstoy and Dostoevsky: while Tolstoy embraces the idealistic hope that humans can create a Kingdom of God on this earth, Dostoevsky argues that this kind of idealism leads only to political bestiality and to the destruction of the idea of God. Within the context of his comparison, Steiner refers to Nazism and Soviet Communism. At this point in time, he seems convinced of Norman Cohn's argument that these two totalitarian systems are modern manifestations of revolutionary messianism.[49] Here, again, Nazism is viewed as part of a larger continuity within European culture:

> The "thousand-year" *Reich* of National Socialism and the classless, ultimately disappearing, state of Soviet Communism are eschatological images and new goals in the ancient pursuit of the millennium. The eschatology is secular in that it arises out of a denial of God. But the underlying vision is that of all chiliastic and utopian movements: man must either create the good life here on earth or resign himself to suffering his term in a chaotic, unjust, and frequently incomprehensible journey between two poles of darkness. The Kingdom of God must be realized as the Kingdom of Man. This is the theology of the totalitarian utopias.[50]

This brief but emphatic interpretation of totalitarianism reappears later in a series of lectures in 1974 in which Steiner discusses the void left in Western culture by the collapse of formal religion. Steiner does not however continue to pursue the view that Nazism is utopian by nature or that it has the same underlying structure as Soviet Communism.

The Death of Tragedy (1961)

Steiner's second book, *The Death of Tragedy*,[51] had its beginnings as his first doctoral thesis, which was rejected by Oxford in 1950 for its comparative nature. Steiner shelved the work and returned to it years later, presenting it at the Gauss Seminar at Princeton before finally publishing it in 1961.[52] In the dedication, Steiner acknowledges the determinative influence of his father: "Principally, however, this essay belongs to my father. The plays I discuss in it are those which he first read to me and took me to see. If I am able to deal with literature in more than one language, it is because my father, from the outset, refused to recognize provincialism in the affairs of the mind. Above all, he taught me by the example of his own life that great art is not reserved to the specialist or the professional scholar, but that it is best known and loved by those who live most intensely."[53]

The Death of Tragedy is a study of the tragic form of drama invented by the Greeks and an attempt to explain its decline after Shakespeare. The book begins with a discussion of the two cultural foundations of Western culture, Athens and Jerusalem, and their opposed conceptions of the workings of the universe. Representations of personal suffering and heroism are not universal across human culture, Steiner tells us, but are the product of the Greek imagination in which human beings are not compensated in the face of catastrophe or given justice after the fact. In the Greek world, "human hatreds and the wanton mysterious choice of destiny" determine reality. The Greeks believed that "the spheres of reason, order, and justice are terribly limited . . . [where] the doom of Thebes was predestined. There is no use asking for rational explanation or mercy. Things are as they are, unrelenting and absurd. We are punished far in excess of our guilt."[54]

This view of human existence as irrational and anarchic, upon which the art of tragedy depends, is alien to the Judaic conception of the world, where there is a demand for, and expectation of, divine justice. Referring to *The Book of Job,* in which God compensates Job for his suffering, Steiner argues, "where there is compensation, there is justice, not tragedy."[55] God's justice is also rational: "The Judaic spirit is vehement in its conviction that the order of the universe and of man's estate is accessible to reason. The ways of the Lord are neither wanton nor absurd."[56] In Judaism, there is a relationship between knowledge and action so human suffering is recognized as the result of moral failing. In the Greek world, the forces that determine our destiny lie outside the control of reason or justice in an "ironic abyss" where humans are left vulnerable to anarchic and demonic energy.[57]

Absolute tragedy, then, is the unique product of fifth-century Greece.[58] From this point forward in Western culture, Steiner argues, there are only variations of (tempered) tragedy mitigated by different cultural and religious traditions. The main chapters of the book trace the conflicting definitions of tragedy in European art and literature from Periclean Athens, England (1580–1640), seventeenth-century Spain, France (1630–90), Germany (1790–1840), and finally, to twentieth-century Scandinavia and Russia. According to Steiner, the dividing line in the history of tragedy is the seventeenth century, a time in which the neoclassical conception of tragedy is abandoned for a more popular, romantic ideal of drama. The prime example of this shift is Shakespeare, whose plays "violated every precept of neo-classicism. They broke with the unities, dispensed with the chorus, and combined tragic and comic plots with indiscriminate power. . . . They took from [Seneca] his rhetoric, his ghosts, his sententious morality, his flair for horror and blood-vengeance; but not the austere, artificial practices of the neo-classic stage. To the genius of Greek tragedy, or rather to its inferior Latin version, Shakespeare opposed a rival conception of tragic form and a rival magnificence of execution."[59]

The French novel, German opera, and Russian drama are the subsequent forms Steiner discusses in the history of tragic drama. In his final chapter, Steiner argues that twentieth-century variations of tragedy are in crisis for a variety of reasons. The basic foundation of European culture remains Christian, which is antitragic by nature because of its redemption of humanity through the death and resurrection of Jesus. Then there is the influence of an equally antitragic modern political ideology, Marxism, which argues that humanity is "advancing toward the justice, equality, and leisure of the classless society . . . [and where] final victory is as certain as the coming dawn."[60] But the deepest level of explanation is related to the Holocaust. The final blow is dealt to tragedy by the violence of the twentieth century, and this is accomplished via language:

> The political inhumanity of our time . . . has demeaned and brutalized language beyond any precedent . . . [that] we grow insensible to fresh outrage. This numbness has a crucial bearing on the possibility of tragic style. . . . Compared with the realities of war and oppression that surround us, the gravest imaginings of the poets are diminished to a scale of private or artificial terror . . . [In classic tragedy], cruelty was still commensurate to the scope or response of the imagination. I wonder whether this is still the case. What work of art could give adequate expression to our immediate past? The last war has had neither its *Iliad* nor its *War and Peace.* None who have dealt with it have matched the control of remembrance achieved by Robert Graves or Sassoon in their accounts of 1914–18. Language seems to choke on the facts. The only array of words still able to get near the quick of feeling is the kind of naked and prosaic record set down in *The Diary of Anne Frank.* Given the abuses of language by political terror and by the illiteracy of mass consumption, can we look to a return of that mystery in words which lies at the source of tragic poetry? I think not.[61]

For Steiner, tragedy is dependent upon a certain standard of language and poetic imagination. Both must be intact to allow for the articulation of a tragic view of man: the contradiction between human existence and the workings of the universe, or, in Steiner's words, the sense that human beings are unwelcome guests in the world. The facts of the Holocaust overwhelm both language and imagination, making the act of legitimate representation unlikely, if not impossible. This passage inaugurates what will become a major Steinerian focus: the question of whether or not it is possible to represent adequately the events of the Holocaust or whether the Holocaust experience lies outside human language and all other means of representation.

In the epilogue, Steiner uses a personal recollection related to the Holocaust to illuminate his argument that tragedy is dead, which I will quote in its entirety:

> I was taking a train journey through southern Poland not long ago. We passed a gutted ruin on a comb of a hill. One of the Poles in my compartment told me what had taken place there. It had been a monastery, and the Germans had used it as a prison for captured Russian officers. In the last year of the war, when the German armies began receding from the east, no more food reached the prison. The guards pillaged what they could off the land, but soon their police dogs turned dangerous with hunger. After some hesitation, the Germans loosed the dogs on the prisoners, and maddened by hunger, the dogs ate several of them alive. When the garrison fled, they left the survivors locked in the cellar. Two of them managed to keep alive by killing and devouring their companions. Finally, the advancing Soviet army found them. The two men were given a decent meal and then shot lest the soldiers see to what abjection their former officers had been reduced. After that, the monastery was burnt to the ground. The other travellers in our compartment had listened, and now each in turn recounted some incident comparable or worse. One woman told of what had been done to her sister in the death-camp at Matthausen. *I will not set it down here, for it is the kind of thing under which language breaks.* (Italics mine)[62]

This passage announces several things. As of the early sixties, Steiner has traveled to the Nazi killing grounds in Poland, and he has met survivors of the camps.[63] In this recollection, we hear Steiner sifting human experiences into hierarchical categories like "comparable or worse." There are human experiences that language can describe, even those of the Russian soldiers who survived by eating their comrades, but there are other experiences, death camp experiences, which are met with silence. Steiner tells us, "I will not set it down here, for it is the kind of thing under which language breaks."[64] For Steiner, there are now experiences that language cannot carry or even hope to convey. There are crimes so heinous, so outrageous, that there are no words adequate for their description, crimes that are literally unspeakable.

Steiner and the others in his train compartment sat in silence after hearing these stories of suffering. Then an old man recited a medieval parable, which he thought might explain how such things can occur: "In some obscure village in central Poland, there was a small synagogue. One night, when making his rounds, the Rabbi entered and saw God sitting in a dark corner. He fell upon his face and cried out: 'Lord God, what are Thou doing here?' God answered him neither in thunder nor out of a whirlwind, but with a small voice: 'I am tired, Rabbi, I am tired unto death.'"[65] Steiner then offers his interpretation of this allegory of God's exit from the world:

> The bearing of this parable on our theme, I take it is this: God grew weary of the savagery of man. Perhaps He was no longer able to control it and could no longer recognize His image in the mirror of creation. He has left the world to its own inhuman devices and dwells now in some other corner of the universe so remote that His messengers cannot even reach us. I would suppose that He turned away during the seventeenth century, a time which has been the constant dividing line in our argument. In the nineteenth century, Laplace announced that God was a hypothesis of which the rational mind had no further need; God took the astronomer at his word. But tragedy is that form of art which requires the intolerable burden of God's presence. It is now dead because His shadow no longer falls upon us as it fell on Agamemnon or Macbeth or Athalie.[66]

In this discussion the Holocaust is the product of a God-forsaken universe, the exact opposite of the traditional Judaic God-centered world structured along the lines of reason and justice. There is no transcendent power in the secular world, and the implications are troubling not only for the likelihood of ethical behavior but also for the possibility of artistic creation.[67] This subject, related explicitly to Steiner's concern with the Holocaust, evolves over the years into Steiner's diagnosis of the crisis of meaning in Western culture.

As this chapter on Steiner's early work suggests, the mass murder of European Jewry first shadows, and eventually begins to inform, his discussions of language, literature, criticism, and culture during the 1950s. Steiner's first reference to the mass murder of European Jewry is peripheral to the essay *Malice* (1952), which categorizes it under the general heading of human evil. Almost a decade later, Steiner argues that the Nazi murder of Europe's Jews (still not yet referred to as the Holocaust), and the outrageous abuse of humanity and language it represents, has actually made both tragedy and authentic representation, in general, impossible. Language is thought to collapse under the weight of the inhumanity it is now asked to carry and to articulate. By 1959, the Holocaust, and the massive destruction of two world wars, is also seen by Steiner to have precipitated a crisis of confidence in Western culture. Against the New Criticism, a decontextualized American approach to literature (and an example of this same crisis), and the overly optimistic approach to literature that predates the destruction of the twentieth century, Steiner attempts to reorient the discussion of literature so as to protect and preserve Western culture from self-destruction.

During these early years, Steiner establishes himself as a critic whose work both supports, and represents, a serious literary criticism that is central to the preservation of language and culture. Steiner tells us that his approach to culture and literature is influenced by a group of central European Jewish intellectuals, who are also Marxist literary critics: Theodor Adorno, Walter Benjamin, and especially Georg Lukács. As mentioned, there are many points of intellectual contact between these critics and Steiner; however, the most important is their firm belief in the moral purpose of criticism, that "a vital critical tradition, vital even in its polemics, is not a luxury but a rigorous need"[68] and a "militant force toward shaping men's lives."[69]

As demonstrated in the next chapter, Steiner's interest in the Holocaust, and the pressure it increasingly imposes upon his criticism, continues to influence his work throughout the 1960s as the scholarly process of discovery and explication reveals the destruction of European Jewry in ever-increasing detail.

3

Surviving in Cambridge, 1961–1974

Over the last fifty years, the University of Cambridge has been George Steiner's fixed base of intellectual operation, and a significant influence on Steiner's evolution as a thinker. Yet, as a Jew and a European, Steiner has remained an outsider in English academic life. His early study of the Holocaust, placed at the center of his analysis of Western culture, further compounded Steiner's isolation from English colleagues who did not share his interest in the subject. In this chapter I suggest that Steiner's experience of post–World War II Britain reinforces his identity as a central European Jew and first stimulates his investigation into the problem of the nature and condition of the humanities after the Holocaust. We shall discover how the cultural and intellectual exchange between George Steiner and his English environment precipitates the formulation of his theories on the relationship between the Holocaust, antisemitism, and Western culture. However, before examining the work Steiner publishes during this period, I will discuss the cultural clash that separates Steiner from his English colleagues beginning in the 1960s.

George Steiner and Cambridge English

To be a critic is to be critical. To be critical one must observe, discern, find fault and merit, pass judgment, even censure, all with precision. By its very nature criticism is adversarial and has the potential to become antagonistic and combative. Mark Krupnick has argued that literature departments are particularly combative and that arguments between literary scholars too often degenerate into personal attack. He argues that this combativeness can be explained by the "shared disposition among literary academics, who tend to stake their professional and personal identities on their readings . . . [and who] tend to experience alternative approaches to the truth as they see it as a personal affront, and cause for counterattack."[1] Much depends on the personality and style of the individual critic. Some are thought to carp and cavil, others are admired for their deep insights and moral seriousness. George Steiner is both accused of the former by his critics and celebrated for the latter by those who recognize his polymathic virtuosity.

The critical reception of Steiner's work has been divided from the beginning of his career as a public intellectual. It is instructive that the one and only published collection celebrating his work begins with the following admonition: "Surely this veritable priest of reading deserves to be read with a patience and punctiliousness very much greater than what he is sometimes accorded in this way in the English-speaking world."[2] Steiner identifies the bias set against him within the academy as one of widespread resentment over his reluctance to declare only one field of specialization. He feels his belief "that cows have fields but that passions in motion are the privilege of the human mind has long been held against [him]."[3] This may indeed reflect the concerns of some scholars; however, the hostility directed toward Steiner has been especially intense in England, where it became the subject of an article written by John Carroll, one of Steiner's former students.[4]

The long history of animosity between George Steiner, the English Faculty at Cambridge, known simply as "Cambridge English," and the British literary establishment is well known to Steiner's English readers but not necessarily to those outside Great Britain. In 1961, John Cockcroft, the Nobel physicist and member of the UK Atomic Energy Authority, established a new science college at Cambridge named for Sir Winston Churchill. He recruited Steiner from the Institute for Advanced Study at Princeton as a scientifically sensitive humanist to direct English studies at the new college. Steiner became one of Churchill College's founding fellows and was appointed its Director of English Studies from 1962 to 1969. The English Faculty of the University of Cambridge, however, refused to offer him an appointment or to acknowledge him in any formal way.

To understand how George Steiner can be associated with Cambridge and yet remain completely excluded from its English Faculty, one must be familiar with the Oxbridge system and the unique relationship that exists between its university faculties and colleges. Sir James Mountford, in his book *British Universities,* provides the following explanation:

> Each university [composed of its faculties] has its own existence apart from the colleges, it provides some of the teaching, it alone examines and awards degrees, it must concur in any proposed change in the statutes of a college, and no new college can be founded without its sanction. At the same time the colleges have their own very considerable autonomies. They are self-perpetuating and elect their own fellows entirely at their discretion, they own and have absolute control over their own property, they manage their own finances, and, subject to the matriculation regulations of the university, they admit what students they please.[5]

In this system, Steiner taught English at Churchill College but was restricted from examining and supervising graduate students of English. This restriction became a serious problem at Cambridge as more and more students wanted to study under Steiner's tutelage.

The reasons for this hostile position against Steiner were never discussed publicly but were assumed by John Carroll to be the following: "Steiner's work is superficial, some say unscholarly. There is a brilliant gloss, but essentially the analysis never penetrates deeper than journalistic sketchiness. Steiner's popularity among students merely illustrates the ease with which modern youth can be led away from serious, systematic criticism. Within the university he is a corrupting force."[6] These criticisms imposed a chilling effect on Steiner's academic career in the United Kingdom and, as a result, he was forced to look elsewhere for a permanent teaching position. Steiner found an environment more akin to his linguistic needs and scholarly sensibilities when he was offered a Chair in Comparative Literature at the University of Geneva in 1974. For twenty years Steiner taught in Switzerland, returning to his family in Cambridge during the summer months. Today he remains Extraordinary Fellow of Churchill College and continues to work out of his Cambridge study.

The controversy between Steiner and Cambridge English was not simply a manifestation of British antisemitism, as some believe, but was the result of a fundamental cultural and intellectual conflict that continued to smoulder over the years. By arguing that most "literary criticism is ephemeral, bordering on journalism,"[7] Steiner set himself apart early on from his English colleagues. He aligned himself with European critics of "high moral seriousness" such as Georg Lukács and Walter Benjamin, who worked "outward from the particular literary instance to the far reaches of moral and political argument."[8] Though he studied English literature at Oxford and taught the subject at Churchill College, there is no question that the conflict between Cambridge English and George Steiner is one of intellectual style and cultural sensibility. British critics in general have had particular difficulty appreciating George Steiner and his ideas, and their reviews of his work often end in some form of personal attack. For years, critics and scholars in England have accused Steiner of transmitting questionable ideas in an aggressive and haughty manner.[9] They ridicule his way with the English language,[10] and wonder aloud about his intellectual competence and the quality of his scholarship.[11] Likewise, Steiner has not hidden his disdain for certain aspects of British culture. Critical of what he perceives to be the English aversion to philosophical thought,[12] he deeply resents England's monolingual provincialism and the increasing dominance of the English language abroad.[13] Once hopeful that England would open itself to his beloved continent, Steiner continues to be disappointed by Britain's hopeless orientation toward the United States and by what he considers its hostile stance toward Europe.[14] He has also enjoyed confronting and challenging his English hosts and their beloved national symbols. In March 1971, Steiner used a prestigious lecture series, held in honor of the memory of T. S. Eliot, as an opportunity to admonish the poet critic for neglecting to address the Holocaust in his famous book on culture,[15] *Notes Towards the Definition of Culture*,[16] published just three years after World War II. In another lecture, entitled "A Reading Against Shakespeare," Steiner used Ludwig Wittgenstein's critical comments about the Bard as a chisel with which to whittle away the "Shakespeare cult" still so alive in England.[17]

It is important to note that Englishness is intimately connected to the English literary tradition; this connection is reflected by a culture whose national heroes are very often writers and poets. As a matter of course, Steiner's criticism sets English writers against their European counterparts (be they French, German, Italian, or Russian) with a distinct preference for the latter. Kafka, Dostoevsky, Dante, and Racine are all thought to be superior to Shakespeare, while Karl Kraus is in Steiner's opinion "a more incisive observer of the relations between language and power than was Orwell."[18] Steiner's criticism is famous for its great lists and pantheons in which there is a winner and many losers. Over the last five decades Steiner's comparative literary criticism has chipped away at English literary figures and the cultural monuments they have inspired. Undoubtedly, this critical stance, one that privileges European arts and letters over lesser "Anglo-American" equivalents, heightened the animosity between Steiner and his English critics.

The position of Cambridge English however was made difficult by the fact that Steiner's lectures, on subjects completely foreign to the study of English literature at the time, attracted more students than any other at Cambridge. Sometimes attracting as many as one thousand students out of a university population of ten thousand, his lectures on Marx, Freud, Lévi Strauss, and Brecht were a novelty in this provincial English environment.[19] These were part of an annual series of eight lectures sponsored by the English Faculty for a nominal fee of £100. In 1970, the Faculty revoked its invitation for Steiner to lecture at Cambridge and only through student protest was Steiner reinstated. In a context in which students complained that the method of "cold academic dissection" embraced by Cambridge English destroyed their interest in literature and their love of reading, students left Steiner's lectures "inspired, talking, arguing, going away to read the books which [had] been discussed."[20] As John Carroll argues, Steiner's pedagogical virtuosity in such a wide range of subjects was a threat to the traditional literary establishment: "The presence of a central European Jew as fluent in German, French, and Italian as in English, is not only alien in this provincial country town but also threatening. There is a power in his vast erudition and culture which appears to have made some of those who have confined their interest to the English tradition uncomfortable."[21]

As difficult as English life has been for Steiner, he relishes his outsider status and claims to be most comfortable just outside consensus. The literary critic Bryan Cheyette reminds us of this when he contrasts George Steiner with Sir Isaiah Berlin, another prominent European Jewish intellectual living in England, who "was prepared to acculturate and become a member of the British establishment, and was rewarded. Steiner has always refused to play that game."[22] Isaiah Berlin was an avowed liberal anglophile, whose work is viewed as a celebration of the philosophic and political traditions of Great Britain. Many, by contrast, perceive Steiner as a continental outsider who embraces an intellectual style and critical perspective at odds with the specific hallowed conventions of English literature. Steiner's continental cultural criticism is comparative and interdisciplinary by nature, whereas English literary criticism is traditionally just that: English and strictly concerned with literature or "The Great Tradition." By excluding Steiner from the English literary establishment, the dons made clear that Steiner's philosophical and sociological, in other words, *Germanic,* approach to literature was not welcome at Cambridge.

The counterexample of Sir Isaiah Berlin is instructive and demonstrates my argument that the conflict between Steiner and Cambridge English is not only the result of British antisemitism, but is also the product of a complicated conflict between English and continental intellectual styles and cultural sensibilities, not to mention individual personalities. The difference between the English reception of Isaiah Berlin, the liberal philosopher, and that of George Steiner, a continental cultural critic, is striking. While Steiner has suffered exclusion, Berlin is celebrated as one of Britain's foremost philosophers, who served in the British Embassy in Washington during World War II and provided Winston Churchill with a weekly summary of American opinion, which was said to be the prime minister's favorite reading.[23] Whereas George Steiner has been an outsider *par excellence,* Sir Isaiah Berlin was a knighted Oxford insider, whose BBC obituary remembered him as "the dominant scholar of his generation . . . an extraordinary, life-loving man with a mind like an encyclopedia, [whose death] leaves a hole in the intellectual life of Britain [that is] impossible to fill."[24]

Both men are Jews who left Europe as children, who then studied at Oxford and came to reside in England for most of their lives. Isaiah Berlin was born in Riga, the capital of Latvia, to a Jewish family of timber merchants.[25] The Berlins arrived in England in 1919, when Isaiah was just ten years old, and they never looked back. They were anglophiles from the beginning, whose transition into English culture was remembered as "a smooth and straight road."[26] Antisemitism does not appear to have seriously affected Berlin's existence in Great Britain, whether in his personal life or in his celebrated career as an Oxford don and leading public intellectual. In his biography of Berlin, Michael Ignatieff explains how Isaiah Berlin assimilated quite easily into the fabric of English life and the reasons for this high level of integration:

> Isaiah more or less accepted everything the English liked to believe about themselves: that they were practical, untidy, eccentric, fair-minded, empirical, common-sensical and that ubiquitous word, decent. His was a version of Englishness frozen in the moment when he first encountered it in the 1920s: the England of Kipling, King George, G. K. Chesterton, the gold standard, empire and victory. The long slide into imperial decline and self-doubt lay decades ahead. Narrow-minded provincialism, philistinism and insularity played no part in his idea of England. If the English took to him, it was because he offered them back their most self-approving myths.[27]

Instead of reflecting back to the English their "self-approving myths," as Berlin is thought to have done, Steiner does quite the opposite. Critics charge Steiner with being an ungrateful guest, who never tires of criticizing England, its institutions, traditions, and ways of life, as a lesser version of his beloved Europe. It is clear that George Steiner isolated himself from his English colleagues by refusing to assimilate the dominant intellectual and cultural norms of English academic life. Instead, Steiner insisted on approaching the study of English literature, like Georg Lukács, as a *Geisteswissenschaftler*.[28]

Another important difference between these two public intellectuals is the fact that, while George Steiner's work focused increasingly on the Holocaust, Berlin did not pursue the subject publicly. There are twenty years between these men, and while they both experience the Holocaust in personal ways, losing family and friends who had not escaped Nazi-occupied Europe, they do so at different times in their lives. As discussed, the war destroys the Steiners' European Jewish existence and forces them to relocate to New York City. The experience of coerced exile and its aftermath defines George Steiner's late childhood and adolescence, whereas Isaiah Berlin had by then left Riga, grown up in (and embraced the culture and ideals of) Great Britain, studied at Oxford, and was working for the British government in Washington during the war. Unlike Berlin, Steiner's formative years are dominated by the growth of Nazism in neighboring Germany, by the war itself, and by the unfolding news of the mass destruction of European

Jewry afterward. While it is easy to see why the Holocaust becomes central to Steiner's thinking about culture, the reasons for Isaiah Berlin's avoidance of the subject in his philosophical work are not as obvious.[29]

The Nature and Purpose of the Humanities

The conflict between Steiner and Cambridge English was only exacerbated by Steiner's growing interest in the Holocaust during the 1960s. To understand the reaction of Steiner's literary colleagues to his writings on the Holocaust and the humanities, a brief discussion of English Studies and its humanistic assumptions is necessary. Oxford was the first to establish a School of English Language and Literature in 1893. Its students were mostly young women until World War I as English was seen as a "soft" subject appropriate only for females and the lower orders of society, whereas university students, composed of the upper classes, studied the traditionally learned subjects of classics and mathematics. Before 1919, English Studies at Cambridge was restricted to the field of modern and medieval languages.[30] In 1927, the Faculty of English was established and with it the independence of English literature as an academic discipline. The first members of the Faculty, however, were drawn from history (Mansfield Forbes), classics (E. M. Tillyard), and philosophy (I. A. Richards). The faculty began with only twelve permanent lecturers, soon adding six probationary faculty lecturers, among them Frank Raymond Leavis.[31]

During these early years, several forces were at play upon the development of English Studies. As mentioned, English was traditionally associated with women and the middle class as the vehicle through which these groups were educated in the English system. In their attempt to establish English as a legitimate academic discipline, the founding scholars at Cambridge worked hard to masculinize and professionalize the study of English literature.[32] The patriotism of the First World War had a major impact on this process. The history of the English language was believed to reflect the history of the English people, and English literature was viewed as the repository of English genius. English literary history, a product of biography, bibliography, and philology, revealed the unified process of national evolution and the natural harmony assumed to exist between "human character, literary quality, and a culture of Englishness."[33] The war also allowed men of various social and economic backgrounds to mingle and to join together in common cause. This interaction had profound effects on English society and directly affected the development of Cambridge English:

> many students . . . were bourgeois rather than upper class and . . . newly returned from the war, older, more independent, with a weight of experience the conventional students were unable to match. The wartime experiences of many had been cataclysmic, and had roused in them a spirit of seriousness and idealism; a need to find point and value in human life and to work actively for a better society. This search, combined with long-held notions about the value of English Studies, invested many of the students of the new subject with an almost religious belief in its value as a civilising, humanizing force outside the confines of the academy.[34]

This wholehearted trust in the humanizing tendencies of literature and culture continued throughout World War II, into the 1960s and 1970s, when Great Britain was in the process of democratizing the tripartite English educational system.[35] Many elites, especially those at Oxford and Cambridge, perceived these educational reforms as an attack on long-standing values and cherished institutions. Concerns about falling academic standards and the declining state of literacy in Great Britain began to dominate debate in the humanities. Led by F. R. Leavis, English dons were desperate to reassert the central importance of the humanities, particularly literature, for the survival of English culture.[36]

This then, is the context into which Steiner contributed his first essay collection, originally published in 1967 and entitled *Language and Silence: Essays on Language, Literature, and the Inhuman*,[37] which begins by stating that the Holocaust:

> puts in question the primary concepts of a literary, humanistic culture. The ultimate of political barbarism grew from the core of Europe. . . . Not only did the general dissemination of literary, cultural values prove no barrier to totalitarianism; but in notable instances the high places of humanistic learning and art actually welcomed and aided the new terror. Barbarism prevailed on the very ground of Christian humanism, of Renaissance culture and classic rationalism. . . . [This] compels us to ask whether

> knowledge of the best that has been thought and said does, as Matthew Arnold asserted, broaden and refine the resources of the human spirit. . . . Assumptions regarding the value of literate culture to the moral perception of the individual and society, [which] were self-evident to Johnson, Coleridge, and Arnold . . . are now in doubt.[38]

Language and Silence works hard to convince Steiner's English colleagues that they too, as members of Western civilization, must wrestle with the meaning of the Holocaust in their evaluation of the function of literature and the humanities. The essay "Humane Literacy" argues this point explicitly, while at the same time acknowledging that such an inquiry is deemed "bizarre or subversive" by many in the English literary establishment. Whoever teaches or interprets literature must, according to Steiner, examine their reasons for doing so and "ask of himself what he is about."[39] After the Holocaust, we can no longer simply assume "the value of literate culture to the moral perception of the individual and society."[40]

In reaction to this crisis, however, Steiner does not abandon culture altogether but calls for a reconstitution of humane literacy. And the literary critic, he writes, is in the uniquely important position to "help us read as total human beings, by example of precision, fear, and delight."[41] As part of this reconstitution, Steiner enters the British debate over the larger purpose of the humanities. *Language and Silence* includes essays that discuss the English concern with maintaining the standards of high literacy under the pressures of contemporary educational reform. Essays like "The Retreat from the Word" and "To Civilize Our Gentlemen" criticize the democratic reforms to British education for their effects on literacy: "Surely there can be no doubt that the access to economic and political power of the semi-educated has brought with it a drastic reduction in the wealth and dignity of speech."[42] Additionally, Steiner argues that the mass media and consumerism in England and the United States are corrosive influences upon the English language, just as Nazism and Soviet communism were on German.[43]

Another possible reason for the malaise in English literature, suggests Steiner, is the unwillingness on the part of its practitioners to wrestle with the "realities of our intellectual and psychological situation."[44] This unwillingness leads Steiner to further discuss the effects of the Holocaust on the humanities. The essay "To Civilize Our Gentlemen" expands his original argument, that the old assumptions about the humanities no longer hold after Auschwitz, to include the suggestion that the literary imagination may actually welcome political bestiality:

> Unlike Matthew Arnold and unlike Dr. Leavis, I find myself unable to assert confidently that the humanities humanize. Indeed, I would go further: it is at least conceivable that the focusing of consciousness on a written text, which is the substance of our training and pursuit, diminishes the sharpness and readiness of our actual moral response. . . . The capacity . . . for moral risk in any human being is not limitless; on the contrary, it can be rapidly absorbed by fictions, and thus the cry in the poem may come to sound louder, more urgent, more real than the cry in the street outside. The death in the novel may move us more potently than the death in the next room. Thus there may be a covert, betraying link between the cultivation of aesthetic response and the potential of personal inhumanity. What then are we doing when we study and teach literature?[45]

Steiner's literary criticism, focused on the Nazi murder of European Jewry, was perceived by those at Cambridge to be a completely bizarre pursuit, based upon a combination of totally unrelated subjects. Steiner admits to being asked by one of his colleagues at Cambridge, who was baffled by Steiner's concerns, "why someone trying to establish himself in an English literature faculty should refer so often to the concentration camps; why they were in any way relevant."[46] Bryan Cheyette is quite right when he states that in general Steiner was "working against the grain: Britain, until recently, didn't think it had a relationship to the Holocaust; its mythology of the war was rooted in the Blitz, Dunkirk, [and] the Battle of Britain."[47] It is also the case that during the 1960s and 1970s there was little public discussion in Britain about the Holocaust in general.

I would argue that Steiner's English colleagues perceived his admonishment of Great Britain after the Holocaust as fundamentally flawed and even quite outrageous given the fact that England was responsible for resisting and finally defeating Nazi Germany, putting an end to Hitler's murderous regime. Within this postwar English mindset, where Nazism was seen as both anti-human and anti-Western, Steiner's generic category of "Western culture" made no sense whatsoever. To implicate England, and English literature, of all things, in a generalized failure of the humanities symbolized by the specific Nazi crimes against the Jewish people was seen as truly peculiar. Still more curious, and infuriating to some, was Steiner's apparent neglect of the Germans in his interrogation of Western culture after the Holocaust. With the exception of his early essay on the nazification of the German language, "The Hollow Miracle," Steiner did not discuss Germany. The Church, high culture, and Western culture are implicated in Steiner's work for their role in the Shoah, but the Germans, the specific culture and history of Germany, are somehow neglected. Instead of interrogating Germanic culture, thought by the British to be the proper context in which to study Hitler's Holocaust, Steiner's work was read as a misguided and irrelevant, yet still offensive, attack on the English and their literary tradition. And this, while Steiner was perceived to be promoting a "Germanic model of criticism" and insisting upon teaching young Cambridge English students the work of Germanic thinkers like Hegel, Marx, and Freud.

There is no question that Steiner alienated himself from the English literary establishment by discussing the Holocaust and its relationship to Western culture at a time when the Jewish experience under Nazism was simply not a topic of discussion in English society or academia. It is here that one can characterize George Steiner as a pioneer. The work he produced at Cambridge during the 1960s asks trenchant questions about the nature of Western culture and the meaning of the humanities, questions that continue to trouble some of us today. Indeed, this important period establishes many of the lifelong concerns of his career as an intellectual.[48]

A Kind of Survivor

The essays in *Language and Silence* reveal Steiner's existential, intellectual, and emotional struggle with the mass murder of European Jewry as the experiences of survivors and the historical facts gradually filter into public consciousness. Like other pioneering scholars, Steiner's interest in the Holocaust develops years after the fact, during the long period of reflection and aftermath in which the Holocaust becomes the historical event we know today. As such, his perceptions change over time, especially those related to the questions of uniqueness, representation, and explicability.

Reading his work on the Holocaust within the larger cross-cultural context of its aftermath allows the reader to recognize Steiner's role as an international interlocutor in the process of discovery, examination, and explanation of the Holocaust.

By the 1960s interest in the Nazi Final Solution was growing, and scholars who had either escaped or survived its devastation began publishing their work on the subject. Theodor Adorno returned to Germany after the war and was by this time speaking publicly about the mass murder of European Jewry.[49] Hannah Arendt stayed in the United States after World War II and covered the Eichmann Trial of 1961 for the *New Yorker,* later published as *Eichmann in Jerusalem* in 1963.[50] By the mid-sixties, the personal accounts of Viktor Frankl, Elie Wiesel, Primo Levi, and Bruno Bettelheim, all Jews who survived the Nazi occupation of Europe, had been translated into English.[51] *The Diary of Anne Frank* had been translated into many languages, and the work of pioneering scholars such as Léon Poliakov, Gerald Reitlinger, Alan Bullock, Raul Hilberg, Fritz Stern, Stanley Milgram, George Mosse, and Richard L. Rubenstein was published.[52] To accommodate this growing interest in the mass murder of European Jewry, as reflected by a burgeoning scholarly literature, the Library of Congress adopted a subject heading for the Holocaust in 1968. Beginning in the early 1950s and continuing through the 1960s, Holocaust-related institutions and events were publicized by governments and the media: *Yad Vashem,* the Holocaust Martyrs' and Heroes' Remembrance Authority, was established by the State of Israel in 1953; the first death camp trials began in Germany in 1963;[53] in 1964, Rolf Hochhuth's play *The Deputy,* about Pius XII's silence during the war, appeared on Broadway; and Vatican II released *Nostra Aetate* in 1965, which condemned antisemitism and absolved the Jewish people as a group of the charge of deicide.

As discussed in the introduction, the question of when, how, and why the Holocaust enters public consciousness is currently a growing area of investigation, still in its early stages.[54] In Steiner's case, the reasons are both personal and intellectual, and the two are related. The basic biographical facts, wherein he and his family escaped soon-to-be-occupied France in January 1940, and lost family members and friends to the Holocaust, combine with the aforementioned Holocaust-related cultural developments taking place in Western societies throughout the 1950s and 1960s to produce in him an ever-increasing awareness of, and concern with, the Holocaust.[55] Unlike most critics in the English-speaking world during this time, Steiner is particularly sensitive, and open, to these international developments for three major reasons: his personal relationship to the Holocaust; his interest in the work of central European Jews like Theodor Adorno and Hannah Arendt who deal with the subject of the Holocaust early and explicitly; and, his multilingual and multicultural range by which he was exposed to Holocaust-related events and material produced outside England and the United States. Like his father before him in 1930s France, few of Steiner's colleagues, especially those personally untouched by the Holocaust, shared or even understood his concerns during this period. In the larger societies in which Steiner moved, particularly Great Britain, the public would have to "catch up" to Steiner before his work on these questions would truly resonate in any meaningful way. Ironically, in England at least, his pioneering work on questions related to the Holocaust injected the subject into public discourse and thereby helped bring it into British consciousness.

Steiner admits to becoming engrossed with thoughts about his own survival and that of his immediate family during the early sixties. Some of his writings, which he characterizes as "stagings of ideas,"[56] begin to deal with the guilt he feels for living comfortably in New York during the war. Steiner published a collection of short stories in 1964, entitled *Anno Domini: Three Stories of the War*, which explore his interest in the Holocaust and his strange feelings of envy for those who were there.[57] One story, "Cake," involves a Harvard doctoral student who finds himself in Paris as World War II breaks out. All around him, Jews are harassed and tortured but all he can feel toward them is envy:

> But my envy grew like a cancer. It made my very soul itch. Looking back on that time (and nothing in my life has been more vivid) . . . I wanted to be that man. I cried out in the prim solitude for those heavy blows. . . . The military were beginning to put up placards with the names and pictures of those executed. I stood before them in mournful lust. I memorized their features and relived, in the privacy of my room, what I could conceive of the obscene torment of their several deaths. I envied them crazily. . . . It seemed

> to me a deprivation, the omission of a rare chance, that I should not have visited on my own flesh and nerve the hideous contrivances they had experienced. We live at the airy top of the spiral staircase of our inward; only the great fears and pains can force us to the long descent. Yet who has not been in the well of his being, in the foul lightless place, has taken no journey. Not to know how you will behave when you are strung on the bench and they walk towards you with their gloves, is to know little. It is to live with yourself as spinsters do, in the brittle familiarity of mere acquaintance.[58]

Steiner is in a complicated position. He missed the event that comes to define his adult life, work, and identity as a Jew, but had he been in Paris during the Nazi occupation he would likely have perished: "Of the Jewish boys and girls in my school class and circle, two have survived (of whom I am one). The unmerited scandal of this survival, the pathological bent toward some immediate sharing of their hideous fate (how would I have behaved, how abject would my fears have been?) is with me always. It is inherent in my sense of lamed self and of my assignment. Which is that of 'remembrancer' . . . of one who learns by heart in order to hand on what would otherwise be ash."[59]

One might ask, what is the relationship between someone like Steiner, a Jewish child whose family escaped the Nazi assault and lived comfortably in New York City during the war, and the Holocaust? The answer to this question goes to the heart of Steiner's Jewish identity and his dedicated attempt to become a remembrancer. In 1965, Steiner published an essay in *Commentary* entitled "A Kind of Survivor" and dedicated it to Elie Wiesel. The essay, included in *Language and Silence,* is an intimate portrait of Steiner's Jewish identity as he understands it and also appears to be a response to questions about his reluctance to settle in Israel. He begins by explaining that although he escaped the Holocaust by "an accident of good fortune," he is still a product of this catastrophe: "But in another sense, I am a survivor, and not intact. If I am often out of touch with my own generation, if that which haunts me and controls my habits of feeling strikes many of those I should be intimate and working with in my present world as remotely sinister and artificial, it is because the black mystery of what happened in Europe is to me indivisible from my own identity. Precisely because I was not there, because an accident of good fortune struck my name from the roll."[60]

The Holocaust forces Steiner to reexamine his Jewish identity. Neither a religious man nor a Zionist, George Steiner is a Jew because his parents are Jews, and he believes this heritage "puts on [the backs of his own children] a burden of ancient loathing and set[s] savagery at their heels."[61] The threat of anti-Jewish violence and the fear that accompanies it, termed by Steiner "the darkness we carry," unifies the Jewish people and brings Steiner into the fold.

The last half of the essay stakes out Steiner's Jewish identity by introducing his conception of "Central European Judaism" and discussing his personal relationship to it. Somewhat defensively, he defines himself against Jewish orthodoxy, Israeli Zionism, and what he calls American Jewish conservatism, arguing, "That which has been destroyed . . . embodied a particular genius, a quality of intelligence and feeling which none of the major Jewish communities now surviving has preserved or recaptured. Because I feel that specific inheritance urgent in my own reflexes, in the work I try to do, I am a kind of survivor."[62] George Steiner is a "kind of survivor" in two senses: he is a European Jew who escaped death in the Holocaust, and he is also one of the last representatives of the central European Jewish world destroyed by the Shoah. Steiner is vocal about his independent status as an outsider in both academe and the contemporary Jewish world. Even though he grew up in the United States, Steiner does not identify as an American nor does he identify with the concerns of American Jewry. His Judaism, annihilated by Nazism and Stalinism, is that of his father, "Central European Judaism":

> They had a quick way with languages. . . . The habits of reference of this European Jewish generation often point to the Greek and Latin classics; but these were seen through the special focus of Winckelmann, Lessing, and Goethe. . . . The Central European Jewish bourgeoisie was frequently intimate with the plays of Shakespeare . . . It read Balzac and Stendhal . . . Tolstoy, Ibsen, and Zola. . . . Jewish taste, in the guise of dealer, patron, and critic, backed Impressionism and the blaze of the modern. . . . In its golden period, from 1870 to 1914, then again in the 1920's, the Jewish leaven gave to Prague and Berlin, to Vienna and Paris a specific vitality of feeling and expression, an atmosphere both quintessentially European and "off-center."[63]

Steiner associates himself with a wide range of central European Jewish intellectuals by identifying himself as a surviving son, the next generation, as it were, of the culture that produced these brilliant individuals. This self-definition presents Steiner with a momentous challenge. The impressive line of assimilated Jewish intellectuals of central European ancestry he claims to represent includes some of the most important writers and thinkers of the nineteenth and twentieth centuries: Marx, Freud, Einstein, Kafka, Wittgenstein, Hofmannsthal, Benjamin, Lévi Strauss, Adorno, and Arendt. Steiner maintains that this esteemed group of people and their common practice of what he terms "radical humanism" provides his sense of vocation. And more important, he shares the specific concerns of the Jewish intellectuals who escaped Nazi Europe. In particular, the work of Hannah Arendt, Theodor Adorno, and Claude Lévi Strauss is "indispensable to [his] understanding of the philosophic, political, aesthetic roots of the inhuman; of the paradox that modern barbarism sprang, in some intimate, perhaps necessary way, from the very core and locale of humanistic civilization."[64]

In a review of Steiner's *Language and Silence,* Theodore Solotaroff suggests that Steiner's passionate identification with this "pantheon of modern genius" "means to Steiner, I think, to stand in a deep sense for the whole generation of his peers—these children who did not survive, who left this great tradition bereft of its natural protégés, who make such a haunting absence today in the life of the European mind."[65]

George Steiner *does* feel obligated to both memorialize and continue this intellectual tradition annihilated in its prime. He states his purpose unambiguously: "I am a remembrancer. At the centre of my work is an attempt to come *after* the Shoah, culturally, philosophically, in a literary sense: to be somewhere around with all the shadows and the ghosts and the ash, which are so enormous here. . . . There should be a few impractical Jews left in the great shadow world of Europe who at least remember what the civilization here was."[66] Steiner is not however simply engaged in memorializing this lost world; his work is also an act of *resuscitation.* Since the Holocaust, many have questioned the nature of the Jewish encounter with European culture, especially that of the so-called German Jewish symbiosis.[67] Some have criticized German Jews for not recognizing the hostility radiating toward them, while others deny that any productive exchange occurred at all. Opposing these criticisms, Steiner's conception of "Central European Judaism" reinvests this discredited dialogue with meaning. Instead of ridiculing or judging Jews engaged in dialogue with European culture, Steiner models his very conceptions of Judaism and humanism entirely upon their example.

In "A Kind of Survivor" Steiner introduces his critique of nationalism and his view of Jewish homelessness as the secret strength of Judaism. While acknowledging the historically imposed nature of Jewish exile, he argues that it may have an exemplary role to play in modern history: "to show that whereas trees have roots, men have legs and are each other's guests."[68] Here Steiner suggests that the Jewish people may have a special obligation to humanity when it comes to nationalism, arguing, "When a Jew opposes the parochial ferocity into which nationalism so easily (inevitably) degenerates, he is paying an old debt. By one of the cruel, deep ironies of history, the concept of a chosen people, of a nation exalted above others by particular destiny, was born in Israel."[69] He then suggests that National Socialism modeled itself upon this Jewish precedent: "In the vocabulary of Nazism there were elements of a vengeful parody on the Judaic claim. The theological motif of a people elected at Sinai is echoed in the pretence of the master race and its chiliastic domination. Thus there was in the obsessed relation of Nazi to Jew a minute but fearful grain of logic."[70] This argument is not pursued by Steiner in subsequent writings although, as we shall see in the next chapter, it does reappear as part of Hitler's speech in *The Portage to San Cristóbal of A.H.*

The first essay in which Steiner addresses the Holocaust at length is "Postscript," which was first published in 1966 and later included in *Language and Silence.* This essay relates Steiner's recent reading of two books about the Holocaust, *Scroll of Agony: The Warsaw Diary of Chaim Kaplan* and Jean François Steiner's *Treblinka,* which both reveal the sadistic and sordid behavior of the Nazis in great detail. Feelings of outrage and utter disgust are palpable in Steiner's response to these texts, and it is here that he begins to identify explicitly with the victims of the Holocaust. Clearly, the individuals described in these texts are no different from the people found in his own family: "At a previous point in rational time, Professor Mehring was sitting in his study, speaking to his children, reading books, passing his hand over a white tablecloth on Friday evening. And flayed alive, 'blood splashing slowly from his hair,' Langner was . . . the same human being who had, a year earlier . . . walked the daylight street, done business, looked forward to a good meal, read an intellectual monthly."[71] Steiner admits to feeling guilty about the good fortune of his family to have survived in such a normal environment when children his age suffered deportation and murder in Europe. "A Kind of Survivor" told us in dramatic terms that it was "[d]ue to [his] father's foresight . . . [that he] happened not to be there when the names were called out. [He] did not stand in the public square with the other children, those [he] had grown up with. Or see [his] father and mother disappear when the train doors were torn open."[72] A sense of guilty association is laid bare in "Postscript":

> One of the things I cannot grasp, though I have often written about them, trying to get them into some kind of bearable perspective, is the time relation. . . . Precisely at the same hour in which Mehring or Langner were being done to death, the overwhelming plurality of human beings, two miles away on the Polish farms, *five thousand miles away in New York,* were sleeping and eating or going to a film or making love or worrying about the dentist. This is where my imagination balks. The two orders of simultaneous experience are so different, so irreconcilable to any common norm of human values, their coexistence is so hideous a paradox—Treblinka *is* both because some men have built it and almost all other men let it be—that I puzzle over time. (Italics mine)[73]

At this point in time, Steiner has difficulty accepting the fact that his life in Manhattan, between the ages of eleven and sixteen, was lived "as if on another planet" compared with that of European Jewry as a whole. He asserts that we must discover the relation between these two experiences to "locate . . . the measure of unknowing, indifference, complicity, commission which relates the contemporary or survivor to the slain."[74] In this passage, Steiner includes himself among those who, at the time, were ignorant, complicit, or indifferent to the fate of Europe's Jews. Concluding the essay on a personal note, he realizes that while other children suffered, "[he] was fed, beyond [his] need, and slept warm, and was silent."[75]

"Postscript" conveys Steiner's frustration and anger over the Holocaust and the inordinate amount of suffering it forced upon millions of innocent people with whom he personally identifies. The finger of judgment is pointed in several directions. The contemporary world, and its reaction to the Shoah, frustrates Steiner: "We who come after are shrill and discomfort each other with claims of anger or impartial perception. Monsieur Poliakov speaks of the successive 'scandals' which attend all books on the murder of the Jews from Schwarz-Bart's *The Last of the Just* to Hochhuth's *The Deputy* and now *Treblinka*. Silence during the murder, but scandal over the books."[76] Hannah Arendt's thesis on the failure of Jews to violently resist the Nazis is the result, according to Steiner, of her own failure to imagine the living conditions of unarmed, starving Jews. He concludes that this failure of imagination leads her to ask "a radically indecent question."[77] Steiner chastises the non-Jewish world for the failure of Western governments to bomb the Nazi death camps and railway lines and for failing to save Jewish children during the 1930s. The Poles and Ukrainians are highlighted specifically for their enthusiastic cooperation with the Nazis and their collaboration against Jews. In dramatic opposition to his earlier assertion, that "indifference yields no malice, and vessels gliding past one another in the night exchange neither shot nor salutation,"[78] the silence of Christianity and Western civilization, Steiner now charges, "makes all who were indifferent accomplice to the Nazis."[79]

In this essay, Steiner refers to the work of Holocaust historians for the first time, stating that although historians have done a vast amount of work, certain questions "remain obscure or unanswered."[80] Chaim Kaplan, the author of the diary discussed here, is celebrated for his "utopian commitment to reason and historical analysis."[81] Kaplan's attempt to try to understand and explain the events of the Holocaust "without exaggerations and distortions," with extreme precision and honesty, admitting even moments of humanity he witnessed on the part of the Germans, is according to Steiner a model for how we are to proceed in our confrontation with the Holocaust.[82]

Why are we to continue reading these "literally unbearable records?" Steiner asks. He tells us it is so that we make ourselves aware that the "solution" was not "final" but "spills over into our present lives."[83] Jews must become cognizant of the degree to which, after the Holocaust, "everything is possible, that starting next Monday morning at, say, 11:20 a.m. time can change for oneself and one's children and drop out of humanity."[84] The drive to annihilate the Jewish people has survived Nazism, and this fact forces

Steiner to try to understand the phenomenon of antisemitism. Steiner tells us here that there are elements of antisemitism "deeper than sociology or economics or even historical superstition. The Jew sticks like a bone in the throat of any other nationalism."[85] Referring to Kaplan, Steiner writes, "He knew what not very many, as yet, are prepared to see plainly: that Nazi anti-Semitism is the logical culmination of the millennial Christian vision and teaching of the Jew as killer of God."[86] As we shall see, this idea becomes central to Steiner's attempt to explain the phenomenon of antisemitism.

Holocaust Representation

In the late sixties, Steiner begins to assert that if we are to understand the Holocaust it must be in terms of its own unique history and characteristics, rather than as another general example of human evil. By comparing two reviews Steiner wrote on the poetry of Sylvia Plath, this major shift in perception becomes apparent. In 1965, Steiner praised Plath's poetry, calling "Daddy" "one of the very few poems I know of in any language to come near the last horror. It achieves the classic act of generalization, translating a private, obviously intolerable hurt into a code of plain statement, of instantaneously public images which concern us all."[87] He goes so far as to call "Daddy" the "'Guernica' of modern poetry" and salutes Sylvia Plath's "desperate integrity" as "only one of a number of young contemporary poets, novelists, and playwrights, themselves in no way implicated in the actual holocaust, who have done most to counter the general inclination to forget the death camps."[88] Steiner then wonders aloud if it is only those, like Plath, "who had no part in the events who *can* focus on them rationally and imaginatively; to those who experienced the thing, it has lost the hard edges of possibility, it has stepped outside the real."[89]

Four years later, in 1969, Steiner returned to these same poems, published under the title *Ariel* in 1965, except now he asks provocatively, "What extra-territorial right had Sylvia Plath—she was a child, plump and golden in America, when the trains actually went—to draw on the reserves of animate horror in the ash and the children's shoes? . . . Do any of us have license to locate our personal disasters, raw as these may be, in Auschwitz?"[90] He goes on to state, "Sylvia Plath was not a Jew. So far as I know, she had no personal connections with the holocaust. But Daddy became a 'panzer-man', the swastika replaced the sky, and the poet rode the death-cars to the ovens. I am not concerned with the private, domestic agonies which may have triggered this black piece of mimicry."[91] How do we account for such a distinct change in Steiner's attitude and perception within the span of only four years?

It appears that between 1965 and 1969, Steiner moves from feelings of respect and gratitude for a non-Jewish poet's interest in the Holocaust to a feeling of resentment for this same poet's use of Holocaust imagery. Steiner is offended by the same poems four years later for what he feels is their appropriation, not memorialization, of the Holocaust experience. Sylvia Plath is now seen as an artist who appropriates the horrific imagery of the Holocaust and uses it in her poetry in an attempt to express her own feelings of victimization, thereby dissolving the specificity of the Holocaust into general human experience. In subsequent years, Steiner defends artists, like William Styron for instance,[92] who attempt a meaningful approximation of the Shoah experience itself; however, he maintains that it is wholly inappropriate to use the horror of the Holocaust as a metaphor to communicate something unrelated to it (as Plath is believed to do in her poetry). This position is consistent with Steiner's rejection of an abstract universalism that subsumes the specificity of the Holocaust.

The Holocaust, Antisemitism, and Western Culture

Steiner first sets out an explicit understanding of the specific nature of the Holocaust and antisemitism in his *T. S. Eliot Memorial Lectures* for 1970, which he delivered at the University of Kent at Canterbury and published under the title *In Bluebeard's Castle: Some Notes Towards the Redefinition of Culture*. The first lecture, entitled "The Great Ennui," discusses the origins of the inhuman and the crises experienced by Europe in the twentieth century as rooted in the "long peace" of its nineteenth century (1815–1915). The second lecture, entitled "A Season in Hell," begins with the following declaration: "Much of my work has concerned itself, directly or indirectly, with trying to understand, to articulate, causal and teleological aspects of the holocaust. My own feelings are patently implicated. But so is the conviction that an analysis of the idea and ideal of culture demands the fullest possible understanding of the phenomenology of mass murder as it took place in Europe, from the Spanish south to the frontiers of Russian Asia between

1936 and 1945."[93] Given the hostility in England directed toward Steiner's interests, it is possible that his replacement of the Holocaust (as of 1971 the word is still not capitalized in Steiner's work) with a more inclusive concept of mass murder from Spain to Russia between 1936 and 1945 is an attempt to appeal to the interests of his English audience and bridge the gap between them. It is soon made clear however that the central focus of Steiner's concern in these lectures is the murder of European Jewry, not the Spanish Civil War, the Nazi occupation of Europe, or Stalin's great purges.

Steiner opened the lecture series by referring to T. S. Eliot's *Notes Towards a Definition of Culture*,[94] which Steiner's subtitle echoes, in the following terms: "Not an attractive book. One that is gray with the recent shock of barbarism, but a barbarism whose actual sources and forms the argument leaves fastidiously vague."[95] In the early moments of the second lecture, Steiner admits to finding Eliot's failure to face the issue in this respected text on culture "acutely disturbing."[96] He asks, "How, only three years after the event, after the publication to the world of facts and pictures that have surely, altered our sense of the limits of human behavior, was it possible to write a book on culture and say nothing?"[97] To his British Christian audience, Steiner bravely asserts that the mass murder of European Jewry puts "in question the very nature of Christianity and . . . its role in European history."[98] How, then, he asks, was it possible for Eliot "to detail and plead for a Christian order" after the Holocaust?[99] One explanation for Eliot's apparent lack of concern for the fate of Europe's Jews, Steiner suggests, rather gingerly, is related to the "ambiguities on the theme of the Jew in Eliot's poetry and thought."[100]

In spite of this failure, however, Steiner is convinced by the basic argument of Eliot's text, which is his "insistence on the religious character of genuine civilization, and his 'conception of culture and religion as being, when each term is taken in the right context, different aspects of the same thing.'"[101] However, Steiner also believes that the Holocaust must be set within the framework of the psychology of religion, and that "an understanding of this framework is vital to an argument on culture."[102] Given Eliot's religious definition of culture, and Steiner's understanding of the religious foundations of the Holocaust (as laid out in this lecture series), one can see how Steiner interprets Eliot's neglect of the Holocaust, in a book that attempts to define culture, as a fatal error in conception and analysis. And so, Steiner attempts to compose his own "notes towards the *re*-definition of culture."

Steiner begins by explaining to his English colleagues his own conception of the Holocaust. Stating that the mass murder of European Jewry "was not the result of merely individual pathology or of the neuroses of one nation-state" nor "some monstrous accident of modern social history,"[103] Steiner tells his audience that the Holocaust is neither a German phenomenon, as the British believe, nor simply the brainchild of Adolf Hitler. The Holocaust differs from other massacres in human history; it is unique "at the level of philosophic intent" and this intent "takes us to the heart of certain instabilities in the fabric of Western culture, in the relations between instinctual and religious life."[104] It is then a phenomenon of Western culture, specifically the religious foundations of the West, and therefore has a direct connection to Great Britain as well. One of the underlying appeals Steiner makes in this lecture series is for his English colleagues to engage with the Holocaust and to wrestle with the crisis of conscience it creates for all people touched by the Western religious and cultural heritage. At this time, in this specific national context, in which Steiner consciously remains an outsider, his questions and concerns are unique, uncomfortable for many, offensive to some, and incomprehensible still to others.

Ultimately, Steiner interprets the Holocaust as a "reflex . . . of natural sensory consciousness, of instinctual polytheistic and animistic needs," resulting from what he terms *the blackmail of transcendence*, the unrelenting demands of morality imposed by the Jews upon humanity.[105] His second lecture, entitled "A Season in Hell," outlines the unique nature and specific dynamics of antisemitism, which delineate the Shoah and separate it from other acts of atrocity in human history. According to Steiner, the Jewish people are responsible for creating three separate systems of human perfectibility by which they are perceived to blackmail humanity: Mosaic monotheism, Christianity, and Marxism. All three paradigms place stringent moral demands, and a psychologically unrealistic imperative of perfection, upon humanity. Jewish ethical demands, which flow from these three systems, are beyond the grasp of humanity and the psychic stress produced by this failure eventually leads to resentment and hatred for the people responsible for it. This antagonistic process, forced upon the world by the Jews,[106] is *the blackmail of transcendence:* "'Surmount yourself. Surpass the opaque barriers of the mind to attain pure abstraction. Lose your life in order to gain it. Give up property, rank, worldly comfort. Love your neighbor as you do yourself—no, much more, for self-love is sin. Make any sacrifice, endure any assault, even self-denunciation, so that justice may prevail.' Unceasingly, the blackmail of perfection has hammered at the confused, mundane, egotistical fabric of common, instinctual behaviour."[107] Steiner argues that monotheism "tore up the human psyche by its most ancient roots"[108] by replacing polytheism, which allowed for a diversity of human belief and easy ritual practice in which the gods were a consistent and tangible presence in our lives, with one supreme God who is all powerful, all knowing, judgmental, and demanding, yet absent from the daily lives of human beings. The Jewish God forbids the pronunciation of His name and any representations of His image. In this context, Steiner quotes Nietzsche, who argued that monotheism was "the most monstrous of all human errors" because it destroyed polytheism, which freed the human spirit and celebrated diversity.[109] Freud also understood the problems that attend the birth of monotheism, suggests Steiner, by shifting its creation from the Jews to the Egyptians in his famous work *Moses and Monotheism.* Steiner reads this text as Freud's unconscious attempt to "wrench the lightening rod out of the hands of the Jewish people" during the first years of Nazi rule.[110]

Christianity continues to blackmail humanity with the claims of the ideal.[111] The Sermon on the Mount and the parables of Jesus demand that human beings "make [themselves] new, and in so doing stifle the elemental desires, weaknesses, and claims of the ego . . . By their simple presence, at every occasion of Christian worship, these fantastic moral requirements mock and undermine mundane values."[112] Marxism, the final stage in Steiner's theory of antisemitism, transforms the prophetic rage against injustice into "the socialist vision of the destruction of the bourgeois Gomorrah and the creation of a new, clean city for man."[113] This unrelenting dialectic between moral demands and human inadequacy creates a "profound unbalance at the pivot of Western culture, a corrosive pressure on the subconscious" that results in deep loathing for the Jewish people as the inventors of God and His Law.[114] Steiner argues that the Jew is the "bad conscience" of Western man who "[keeps] alive and visible" the "abandonments of spiritual and moral perfection, the hypocrisies of an established, mundane religiosity, [and] the Absences of a disappointed, potentially vengeful God."[115]

It is this enduring animosity, according to Steiner, that motivates the Nazi desire to exterminate the Jewish people, and it also accounts in his view for the indifference to Jewish suffering felt by so many others. In this sense, the Holocaust is an attempt to kill those who not only murdered God but who first created Him: "Deep loathings built up in the social subconscious, murderous resentments. The mechanism is simple but primordial. *We hate most those who hold out to us a goal, an ideal, a visionary promise which, even though we have stretched our muscles to the utmost, we cannot reach, which slips, again and again, just out of range of our racked fingers—yet, and this is crucial, which remains profoundly desirable, which we cannot reject because we fully acknowledge its supreme value.*"[116] The Holocaust, then, is a revolt against the pressures of morality, a reversion to the base instincts of natural man:

> The genocide that took place in Europe and the Soviet Union during the period 1936–45 . . . was far more than a political tactic, an eruption of lower-middle-class malaise, or a product of declining capitalism. It was no mere secular, socio-economic phenomenon. It enacted a suicidal impulse in Western civilization. It was an attempt to level the future—or, more precisely, to make history commensurate with the natural savageries, intellectual torpor, and material instincts of unextended man. Using theological metaphors, and there is no need to apologize for them in an essay on culture, the holocaust may be said to mark a second Fall. We can interpret it as a voluntary exit from the Garden and a programmatic attempt to burn the Garden behind us. Lest its remembrance continue to infect the health of barbarism with debilitating dreams or with remorse.[117]

One may wonder why this reversion happens in the middle of the twentieth century. Steiner's answer is twofold. The primary explanation deals specifically with Nazism, and explains the phenomenon as a vicious chapter in the ongoing attempt of Western culture to divorce itself from religion. This reflects *the blackmail of transcendence,* the process by which Steiner sees humanity resisting the imposition of Jewish ethics in the forms of monotheism and Christianity. In Nazism, Steiner argues, "an extinct theology is at work . . . [whose] slow, incomplete death has produced surrogate, parodistic forms.

The epilogue to belief, the passage of religious belief into hollow convention, seems to be a more dangerous process than the philosophes anticipated. The structures of decay are toxic."[118] Here, Steiner directly relates *L'univers concentrationnaire* to the Christian conception of Hell by asserting that the *Arschloch der Welt,*[119] "that hideously exact and allegoric German term for Auschwitz and Treblinka . . . is *Hell made immanent.*"[120] He believes that post-Christian culture continues to need Hell, a place that has gripped the Christian European imagination for centuries, so it learned "to build and run it on earth. A few miles from Goethe's Weimar or on the isles of Greece."[121] And it is through our locating "Hell above ground, [that] we have passed out of the major order and symmetries of Western civilization."[122]

The second part of Steiner's explanation focuses on the broader origins of this voluntary exit from civilization, and locates them in Europe's *long summer of 1815–1915,* during which bourgeois high culture hit its zenith of humane literacy. In his first lecture, "The Great Ennui," Steiner argues that "this hundred years' peace . . . established the criteria of culture which have, until very recently, been ours."[123] During this time, human hopes were embodied by the rational and progressive humanism of the Enlightenment. Rationalism and human reason were to replace the violent tribalism and superstitious persecution associated with religion. The French Revolution and the Napoleonic period inaugurated:

> an overwhelming immanence, a deep, emotionally stressed change in the quality of hope. Expectations of progress, of personal and social enfranchisement, which had formerly had a conventional, often allegoric character, as of a millenary horizon, suddenly moved very close. The great metaphor of renewal, of the creation, as by a second coming of secular grace, of a just, rational city for man, took on the urgent drama of concrete possibility. The eternal "tomorrow" of utopian political vision became, as it were, Monday morning. . . . The crowning statement, perhaps, is to be found in Marx's economic and political manuscripts of 1844. Not since early Christianity had men felt so near to renovation and to the end of night.[124]

But alongside these humane hopes for the European future, argues Steiner, there existed a vast reservoir of frustration and ennui[125] resulting from the failure of real revolutionary change:

> What followed was, of course, a long spell of reaction and stasis. Depending on one's political idiom, one can see it either as a century of repression by a bourgeoisie that had turned the French Revolution and the Napoleonic extravaganza to its own economic advantage, or as a hundred years of liberal gradualism and civilized order. . . . The collapse of revolutionary hopes after 1815, the brutal deceleration of time and radical expectation, left a reservoir of unused, turbulent energies. . . . the economic-industrial growth released by continental war and the centralized consciousness of the new nation-states took place exponentially. . . . It is in the early and mid-nineteenth century that occur both the dehumanization of laboring men and women in the assembly-line system, and the dissociation between ordinary educated sensibility and the increasingly complex, technological artifacts of daily life. . . . The conjunction of extreme economic-technical dynamism with a large measure of enforced social immobility, a conjunction on which a century of liberal, bourgeois civilization was built, made for an explosive mixture.[126]

By 1900 Europe was dominated by a gray bourgeois culture and middle-class ideals of respectability, which Steiner argues nurtured a frustrated feeling of stasis and eventually resulted in a unanimous thirst for war and destruction. Referring to Freud's conception of the death wish, Steiner is convinced by Freud's "portrayal of the tensions which civilized manners impose on central, unfulfilled human instincts."[127] Just as in *the blackmail of transcendence,* the base instincts of humanity reveal themselves here in a "perverse longing . . . or itch for chaos . . . and violent dissolution."[128] European society, according to Steiner, squandered its utopia by succumbing to the suicidal impulse inherent in culture itself. Steiner concludes that the unprecedented killing and destruction unleashed by the First World War conditioned Europe for the methodical massacre of World War II. The difference was, however, that "what had been miscalculation and uncontrollable mishap during the first World War became method during the second."[129]

The Problem of Secularized Culture

As we have seen in *Tolstoy or Dostoevsky* and *In Bluebeard's Castle,* Steiner locates both aesthetic inspiration and ethical behavior in the sacred demands of the Western religious tradition. The rejection of religious belief and the process of secularization in Western culture, seen by Steiner to be extensions of *the blackmail of transcendence,* do not result in our liberation from violence and superstition as promised by the philosophes of the Enlightenment. Instead, the absence of formal religion creates a feeling of emptiness in the lives of people, a void of meaning and purpose, which they attempt to fill with secular imitations. Steiner's Massey Lectures, delivered on CBC Radio in 1974 and published that same year as *Nostalgia for the Absolute,*[130] argue that Marxism; Freudian psychoanalysis; Lévi Straussian anthropology; and the irrational fads of astrology, occultism, and Orientalism should be understood as attempts to fill the void left by the waning of formal religious systems in Western culture. Specifically, Steiner argues, "the decay of a comprehensive Christian doctrine had left in disorder, or had left blank, essential perceptions of social justice, of the meaning of human history, of the relations between mind and body, of the place of knowledge in our moral conduct."[131] The "meta-religions," "surrogate creeds," or "substitute theologies" of Marx, Freud, and Lévi Strauss all claim to explain the totality of human history, including theories of the future and the meaning of life, offering adherents "a complete picture of 'man in the world.'"[132] Even though these systems of belief may be hostile toward religion and deny the existence of God and an afterlife, Steiner argues that their "structure, . . . aspirations, [and] . . . claims on the believer, are profoundly religious in strategy and in effect."[133] Steiner believes the waning of Western religion and its moral certitude creates a "deep-seated nostalgia for the absolute."[134] The attraction people have for these surrogate creeds demonstrates the human hunger for mythology and our need for something to explain the world and our place within it.

The fact that Marx, Freud, and Lévi Strauss all share Jewish ancestry, while at the same time having very different relationships and attitudes toward this heritage, is of significance for Steiner. He argues that Judaism influences Marx's prophetic rage and faith in logical history; Freud's intellectuality, severe ethicism, and trust in the power of language; and Lévi Strauss's biblical sense of retribution for our failure to observe our "contractual responsibilities to creation."[135] For Steiner, Marxism, Freudian psychoanalysis, and Lévi Straussian anthropology are Jewish attempts to "replace a dying Christianity," and are all manifestations of *the blackmail of transcendence,* although ones that impose a secularized variation of Jewish ethics.

Like any religion, Steiner tells us, Marxism has its prophet, apostles, and canonic texts, its own emblems, legends, and language. It demands total commitment, offers a complete explanation of man's function and history in the world, and "offers a contract of messianic promise concerning the future."[136] In an attempt to understand the barbarism that has occurred when Marxism has been put into practice, Steiner explains that the Marxist dream for the future is dependent upon a period of class conflict that eventually transforms itself into a utopian society. Steiner believes this secular messianic doctrine allows people to tolerate inhuman treatment and conditions as a difficult but temporary part of the emancipatory process:

> surely one of the clues to the mystery of why it should be that many of the most valuable young men and women in past generations, in the face of the most overwhelming evidence about the concentration camps, about perhaps the most brutal police state ever established, about the Asiatic Caesarism of Stalin, nevertheless continued to serve, to believe, and to die. If one wishes to understand the phenomenon of this kind of behaviour, it can only be in the light of a religious and messianic vision, of the great promise which says you shall wade through hell up to your eyeballs if necessary because you are on the destined, the prophetic way to the resurrection of man in the kingdom of justice. It is just because the millenarian scenario of the redemption of man and of the establishment of the kingdom of justice on earth continues to grip the human spirit (having long survived its theological premises), that every experiment in hope fires the imagination far beyond the political facts.[137]

Steiner concludes his lecture on Marx by characterizing Marxism as a failure. It has failed in its explanation of the human condition; it has been proven wrong in its view of the "pauperization of the working class" and the imminent collapse of capitalism; and its promised future is now seen to be only an illusion. "So, [Steiner writes,] on grounds of prophecy as well as on grounds of history, it has failed. Worse, where it is in power it has not brought liberation but bureaucratic terror. . . . Marxism, too, is beginning to look today like one of the great, empty churches."[138]

Freudian psychoanalysis is also a surrogate for Christianity, according to Steiner, who interprets Freud's work as an attempt to "remove from the human psyche the infantile illusions . . . of religion" and to "reconcile man to a godless reality" in a post-Christian world.[139] Like Marx, Freud also conceived of his psychological philosophy as scientific in nature. Steiner argues that Freud desperately hoped to be able to prove that the existence of key concepts such as the libido, the castration complex, and the id was based upon clinical biological evidence. "No such clinical, experimental confirmation has been forthcoming," and Steiner argues that this fact demonstrates the "essential tragedy of the Freudian enterprise."[140] And as far as banishing "the archaic shadows of irrationalism, of faith in the supernatural," Freud's goal remains out of reach.[141] However, Freudian models and concepts, classifications and categories, are still valued by Steiner as "inspired readings of, and projections from, the very special economic, familial, sexual conditions of bourgeois existence in central and western Europe between . . . the 1880s and the 1920s."[142] The truths provided by the Freudian enterprise are not scientific, but are "of an intuitive, aesthetic order such as we find in philosophy and in literature" and are equally valuable.

What interests Steiner about the work of Claude Lévi Strauss is his view of Western culture as the destroyer of natural humanity. The central polarity of human existence is that of nature and culture according to Lévi Strauss. Humanity is a "divided composite of biological and socially-culturally acquired elements [and it] is the interplay between biological constraints on the one hand, and social-cultural variables on the other, which determines our condition."[143] Lévi Strauss charges the Western white man with the destruction of other peoples through military conquest, economic exploitation, religious proselytization, and the continued devastation of the natural environment we all share. He argues that the barbarism of the twentieth century is simply an extension of this "murderous treatment of ecology," which will inevitably result in the extinction of humanity.[144] Steiner recognizes the paradox between Western humanism and barbarism as it echoes in the work of Lévi Strauss:

> The notion of travelling to far places in order to study alien peoples and cultures, is unique to Western man; it springs from the predatory genius

> of the Greeks; no primitive peoples have ever come to study us. This is, on the one hand, a disinterested, intellectually inspired impulse. It is one of our glories. But it is, on the other, part and parcel of exploitation. . . . The Western obsession with inquiry, with analysis, with the classification of all living forms, is itself a mode of subjugation, of psychological and technical mastery. Fatally, analytic thought will adulterate or destroy the vitality of its object.[145]

Steiner's last lecture continues on this theme of the uniquely Western pursuit of disinterested truth, an obsession that Europeans inherited from ancient Greece. He argues that truth, like education and culture, is assumed by those in the West to benefit humanity, to set us free, as it were. What if, Steiner asks, the truth about human nature actually works against our survival and contributes to the destruction of humanity? What if, for instance, human beings are unable to endure long periods of peace without resorting to war? And, what if, hypothetically, "80% or more of what you and I *are* is programmed genetically and by racial inheritance. *Suppose* this were true—what do we do with that kind of knowledge?"[146] Steiner believes that "we, in the West, are an animal built to ask questions and to try to get answers regardless of the cost . . . we are a fairly cruel carnivore built to move forward, and built to move over and against obstacles."[147] The truth, Steiner concludes, is "more complex than man's needs [and] and may in fact be wholly extraneous and even inimical to these needs . . . The truth, I believe, does have a future; whether man does is much less clear. But I cannot help having a hunch as to which of the two is the more important."[148]

There is a deeper level to this emptiness at the heart of Western culture, however, that Steiner believes deals the final blow to our religious foundations. He asserts that there is, at the center of Western culture, a "dramatic crisis of confidence." In a discussion of contemporary Orientalism in his fourth lecture, Steiner interprets the adoption of Eastern fads by the flower children of the counterculture as a symptom of this larger crisis.[149] The cause of this crisis of confidence in the Western heritage is the barbarism unleashed by the two world wars, in which "the holocaust was only the most bestial example."[150] The churches did little to prevent or to stop the violence of World War I, and they did not combat the totalitarianism and genocide of

World War II. Therefore, "those who realize that the same church blessed the killer and the victim, that the churches refused to speak out and pursued, under the worst terror ever visited upon civilized man, a policy of unctuous silence, those who know these things are not surprised by the bankruptcy of any theological stands since."[151] Steiner believes that our resulting sense of failure has made people in the West begin to question and reject previous beliefs about Western cultural and ethical superiority over other parts of the world. In fact, in the Western "quest for innocence" after such destruction, people are turning to Asia, to Africa, and to the indigenous cultures of the Americas for the "qualities of dignity, communal solidarity, mythological invention, involvement in the vegetable and animal orders, which Western man has lost or brutally eradicated."[152] These developments, which Steiner calls "reflexes of fear and compensation in the damaged sensibility of the West" are also interpreted as part of the ongoing attempt to reconcile the haunting absence of religion in Western culture.

During the "Cambridge Years," between 1961 and 1974, George Steiner establishes the dominant themes of his career as an intellectual. Living and working in Great Britain presented many challenges for Steiner and his family; however, it also seems to have forced Steiner to further define his identity as a central European Jew. Great Britain challenged Steiner culturally and intellectually and, against its grain, he developed unique analyses of the nature of literary criticism, the humanities, antisemitism, and Western culture. Defining himself and his intellectual interests against the cultural and intellectual norms of English academic life created a hostile reaction from his colleagues in "Cambridge English" but it also, no doubt, introduced important questions related to the Holocaust and antisemitism into Britain. Steiner's flexibility as an academic, who also writes book reviews and essays for the Sunday papers, broadened his reach and allowed him to influence public culture as well as that of the university.

The essays written during this period, especially those of *Language and Silence,* reflect the personal and intellectual odyssey upon which Steiner found himself during the 1960s. The mass murder of European Jewry is central to this journey. Over the years, Steiner's increasing interest in the Holocaust, and its meaning as a product of Western culture, affects almost every subject he pursues from tragedy to language, the humanities to poetry, the nature of culture to that of criticism. Steiner dedicates himself to the role of remembrancer. He interprets his work as a memorialization of, and tribute to, the central European Jewish culture that contributed so much to modern European society before its destruction by Nazism. Steiner's essays and his book reviews, written for a broad English-language audience, work hard to resuscitate the German Jewish cultural and intellectual exchange of which he is a product. His thought on the Holocaust evolves over time, in its encounter with major works of Holocaust-related art, history, and witnessing beginning in the 1950s and continuing thereafter. Well before many recognized the murder of European Jewry as the central historical event we know today, George Steiner placed it at the center of his analysis of Western culture, and as a result, he can be interpreted as one of the key international interlocutors involved in the early study of the Holocaust.

4

Translation and Treason, 1974–1985

The hostility directed toward George Steiner in Great Britain during the 1960s and 1970s compelled him to go abroad for an academic position. In 1974, Steiner accepted a Chair in Comparative Literature at the University of Geneva, one of the oldest in Europe, and taught in Switzerland for the next twenty years. The multilingual nature of teaching comparative literature at a Swiss university offered Steiner the unique opportunity to live in four languages, a crucial condition central to his work. Switzerland also allowed Steiner to cultivate several important intellectual friendships with scholars such as Gershom Scholem and Alexis Philonenko, who in turn introduced Steiner to Pierre Boutang.[1]

During this period Steiner invests intellectual energy in his ongoing investigation of the humanism-barbarism nexus via his study of language and linguistics. A number of studies result from his examination of the relations between language, literature, and the inhuman, including a book (and two articles) on Martin Heidegger and a novel about Hitler. In the course of several years Steiner confronts the Heidegger controversy, as he does the Anthony Blunt scandal in England, recognizing both as powerful examples of intellectual treason. Steiner's analyses of these two case studies do not however result in a conclusive answer to the question of why the humanities do not humanize. Instead, Steiner attempts to further refine his conceptions of clerisy, truth, and treason by relating them directly to his conception of Judaism in an essay entitled "Our Homeland: The Text." These essays, written between 1980 and 1989, demonstrate that the collusion between art, culture, and inhumanity remains one of Steiner's central preoccupations in his vocation as critic of Western culture.

Literature and Language

In an early essay, entitled "To Civilize Our Gentlemen," Steiner asked his English colleagues, "To a contemporary student of literature the latest recension of Dryden or essay on the point of view in *Nostromo* are certainly of interest. But is the work of Jakobson on the structure of speech or of Lévi-Strauss on the relations between myth, syntax, and culture not as important, or dare I say even more so?"[2] During the 1970s Steiner embarks upon the production and promotion of a literary criticism informed by the study of linguistics, which understands literature as a form and function of language. Steiner's work can be seen as part of the general "linguistic turn" during the 1970s, in which scholars in the humanities integrated the study of language into their established fields of inquiry.[3]

In 1971 Steiner publishes a collection of book reviews and essays entitled *Extraterritorial: Papers on Literature and the Language Revolution*,[4] in which he traces the current "language revolution" to earlier developments in linguistics, symbolic logic, and mathematical philosophy that occurred in central Europe at the turn of the twentieth century. In the central essay, "The Language Animal," Steiner focuses on the effects of World War I as the impetus for a new examination of language, an attempt to locate a new semantic center. After the First World War, he argues, philosophers, poets, and critics realized that humanism, "as it had energized European consciousness since the Renaissance, was in a process of collapse. Karl Kraus's premonition of new dark ages, Kafka's eerily exact pre-vision of the Holocaust, spring from an acute diagnosis of the breakdown of liberal humanism."[5] Steiner argues that because language was the medium of humane literacy and learning, it was understood as the root of the present crisis: "In the hollowness and death of the word, Mauthner, Wittgenstein, and Broch observed the malady of a whole civilization."[6]

The implications of our continuing language crisis are, for Steiner, deeply troubling because he believes that it is our ability to create language that determines our humanity:

> Much of the best that we have known of man, much of that which relates the human to the humane—and our future turns on that equation—has been immediately related to the miracle of speech. Humanity and that miracle are, or have been hitherto, indivisible. Should language lose an appreciable measure of its dynamism, man will, in some radical way, be less man, less himself. Recent history and the breakdown of effective communication between enemies and generations, as it harries us now, shows what this diminution of humanity is like. There was a loud organic and animal world before man, a world full of non-human messages. There can be such a world after him.[7]

Steiner argues, "The least inadequate definition we can arrive at of the genus *homo,* the definition that fully distinguishes him from all neighbouring life-forms, is this: man is a *zoon phonanta,* a language-animal. And there is no other like him."[8] Hence, the study of human language and its origin is, in Steiner's thinking, an investigation into the very origins of human existence, and perhaps holds the key to understanding the human capacity for the paradoxical combination of humanism and barbarism.[9]

In an essay entitled "Cry Havoc," Steiner uses the example of Louis Ferdinand Céline, the French novelist credited with influencing many modern writers such as Günter Grass, William Burroughs, and Norman Mailer, to examine this paradox. Between 1937 and 1941, Céline published three antisemitic works, "in which he cried out for the eradication of all Jews from Europe" and blamed the Jewish people for the defeat and *misère* of France.[10] In 1943, when the Nazis were actually putting his brand of lethal antisemitism into action, Céline republished *Bagatelles pour un Massacre* with the addition of antisemitic illustrations. Steiner contends that Céline "was of a piece," that the same "frenetic energy, the populist oratory, the Rabelaisian genius for magnification" animates both his antisemitic pamphlets and his novels, *Journey to the End of Night* and *Death on the Installment Plan.*[11] To have any coherent insight into the man, and the larger problem he embodies, Steiner argues, we must not separate the literature from the antisemitic works, as many scholars appear to do.[12] In Steiner's estimation, Céline was a master of language with a special talent for fierce rhetoric, a man who eventually accepted words as a substitute for reality and could no longer discriminate between them. This "essential abstraction, of a break between word and fulfillment," Steiner suggests, may provide a "clue to the co-existence of a literary talent of the first rank with obvious moral bestiality."[13] Here, however, the problem is referred to as a puzzle and is thought to constitute "what theologians call a 'mystery'."[14] Still, the questions this problem poses for Western culture remain "fundamental" for Steiner, who argues that we must "bring the study of literature back into touch with the darkened fabric of our lives."[15]

Steiner's celebrated examination of translation, entitled *After Babel: Aspects of Language and Translation,* was published four years later in 1975.[16] The title refers to the story of the Tower of Babel, found in chapter 11 of the Book of Genesis, which explains the diversity of human language as a divine punishment in response to humanity's attempt to challenge the supremacy of its Creator. Scholars of language have investigated the continuing "mystery of Babel" in order to determine the origins of human language. Many have attempted to trace the evolution of competing tongues back to one source: a common human language. The work of Noam Chomsky, for example, posits that the underlying structure of all languages is the same and, therefore, common to all. What he terms "deep structures" form the skeletal system of every language, a universal generative grammatical pattern. According to Chomsky, an innate mental structure exists within human beings from which they generate an ability to communicate linguistically with themselves and others. If, as Chomsky argues, there is a basic system to all languages and, therefore, to all human beings, one could assume that translation, or understanding, would be possible between tongues. It is on this issue, Steiner argues, that Chomsky's theory falls short of its promises: "So far, there has been little evidence forthcoming as to genuine 'formal universals' and next to none of any 'substantive' ones. The distinction between 'deep' and 'surface' structures involves a manifest *petitio principii,* and I can observe nothing but a drastic retreat or *non sequitur* in Chomsky's remark that the fact that all languages are cut to the same rule-constrained pattern does not imply 'that there must be some reasonable procedure for translating between them.' Surely, this is exactly what it must imply."[17]

Steiner believes that the main task for linguistics is to account for the enormous variety and diversity of human languages. Chomsky's theory of an innate universal language structure seems to contradict our variegated linguistic reality. Given Chomsky's scheme of universal "deep structures," Steiner argues, we should expect a restricted, interrelated array of human languages. Instead, there are between four and five thousand tongues currently being spoken on earth, and several thousand more are known to have been spoken in the past. Steiner admits that he is "unable to consider intellectually satisfactory or adequate to the truth any model or formula of human verbal behaviour that does not in some way account for this fantastic multiplicity."[18] Steiner and Chomsky differ further over the point of entry into the investigation of the origins of language. The issues of diversity and mutual incomprehensibility are primary and ontological for Steiner, who is especially concerned with the subject of translation, while Chomsky is dismissive of such "surface" concerns and chooses to focus on what he believes to be the deeper universals of language.[19]

After Babel first introduces Steiner's discussion of the messianic quality of the future tense, a concept developed by Ernst Bloch.[20] It is our "'forward-dreaming' . . . our compulsive ability to construe 'that which is now' as being 'that which is not yet' . . . [our] awareness of 'becoming,' [our] capacity to envisage a history of the future, [that] distinguishes [human beings] from all other living species."[21] To this Steiner adds the uniquely human capacity for falsehood and counterfactual statement:

> Language is the main instrument of man's refusal to accept the world as it is. Without that refusal, without the unceasing generation by the mind of "counter-worlds"—a generation which cannot be divorced from the grammar of counter-factual and optative forms—we would turn forever on the treadmill of the present. . . . Ours is the ability, the need, to gainsay or "un-say" the world, to image and speak it otherwise. In that capacity in its biological and social evolution, may lie some of the clues to the question of the origins of human speech and the multiplicity of tongues.[22]

But truth is a "linguistic responsibility" in Western culture and "the entire gamut from black lie to innocent error is to be found on the left and shadow-side of language."[23] Because of this negative view of "alternity," Steiner argues, scholars have overlooked its significance. The exception is Nietzsche, who states in *Will to Power*, "'There is only *one* world and that world is false, cruel, contradictory, misleading, senseless. . . . We need lies to vanquish this reality, this 'truth', we need lies *in order to live.* . . . That lying is a necessity of life is itself a part of the terrifying and problematic character of existence.'"[24] Steiner discusses the positive and creative aspects of falsehood, arguing that language is primarily fictive by nature and is employed by human beings to escape reality. Steiner argues that only "a small portion of human discourse is nakedly veracious or informative" and that this dialectic of "alternity" is actually necessary for human survival. The ability of language to "conceal, misinform, leave ambiguous, hypothesize, [and] invent is indispensable to the equilibrium of human consciousness and to the development of man in society."[25] It is a mistake to assume that language functions primarily as a means of straightforward communication. On the contrary, argues Steiner:

> in actual speech all but a small class of definitional or "unreflective-response" sentences are surrounded, mutely ramified, blurred by an immeasurably dense, individualized field of intention and withholding. Scarcely anything in human speech is what it sounds. Thus it is inaccurate and theoretically spurious to schematize language as "information" or to identify language, be it unspoken or vocalized, with "communication". The latter term will serve only if it includes, if it places emphasis on, what is *not* said in the saying, what is said only partially, allusively or with intent to screen. Human speech conceals far more than it confides; it blurs much more than it defines; it distances more than it connects. The terrain between speaker and hearer . . . is unstable, full of mirage and pitfalls.[26]

After Babel demonstrates that Steiner's view of language is increasingly complex and is characterized by its own paradox. He has written that language is the primary determinant of our humanity, as the medium for the "conveyance of human order which we call law, and the communication of the quick of the human spirit which we call grace."[27] His defense of the humanities and the Western canon project a firm belief in the possibility of human communication, the existence of truth, and the meaning of meaning. Here he interprets language as a medium of human consolation and liberation in its capacity for invention and its ability to unleash the human imagination from the constraints of reality. But, by the same terms, language is also our greatest burden if we require accurate information and meaningful communication.

These things are not impossible but they are perhaps "as difficult as they are rare."[28] It is this possibility that Steiner examines next in a work of fiction focused on the master manipulator of language: Adolf Hitler.

The Portage of Adolf Hitler

Steiner's investigation into the degenerative effects of bestiality upon language and humanity leads him to argue that just as language is the prime carrier of civilization and our collective humanity, it can also be demonically manipulated by a powerful, hateful entity to perpetrate the most heinous crimes against humanity.

These themes converge directly with Steiner's interest in the Holocaust in his second work of fiction, *The Portage to San Cristóbal of A.H.*, published in 1981.[29] The book is Steiner's imaginative interpretation of the aged Adolf Hitler's capture by a group of Israeli commandos in the Amazon jungle. The slim novella is oriented around two competing monologues. The first is by the director of the Israeli operation and a survivor himself, Emmanuel Lieber, while the second is a final word of self-defense by Adolf Hitler. Steiner admits to being fascinated by Hitler's oratorical ability, and by the demonic and deceitful power of his language. Reflecting back on the novel in 1995, Steiner revealed his artistic intentions to Ronald A. Sharp in an interview for the *Paris Review:* "I wanted there to draw attention precisely to the terrible ambiguity in all language, in all speech acts. . . . I tried to show that in Hitler's language there was antimatter, anti-language, that which is transcendentally annihilating of truth and meaning. And that it had to clash with Judaism, which is a faith, a culture, a trust based perhaps excessively on the word, on the articulacy and possibility of meaning and on constant discourse even with God."[30] So, for Steiner, Adolf Hitler is the master manipulator of language and meaning. Emmanuel Lieber's lament, in chapter 6 of *The Portage,* gives form to Steiner's intentions and voices Steiner's own thought on Hitler's use of language:

> His tongue is like no other. It is the tongue of the basilisk, a hundred-forked and quick as a flame. As it is written in the learned Nathaniel of Mainz: there shall come upon the earth in the time of night a man surpassing eloquent. All that is God's, hallowed be His name, must have its

> counterpart, its backside of evil and negation. So it is with the Word . . . He created on the night-side of language a speech for hell. Whose words mean hatred and vomit of life. Few men can learn that speech or speak it for long. It burns their mouths. It draws them into death. But there shall come a man whose mouth shall be as a furnace and whose tongue as a sword laying waste. He will know the grammar of hell and teach it to others. He will know the sounds of madness and loathing and make them seem music . . . he who very nearly did us to death, who deafened God so that the covenant seemed broken and our children given to ash. Do not let him speak freely.[31]

In the book, Lieber and Hitler do not actually confront each other physically. Steiner has them meet on the battlefield of language; each character expresses himself in a single chapter, with Hitler responding to Lieber's accusations and concluding the book. Alvin Rosenfeld, in his review of *The Portage,* makes this same point, while at once confirming Steiner's design of the clash between (Jewish) language and (Hitler's) anti-language: "Since Steiner keeps them physically apart, their encounter is represented as taking place on the level of language, or within language between two distinctly different attitudes toward the word, the one dedicated to representing the truths of history and the Lord of history, the other an apocalyptic assault against historical and theological thinking and the people who carry it forward into the world."[32]

The last chapter of the book is Hitler's sustained monologue of self-defense, his only utterance, in response to Lieber's charges of mass murder. Here we see Steiner's dialectic of "alternity" at work, a clear depiction of language resisting reality through falsification. Hitler's self-defense is based on four points: he claims to have used the Jewish concepts of a "chosen people" and a "promised land" as a model for Nazi racism; he states that the Jews are actually responsible for antisemitism, as it is a reaction to *the blackmail of transcendence* (the Jewish reminder to humanity of a higher moral standard, through Judaism's creation of monotheism, Jesus Christ, and Marxism); he says that Stalin was responsible for more murders, thirty million to be exact, than he himself was; and finally, he believes that he actually helped the Jews because, by perpetrating the Holocaust, he guaranteed the establishment of the State of Israel.

Most reviews of this work have focused on the Hitler chapter. As a result, Steiner has been criticized in a number of reviews for appearing to put some of his own theories and arguments into the mouth of Adolf Hitler and thereby assisting with his defense.[33] Robert Boyers defends Steiner against this charge, reminding readers that this book is a work of fiction, and arguing that *The Portage* demonstrates precisely how a Hitler could appropriate a Steiner for his own nihilistic purposes.[34] The novel has been both dismissed as "an upsetting and misleading piece of anti-Jewish propaganda of a regrettably contemporary kind which may prove to be of aid and comfort to anti-Semites for some years to come"[35] and celebrated as a brave confrontation with the evil meaning and presence of Hitler.[36]

It seems that one's reaction to *The Portage* often depends on which monologue, that of Lieber or Hitler, one places at the center of the novel. The center, for Steiner, however, has always been chapter 6: Lieber's lament over the torture and murder of the Jewish people under Hitler. In hideous detail, Steiner's protagonist recalls the endless crimes committed against individual Jews: children forced to eat excrement, women raped with truncheons, men burned with acid, all kinds of people burned alive or gassed and then incinerated. In the middle of this graphic retelling, Steiner includes himself among the victims: "the one not being Nathaniel Steiner who was taken to America in time but goes maimed nevertheless for not having been at the roll call."[37] In the afterword of the most recent edition of *The Portage,* published in 1999, Steiner describes the book essentially as a parable about pain: "About the abyss of pain endured by the victims of Nazism. Endured by those being 'ethnically cleansed' in a ravaged habitat in Amazonia. It tries to instance language, and with it the fragile chances of truth, when words are racked in rhetoric and madness. First and foremost, this fable engages the pain of remembrance, the imperative but unendurable pain of recall. It was written in pain. It will have failed if this fact is not palpable to its readers."[38]

Steiner, who has forbidden German and Hebrew translations of the novel, admits to being "profoundly worried about it, and [he] would certainly not dare to come back to it."[39] He also believes that while a major act of interpretation comes nearer to the heart of the subject, "it never comes too near."[40] Robert Boyers recognizes this provisional quality in Steiner's work, arguing, "*The Portage* gestures vigorously at what can only be an absent cause, that is, at the totality of human motives and relations that made possible the holocaust but must remain permanently unavailable to the representational enterprise. Where *The Portage* differs . . . from most other political novels is in its conviction that, though the cause is ever worth pursuing, and must ever be sought in the precincts of human motives, ideas, and institutions, it is likely to be elsewhere, in a precinct unamenable to common sense or careful literary design."[41] For Steiner, the meaning and origins of the Shoah are intricately complex. Despite his literary commitment, and his sense that the instability of human language is somehow implicated in the humanism-barbarism nexus, he still maintains that any worthwhile attempt at comprehending the causal dynamics of Jew-hatred and the nightmare world of Auschwitz must lie in the theological-metaphysical realm, in the ambiguous afterlife of religious feeling in Western culture,[42] and hence will remain provisional.

The Clerics of Treason: Martin Heidegger

During the same period of time in which *The Portage* is published, Steiner begins to study Martin Heidegger and Anthony Blunt as case studies in his ongoing investigation of the relationship between humanism and barbarism. In response to his son's questions about the philosophy of Martin Heidegger, Steiner composes an introduction to the subject, which he publishes in 1978. The book, entitled simply *Heidegger,* was written for the Fontana Modern Masters Series, edited by Frank Kermode.[43] Steiner's book on Heidegger includes an introduction, in which he discusses the various perspectives on the man and his work. Here, as in his extended book reviews, Steiner introduces his English readers to the work of a continental philosopher they have likely not yet read. His introduction deciphers the various scholarly perspectives on Heidegger, in Germany and France specifically, and mentions the problem of his involvement with the Nazi Party before the war, and his postwar silence about the Holocaust.

The book demonstrates Steiner's specific interest in Heidegger's approach to language and literature, and (like Hitlerian oratory) the mesmerizing force of his unique German prose:[44] "It literally spellbinds, making the prose of other philosophers and even the work of contemporary poets seem shallow. Heidegger's play on the hidden life of words, his pulsating cadence, his use of metonymy in which concrete attributes stand for abstract entities and abstract segments represent or enact a concrete whole, seem to become simultaneously transparent and hypnotic, like a deep seen through a film of light or lit water."[45] Steiner admits to the massive presence of Heidegger in his three fields of scholarly interest, which he outlines for his readers:

> First there is that of the tragic readings of man and of man's relations to the state which has its dual source in Greek tragedy and in the emblematic episode of the death of Socrates. Secondly, there is the manifold problem of the nature and development of language and, especially, of the possibilities of and constraints on translation both within and between human tongues . . . Thirdly, I have sought to formulate certain questions about the interactions between, the interpretations of, artistic, philosophic and scientific achievements on the one hand, and the totalitarian politics of the twentieth century on the other. To ask such questions is to revert, obsessively perhaps, to the relations between German culture and Nazism, an interweaving in which the German language, of which Goethe and Kant but also Hitler are master-practitioners, plays a determining role.[46]

In this first edition, Steiner states simply that, amid the "veritable blizzard of indictments and apologias by critics and supporters," the two important questions about Heidegger and Nazism have not been asked: "What, if any, are the connections between the doctrines and idiom of *Sein und Zeit* and those of National Socialism? And what explanation can be offered to account for Heidegger's total refusal, *after 1945,* to say anything candid or even intelligible either about his personal record under Nazism or about the general holocaust?"[47] He does not however attempt his own investigation into these questions, suggesting that it is perhaps too early for these questions to be "stringently formulated and pressed home."[48]

The second edition, published in 1980 as *Martin Heidegger,* does include a section specifically on "Heidegger's Silence." This piece asks the same two questions and attempts to reconstruct the facts of the case. Steiner begins by defending or providing the benefit of the doubt to Heidegger, suggesting: it is possible that Heidegger refers to the Holocaust in private correspondence, perhaps with Hannah Arendt; as rector of Freiburg University, Heidegger prohibits the dissemination of antisemitic tracts and forbids a book burning; there is no evidence for the allegation that Heidegger banned Edmund Husserl from the university library; Heidegger refused to ratify the dismissal of two anti-Nazi deans from the university; Heidegger resigns his position before Hitler takes absolute power on 19 August 1934, and then immediately leaves the Nazi Party; and, after his resignation, Heidegger is denounced and his classes are placed under surveillance. Nevertheless, the speeches Heidegger gives between 1933 and 1934 are acknowledged by Steiner to be "vile, turgid, and brutal stuff in which the official jargon of the day blends seamlessly with Heidegger's idiom at its most hypnotic."[49] But then again, Steiner asserts, "there are, in the midst of these brutal effronteries and servilities, some covert but tenacious indirections."[50] Steiner, who has tremendous respect for Heidegger as one of the very greatest masters of thought, oscillates between condemnation and exculpation throughout the essay.

Addressing the first question, about the relationship between Heidegger's philosophy and Nazism, Steiner acknowledges that specific "instrumental connections between the language and vision of *Sein und Zeit,* especially the later sections, and those of Nazism" do in fact exist:

> In both—as in so much of German thought after Nietzsche and Spengler—there is the presumption, at once mesmerized by and acquiescent in, of a nearing apocalypse, of so deep a crisis in human affairs that the norms of personal and institutional morality must be and shall inevitably be brushed aside. . . . Both Nazism and the ontological anthropology of *Sein und Zeit* stress the concreteness of man's function in the world, the primordial sanctity of hand and body. Both exalt the mystical kinship between the labourer and his tools in an existential innocence which must be cleansed of the pretensions and illusions of abstract intellect. . . . Heidegger's rhetoric of "at-homeness", of the organic continuum which knits the living to the ancestral dead buried close by, fits effortlessly into the Nazi cult of "blood and soil." . . . the Hitlerite denunciations of "rootless cosmopolitans", the urban riffraff, and unhoused intelligentsia . . . chime in readily with the Heideggerian critique of "theyness", of technological modernity, of the busy restlessness of the inauthentic.

> Heideggerian "resoluteness" *(Entschlossenheit)* has more than a hint of the mystique of commitment, of self-sacrificial and self-projective élan preached by the Führer and his "hard-clear" acolytes. . . . In both, there is, logically and essentially, an exaltation of death as life's purposed summit and fulfilment. . . . [And] in the Hitlerite recomposition of the historical past, in the apocalyptic imperative of a totally new beginning in German destiny, Heidegger could find a confirmation of his own more technical, more esoteric anti-historicism.[51]

Steiner argues that the correspondence between Heideggerian philosophy and Nazism is also the result of the unstable nature of language specifically, and the German language especially:

> Both, though at obviously different levels, exploit the genius of German for suggestive darkness, its ability to give to (often empty or half-baked) abstractions a physical presence and intensity. There is in Heidegger's supposition, itself at once metaphorical and mesmeric, that it is not man who speaks where language is most fully effective, but "language itself through man" an ominous hint of Hitler's brand of inspiration, of the Nazi use of the human voice as a trumpet played upon by immense, numinous agencies beyond the puny will or judgement of rational man. The motif of dehumanization is key. Nazism comes upon Heidegger precisely at that moment in his thinking when the human person is being edged away from the centre of meaning and of being. The idiom of the purely ontological blends with that of the inhuman.[52]

In approaching the second question, Steiner argues that Heidegger's rectorship, and association with the Nazi Party in the early 1930s, is not the central issue. At this point in time, Steiner understands Heidegger as "caught up in the electric trance of the National Socialist promise" like millions of other Germans, when Nazism was still "masking its essential barbarism."[53] The fact that Heidegger quit after only nine months and before Hitler's assumption of total power convinces Steiner that Heidegger's behavior is mild in comparison to "many eminent intellectuals [who] did far worse."[54] As "nauseating as they are," Steiner argues, "Heidegger's gestures and pronouncements during 1933–4 are tractable. It is his complete silence on Hitlerism and the holocaust after 1945 which is very nearly intolerable."[55] He asks, "Is there anywhere in Heidegger's work a repudiation of Nazism, is there anywhere, from 1945 to his death, a single syllable on the realities and philosophic implications of the world of Auschwitz? These are the questions that count. And the answer would have to be, No."[56]

Steiner cannot find any evidence of specific anti-Jewish feeling in Heidegger's writings or pronouncements, so he avoids a discussion of anti-semitism as a motivating factor for Heidegger's postwar silence. Perhaps, then, Steiner suggests, he refused to say anything at all because the disaster was beyond rational commentary of any kind. Or he simply could not face the "easy collapse of German academic and cultural institutions before the Nazi challenge."[57] Or finally, Steiner asserts that Heidegger possibly saw the disaster in relation to his conception of German destiny, and "to attempt to circumscribe it within bounds of common sense and morality, would be useless. It would be a trivialization of tragic but exemplary *Dasein*."[58]

This last point, however, no longer "seems at all sufficient" nine years later when Steiner reexamines the Heidegger controversy in an essay, entitled "Heidegger, Again," that is later published as the new introduction to the 1991 edition of *Martin Heidegger*. Here Steiner places Heidegger's language, which he still sees as "wholly inseparable from his philosophy and from the problems which that philosophy poses," within the larger context of post–World War I Germany and its social, political, and economic crises. Steiner argues that *Sein und Zeit*, published in 1927, should be seen as part of a unique constellation of books written in German during the decade following World War I, all of which embody a "metaphysical-poetic discourse on chaos."[59] These texts—Ernst Bloch's *Geist der Utopie* (1918), Oswald Spengler's *Decline of the West* (volume 1, 1918), Karl Barth's *Commentary on Romans* (1919), Franz Rosenzweig's *Stern der Erlösung* (1921), Heidegger's *Sein und Zeit* (1927), and Hitler's *Mein Kampf* (two volumes, 1925–27)—are all voluminous, prophetic, utopian, retrospective, apocalyptic, and, as a result, "make for a specific violence," however stylistic.[60] Out of the destruction and humiliation of defeat, these texts suggest that Germans are destined to "undergo some fundamental renovation, some agonizing rebirth out of the ash of a dead past."[61] Language too will be subject to renovation. In their attempt to "make language new," these works "have a singular radicality," according to Steiner. Bloch and Rosenzweig are neologists who subvert traditional grammar, Barth's idiom exemplifies the abyss between human logic and God, and Heideggerian terminology overcomes "the language of the immediate German past and forge[s] a new speech both by virtue of radical invention and by a selective return to 'forgotten' sources."[62] Heidegger's language is interpreted by Steiner as "a characteristic phenomenon arising out of the circumstances of Germany between the cataclysm of 1918 and the rise to power of National Socialism."[63] And, as he has argued previously, Steiner suggests the German language had a specific ability to meet the needs of the age:

> In short: more consciously, more violently than any other language . . . the German language after the first world war seeks a break with its past. Endowed with a peculiarly mobile syntax and with the capacity to fragment or to fuse words and word-roots almost at will, German looks to elect solitaries in its past, to Master Eckhardt, to Böhme, to Hölderlin, and to such innovations as Surrealism and the cinema in its present, for instigations to renewal. The *Stern der Erlösung,* Bloch's messianic tracts, Barth's exegetics and, above all, *Sein und Zeit* are speech-acts of the most revolutionary kind. It is only in this linguistic and emotive context that Heidegger's method becomes intelligible.[64]

The second part of Steiner's essay revisits the Heidegger debate and the controversy unleashed by Victor Farias's work, *Heidegger et le nazisme,*[65] published in 1987.[66] Steiner is critical of Farias for his "vulgarity and imprecision" when dealing with Heideggerian philosophy; however, his research does reveal the following "sombre nuggets": Heidegger lied by concealing his membership in the Nazi Party until 1945; he clarifies the extent of Heidegger's mental collapse after the surrender of the Reich; he documents Heidegger's evasions during the denazification tribunals; and he documents Heidegger's mistreatment of fellow academic colleagues, his admiration for Hitler, and his cunning survival tactics. Steiner is now convinced of Heidegger's "rhetorical and administrative participation in the Nazification of the German university-world in 1933–4" and sees this fact as evidence that "naked power can mesmerize the academic-mandarin temper."[67] Steiner now sees in the Heidegger case evidence of the specific vulnerability intellectuals have to political corruption:

> Unquestionably, Martin Heidegger saw himself as a chosen *praeceptor Germaniae*, as a leader-in-thought who would mould a national resurrection. The Platonic image, not only in reference to Plato's doctrines of philosophic governance but also with regard to Plato's role as advisor to Sicilian despotism, lay to hand. The chapter of the unwisdom of philosophers in regard to matters political is a long one. Voltaire's Jew-hatred was rabid. The racism of Frege was of the blackest hue. Sartre not only sought to evade or find apologia for the world of the Gulag; he deliberately falsified what he knew of the insensate savagery of the Cultural Revolution in Maoist China. It is an ill-kept secret that cloistered intellectuals and men who spend their lives immured in words, in texts, can experience with especial intensity the seductions of violent political proposals, most particularly where such violence does not touch their own person. There can be in the sensibility and outlook of the charismatic teacher, of the philosophical absolutist, more than a touch of surrogate sadism.[68]

This paragraph provides numerous examples of the failure of the humanities to humanize even those who dedicate their lives to the pursuit and cultivation of the humanities. Here, Steiner's suspicion of direct political action (which he inherited from his father), of the risks of secularization and the inevitable crimes of nationalism are all confirmed as threats to the ideals of the intellectual enterprise.

Steiner returns to the problem that he sees as key to the whole Heidegger Affair: "the refusal by the philosopher of Being, by the master-reader of Sophocles and of Hölderlin, to address his conscience, his reflection, his discourse to the inhuman negation of life in which he played a part (however rhetorical, however mandarin)."[69] After briefly discussing the failure of Heidegger to address the Holocaust in conversations with the poet Paul Celan (the effects of which Steiner sees as calamitous for Celan),[70] Steiner concludes his discussion of Heidegger by suggesting that his silence betrayed his philosophy and its understanding of questioning "as the piety of the human spirit."[71] In his final estimation of Heidegger's behavior and its relationship to his philosophy, Steiner focuses on the complete lack of any conception of evil in Heideggerian philosophy. It is the absence of ethics in Heidegger's work, resulting from his renunciation of theology, that cripples both his philosophy and his humanity. Steiner concludes by stating, "Lacking an ethic, self-maimed in the face of the inhuman, Heidegger's Ontology remains an overwhelming fragment."[72]

The Clerics of Treason: Anthony Blunt

A second example of intellectual treason presented itself to Steiner in November 1979, when Prime Minister Margaret Thatcher announced that Sir Anthony Blunt, the highly respected art historian and official surveyor of the royal family's artistic holdings, had been spying for the Soviet Union for more than thirty years. Beginning in 1940, as a member of the MI5 section of the wartime secret service, Blunt is believed to have infiltrated the communications and activities of governments in exile and foreign embassies in London. He is then thought to have passed this information on to the KGB, "doing grave damage to his own country and [possibly sending] other men—Polish and Czech exiles, fellow intelligence agents—to abject death."[73] Steiner's article on Blunt, entitled "The Cleric of Treason," tries to understand both his motivation for betraying his country and how a scholar like Blunt could live a life of deceit. Steiner spends the first half of the essay detailing Blunt's professional development and achievements,[74] and focusing on his professional dedication to the pursuit of truth:

> To his professional colleagues, Blunt is not only an art historian and an analytic critic of great stature. He is one of the principal cataloguers of our time. . . . The *catalogue raisonné*—the chronological listing and precise description of the output of an artist or of his school—is to the historian of art and culture, to the art critic, and to the connoisseur the primary instrument of ordered perception. . . . [In his appraisal of value] Blunt's austerity was above question. His scholarship, his teaching exemplify formidable standards of technical severity and intellectual and moral rigour. . . . At this level of learning and connoisseurship, deception and the exposure that follows would be irreparable. There was hardly a day on which Professor Sir Anthony Blunt, Knight Commander of the Royal Victorian Order and

honoured guest of the Queen, did not make this clear to his colleagues and to his students.[75]

Steiner then adapts Blunt's case to his famous question about the life of the cultured Nazi commandant who commits mass murder the morning after the Beethoven recital or poetry reading: "I would like to think for a moment about a man who in the morning teaches his students that a false attribution of a Watteau drawing or an inaccurate transcription of a fourteenth-century epigraph is a sin against the spirit and in the afternoon or evening transmits to the agents of Soviet intelligence classified, perhaps vital information given to him in sworn trust by his countrymen and intimate colleagues. What are the sources of such a scission?"[76] For Steiner, the Blunt affair illustrates once again the easy collusion of humanism and barbarism in a highly cultivated intellectual. Anthony Blunt's case, like the Heidegger controversy, raises serious questions about the "nature of intellectual-academic obsession, about the co-existence within a single sensibility of utmost truth and falsehood, and about certain germs of the inhuman planted, as it were, at the very roots of excellence in our society."[77]

In his attempt to explain Blunt's behavior, Steiner dismisses his Marxism as a motivating factor, describing it as "parlour-pink talk in the approved nineteen-thirties style."[78] He does however consider the fact that Anthony Blunt was gay, at a time when homosexual behavior was criminalized in England, to be of significance for two reasons. It gave the Soviets the option of blackmailing Blunt and other gay men into counterintelligence work, and could also have contributed to Blunt's actions against a nation inherently homophobic. Steiner argues that Blunt had been educated in a hypocritical heterosexist system, "underwritten by an explicit ideal of masculine friendship, of a masculine intimacy and mutual trust more lasting and radiant than the plebian values of the outside world . . . that was only a transitory phase before the fading of the summer light and a man's responsible entry into the colder climate of matrimony and family life."[79] In the Oxbridge world of the 1930s and 1940s, one's loyalty was to one's friends, perhaps even more so than to the nation.

But these explanations do not enter the "heart of the maze" that, according to Steiner, is "the radical duplicity, the seeming schizophrenia, of the scholar-teacher of impeccable integrity and the professional deceiver and betrayer."[80] He argues that our society does not consider this question seriously. When we consider the scholar at all, he (this still tends to be a masculine image) is a benign creature, a bumbling, forgetful professor who has difficulty functioning in the "real world." Steiner sees the absolute scholar, and his unique vulnerability to political corruption and violence, very differently. He argues that the obsessive nature of academic interest, of the love of knowledge for its own sake, aside from any utility or value it may have to others, sets the mandarin apart from the rest of humanity. This obsessive interest in one's arcane studies, Steiner asserts, may also make the scholar indifferent to the needs and conditions of common humanity, "to the claims of social justice, of familial affection, and of political awareness."[81] Rather than bringing the scholar into contact with "run-of-the-mill humanity," the vocation of scholarship leads one to see the world as a hostile impediment to the life of the mind.

Steiner argues that there is a particular disorientation that affects those in the humanities, who are by their very nature remembrancers: "The numismatician labouring to identify archaic coinage, the musicologist deciphering medieval notations, the philologist at his corrupt codex, or the art historian who is endeavoring to catalogue minor baroque or rococo eighteenth-century drawings not only has entered into the labyrinth and underworld of the esoteric but has, necessarily, inverted time. For him, the pulse of most vivid presence beats from out of the past."[82] Steiner believes that this disorientation caused by absolute scholarship, especially in the humanities, creates two reflexes: the hunger for involvement in the "real world," which is really "nostalgia for action," and a pent-up hostility that has the potential to become violent. The latter reflex usually "stays formal" where "at the ordinary level, [the scholar] will exorcize his spleen in the ad-hominem nastiness of a book review, in the arsenic of a footnote. He will vent his resentments in the soft betrayals of an ambiguous recommendation or examination report and in the scorpion's round of a committee on tenure."[83] However, this kind of sublimation is not always the end result. Just as Martin Heidegger "saw himself as a chosen *praeceptor Germaniae*, as a leader-in-thought who would mould a national resurrection,"[84] Anthony Blunt is seen to have converted these same mandarin "fantasies of virile action, those solicitations of violence, which bubble like marsh gas from the deeps of abstruse thought and erudition," into covert deception, treason, and conspiracy.[85]

Judaism and the Clerical Ideal

In 1985, with the essay "Our Homeland, The Text," Steiner turns toward a deeper investigation of the role of the cleric, and the nature and meaning of scholarship, in Western culture.[86] Here Steiner shifts the focus to Judaism, specifically to its scholarly and ethical sensibilities, which he grounds in its celebrated textuality. His conception of Jewish clerisy is modeled upon Julien Benda's *La Trahison des clercs*,[87] "an inescapably Jewish book which came of the Dreyfus case."[88] The ideas put forward in this essay both complement and enlarge Steiner's initial conception of "Central European Judaism."

According to Steiner, the Jew is a bookkeeper, both in the sense of keeping God's "balance-sheet . . . between merit and recompense" up to date, and as the "keeper of the Book, an archivist of the revealed."[89] The Jew is also a cleric. Steiner argues that the "mystery and the practices of clerisy are fundamental to Judaism. No other tradition or culture has ascribed a comparable aura to the conservation and transcription of texts. In no other has there been an equivalent mystique of the philological."[90] Steiner then applies to Judaism his definition of the absolute scholar, developed in the previous essays on Heidegger and Blunt: "the sometimes hallucinatory techniques and disciplines of attention to the text, the mystique of fidelity to the written word, the reverence bestowed on its expositors and transmitters, concentrated within the Judaic sensibility unique strengths and purities of disinterested purpose."[91] He argues that this cultural historical development is reflected specifically in the lives and work of central European Jewry: "The 'bookish' genius of Marx and of Freud, of Wittgenstein and of Lévi-Strauss, [who represent] the secular deployment of the long schooling in abstract, speculative commentary and clerkship in the exegetic legacy (while being at the same time a psychological-sociological revolt against it). The Jewish presence, often overwhelming, in modern mathematics, physics, economic and social theory, is direct heir to that abstinence from the approximate, from the mundane, which constitutes the ethos of the cleric."[92]

What, if any, negative reflexes are produced by the Judaic obsession with absolute scholarship? The problem for Judaism, according to Steiner, is not absolute scholarship but nationalism. Both Martin Heidegger and Anthony Blunt engage in treasonous activities against their clerical vocation, and they do so in the service of modern nation-states and political ideology. Only very recently, with the birth of the State of Israel, does this same risk to Jewish clerisy present itself. Steiner tells us that what is at stake here is "*a politics of truth*"[93] and the nation-state is "founded on myths of instauration and of militant glory. It perpetuates itself by lies and half-truths."[94] As a result, Steiner is adamant in his rejection of nationalism:

> The sole citizenship of the cleric is that of a critical humanism. He knows not only that nationalism is a sort of madness, a virulent infection edging the species towards mutual massacre. He knows that it signifies an abstention from free and clear thought and from the disinterested pursuit of justice. The man or woman at home in the text is, by definition, a conscientious objector: to the vulgar mystique of the flag and the anthem, to the sleep of reason which proclaims "my country, right or wrong," to the pathos and eloquence of collective mendacities on which the nation-state—be it a mass-consumer mercantile technocracy or a totalitarian oligarchy—builds its power and aggressions. The locus of truth is always extraterritorial.[95]

Steiner has a special dislike for Zionism, as he interprets Jewish nationalism to be a violation of the ethical and cosmopolitan nature of Judaism. Steiner's Jew is a truth seeker and ethical by nature, who is at home not in Israel but in the text. The Jew carries no specific national allegiance as a "citizen of the world." The original cosmopolitan, the authentic Jew is incorruptible by nationalism or chauvinism of any kind. For Steiner, the mysterious beauty and creative nature of Judaism, as well as the miracle of its survival, lies in its physical homelessness on the earth. The exilic or diasporic history of the Jews allows them the opportunity to participate in other cultures and thereby execute their unique mission in the world. The singularity of Jewish survival demonstrates to Steiner that the Jews have an exemplary role to play in human history: "I cannot shake off the conviction that the torment and the mystery of resilience in Judaism exemplify, enact, an arduous truth: that human beings must learn to be each other's guests on this small planet, even as they must learn to be guests of being itself and of the natural world. . . . Man will have to learn [this truth] or he will be made extinct in suicidal waste and violence."[96] For Steiner, "the notion that the appalling road of Jewish life and the ever renewed miracle of survival should have as their end, as their justification, the setting up of a small nation-state in the Middle East, crushed by military burdens, petty and even corrupt in its policies, shrill in its parochialism, is implausible."[97] Steiner's vision of Judaism as intellectual, cosmopolitan, diasporic, secular, and ethical conflicts with what he characterizes as the militant Jewish nationalism of the Israeli enterprise. The following description of Israel makes his position clear:

> Israel is a nation-state to the utmost degree. It lives armed to the teeth. It has been compelled to make other men homeless, servile, disinherited, in order to survive from day to day (it was, during two millennia, the dignity of the Jew that he was *too weak* to make any other human being as unhoused, as wretched as himself). The virtues of Israel are those of beleaguered Sparta. Its propaganda, its rhetoric of self-deception, are as desperate as any contrived in the history of nationalism . . . There is no singular vice in the practices of the State of Israel. These follow ineluctably on the simple institution of the modern nation-state, on the political-military necessities by which it exists with and against its nationalist competitors . . . Where it has traded its homeland in the text for one of the Golan Heights or in Gaza . . . Judaism has become homeless to itself.[98]

At the core of Steiner's anti-Zionism is his concern over what he views as the Israeli destruction of the Jewish ethical spirit. While he fully admits the State of Israel is a heroic national attempt to guarantee the physical survival of the Jewish people after their devastation in the Shoah,[99] he asks nonetheless: does Israel risk the destruction of Judaism? In this context, one can better understand the passages in Steiner's novel *The Portage to San Cristóbal of A.H.*, where "Hitler" states that he is responsible for the creation of Israel:

> It was the Holocaust that gave you the courage of injustice, that made you drive the Arab out of his home, out of his field, because he was lice-eaten and without resource, because he was in your divinely ordered way. That made you endure knowing that those whom you had driven out were rotting in refugee camps not ten miles away, buried alive in despair and lunatic dreams of vengeance. Perhaps *I am* the Messiah, the true Messiah, the new

> Sabbatai whose infamous deeds were allowed by God in order to bring His people home. . . . Should you not honor me who have made you into men of war, who have made of the long, vacuous daydream of Zion a reality?[100]

In response to a critical review of the staged version of *The Portage,* written by historian Martin Gilbert, Steiner admitted, "It is my anguished hunch that the ghost of Hitler cackles in hell each and every time the State of Israel—*compelled to do so in order to survive*—blows up an Arab house, welds the doors of an Arab shop, patrols the Old City of Jerusalem, sub-machine guns at the ready, or suppresses university classes, books and other forms of free communication not only on the West Bank but, inevitably, in its own backyard."[101] The Zionist goal of Jewish normalization is a gross betrayal of Judaism, in Steiner's estimation, as it forces Jews to transform themselves into a nation like any other. He argues that for Jews to "give up the splendour of [their Mosaic and Prophetic] heritage, to renounce [their] pre-eminent *dignitas* 'among the nations', is to humiliate irreparably [their] inmost identity and *raison d'être.*"[102]

But a Jewish nation state not only violates the ethics of Judaism, it destroys the splendid Jewish intelligence and creativity that is the product of Steiner's cosmopolitan, diasporic "Central European Judaism."[103] In a question-and-answer session after Steiner's B'nai B'rith Jerusalem Address of 1986, he makes the following statement:

> There are three fields in which embarrassingly, the Jews are so immensely gifted, and ahead of the rest of the Earth. (It is quite embarrassing, but we are among friends). The first is my own great passion, which is chess. For complicated reasons we push 32 little bits of wood, or bread in the camps, or plastic, around 64 squares, a quite childish pursuit—to a level of depth and magnificence, near to which no other species of *homo sapiens* has ever come. In the Soviet Union, which rates people from their first games to world championship, there are 12 classes, as you know, mathematically graded. Above class 9 the proportion of Jews is over 80%, above class 10 it is 92%, it is embarrassing beyond words, right? This country plays lousy chess!
>
> "Secondo"—roughly from Paul of Tarsus, who founded the profession, to today, journalism has been the genius of the Jew, we are journalists

> like . . . it is almost embarrassing. Most of the senior staff of *Pravda* and *Isvestia* is Jewish. In the *New York Times* a gentile has a very hard time getting a job.
>
> Where is the worst press of any advanced country—Israel. And with quite fantastically low and provincial standards—they couldn't get a by-line in the *Spokane Sports Sheet,* believe me. I worked in this profession for many years on the London *Economist* and I know whereof I speak!
>
> What is the latest figure again, (please this entirely *en famille,* don't let any of this get out of this room), what is the latest figure? Correct me, 66.7% or is it 66.2% of all Nobels in the sciences since 1900 are Jewish. The Weizmann Institute hasn't won one![104]

Steiner believes that to concentrate the Jewish people in one small nation-state is to lock the text "materially in a material homeland" and risk that "the text may, in fact, lose its life-force, and its truth-values may be betrayed."[105] Steiner has no doubt: Jewish ethics and the restless, creative intelligence of Jews are vulnerable in a nationalistic context like Israel. Steiner's clerical vocation, whether Jewish or Gentile, is stringent in its code of ethics, for "whoever, for whatever motives—patriotic, political, religious and even moral—allows himself even the slightest manipulation or adjustment of the truth, must be stricken from the roll of scholars."[106]

This chapter illustrates the wide-ranging scholarly interests of George Steiner, and yet, at the same time, the central convergence of his intellectual energies upon questions directly related to the Holocaust and other related Jewish themes. In his introduction to the first edition of *Heidegger,* Steiner defines his own field as "the study of language, of its relation to literature on the one hand and to the history of ideas and society on the other. Two German terms, for neither of which English has an equivalent, *Sprachphilosoph* and *Kulturkritiker,* more or less cover the ground."[107] Throughout the 1970s Steiner's essays and magnum opus, *After Babel,* establish his approach to the meaning and role of language in human culture. Woven into this study of language however is Steiner's investigation into the connections between humanism and barbarism, as demonstrated with particular acuity by the Holocaust. While he begins the decade with the confident assertion that language is the chief determinant of our humanity, Steiner's study of the degenerative effects of bestiality upon language and humanity forces him to add the following qualification: language is unstable and can also be used to betray humanity. The most extreme example of this nihilistic betrayal is found in Adolf Hitler, who weaponized the German language into a medium of terror and lies, which he then used to destroy his so-called enemies, principally among them the Jewish people. Steiner uses fiction, *The Portage to San Cristobal of A.H.*, as the vehicle by which he attempts to dramatically illustrate this argument. Often, one sees Steiner alternating between the formats of discursive essay and fiction, in an attempt to represent more dramatically or concretely what are often abstract intellectual arguments.

At the same time, Steiner approaches the work of Martin Heidegger primarily from the same two areas of interest: the study of language and the relationship of humanism to barbarism in Western culture. Martin Heidegger and Anthony Blunt, both masters of thought in their respective fields, interest Steiner as "clerics of treason," powerful intellects whose political corruption betrayed the values of scholarship. These case studies demonstrate for Steiner the risks that attend absolute scholarship and the mandarin temperament, both of which create an ache for the application of ideas through political action and the desire for influence and power.[108]

In his effort to further define the vocation of the cleric, Steiner returns to the inspiration for his own ideals of scholarship: "Central European Judaism." Also at work during this time is Steiner's analysis of Zionism, which converges with his investigation into the nature of scholarship in an essay entitled "Our Homeland, The Text" (1985).[109] It seems that Jewish scholars have not been as vulnerable to political corruption as non-Jewish scholars because of the fact that for nearly two thousand years the Jewish people have been living in exile, without a definitive national territory of their own. This is no longer the case with the establishment of the modern State of Israel. Now Jews face the same possibility of corruption as do non-Jews, and risk losing what Steiner sees as a special quality of cosmopolitan, humanistic intelligence, born of the specific historical experience of European Judaism. A careful reader can see that Steiner's critique of Zionism and the State of Israel (whether or not one agrees with it) is rooted in his love for Judaism, as he defines it, rather than in anti-Jewish feeling as some suppose.[110]

5

The Meaning of Meaning, 1985–2007

Religious concepts and questions weave in and out of Steiner's career-long analysis of Western culture: questions about the nature of evil and of humanity are addressed in his first essay, *Malice;* his first book, *Tolstoy or Dostoevsky,* asks if first-rate aesthetic creation can be done in a culture untouched by religion; *The Death of Tragedy,* his second book, asserts that the genre of tragedy can only exist under the burden of God's presence; and *In Bluebeard's Castle* supports T. S. Eliot's contention that genuine high culture has a religious foundation. By the middle of the 1980s, however, Steiner's work begins to manifest theological and metaphysical themes in a more explicit and unapologetic manner. The major factor determining this shift toward transcendence is the challenge presented by Jacques Derrida and his theory of Deconstruction. This radical nihilistic attack on the Western tradition compels Steiner to employ an equally radical, theologically informed defense of humanism. This turn toward the theological, however, is not restricted to the subject of hermeneutics. As we shall see, all the primary subjects that engage Steiner's attention, from the Holocaust to the phenomenon of antisemitism, to the meaning of artistic creation and the possibility of ethics, to the survival of hope and the mysteries of teaching, are conceptualized in relation to questions about God and transcendence during this period.

Both Judaism and Christianity are native to Steiner's central European thought world; however, during this time Christian theology appears to be exerting notable pressure on his thought. The question of a Christianizing influence in Steiner's recent work is something he acknowledges: "Of late two topics, that of the contiguities of the deaths by law of Socrates and of Jesus, and that of the enigmatic fatality of the Jewish refusal of Christ's claims to messianic status, have obsessed me . . . these concerns have brought with them . . . a new coloration that can be perceived as 'Christianizing.' . . . I had not in any way foreseen this modulation, and it troubles me."[1] Steiner explains his attraction to Christian philosophy as the result of his specific intellectual needs during this time:

> the legacy of iconoclasm, of juridical rationalism in Judaism inhibits an idiom that endeavors to come nearer the transcendent possibility, the otherness of informing unreason in the arts. In trying to hammer out some perception, however rudimentary, into the paradoxes of real presence as we meet with them in the aesthetic, I found myself resorting to the pulses of metaphor, to the analytics of mystery in the Augustinian, Thomist, and Pascalian semantics and aura. . . . The tensions between inheritance and underlying syntax, between personal identity and compelled reference, already performative in Benjamin and Celan's uses of Hölderlin and of Heidegger, have, since the *Antigones,* grown palpable in my conjectures and language. Through them I have begun to glimpse the sickening wellspring of Jewish self-refusal in Simone Weil. This is sombre ground.[2]

As a European Jewish intellectual, deeply concerned with the meaning of Western culture after the Holocaust, Steiner is caught between two apparently irreconcilable traditions. Christianity provides Steiner with a language by which he is able to access the study of aesthetics and hermeneutics, but it remains a language (and a tradition) inherently hostile to the Jewish people. At the same time, Judaism, which we know defines Steiner in so many crucial ways, is a tradition that prevents him from engaging "the otherness of informing unreason in the arts," and from perceiving "the paradoxes of real presence . . . in the aesthetic," subjects that increasingly define the later part of his oeuvre as he battles Deconstruction.[3] Betwixt and between, Steiner can too easily be mistaken for a Christian[4] or dismissed as a traitor to Judaism.[5] As the final pages of this chapter shall demonstrate, it is a mistake for readers to assume that Steiner is moving toward the Christian faith or, by the same token, that he may be undergoing a "Judaically-meaningful *tshuvah,* or turning."[6] It is also unlikely that Steiner's embrace of theological categories and terminology is part of a conscious strategy to provide him with the required authority to pronounce judgment on the state and meaning of Western culture.[7] On the contrary, Steiner is well aware of the lack of authority, and legitimacy, theological categories and terminology have in contemporary culture. As we shall see, this is precisely the problem plaguing Western culture.

Real Presences

In November 1985, Steiner delivers the Leslie Stephen Memorial Lecture at Cambridge University. Four years later an expanded version of this lecture is published under the same title, *Real Presences.*[8] Just as *Tolstoy or Dostoevsky* was Steiner's riposte to the New Criticism, this work is Steiner's attempt to confront the current "crisis of sense" embodied by Derridean Deconstruction, especially its equation of text and commentary and its elimination of *auctoritas.*[9] For the Deconstructionist there is no distinction between the primary text and commentary, between the poem and its critique. All writings, be they primary, secondary, or tertiary, are part of a web of intertextuality and no text is privileged above another. All writing is the product of language, which "always precedes its user and always imposes on his usage rules, conventions, opacities for which he is not responsible and over which his control is minimal. No sentence spoken or composed in any intelligible language is, in the rigorous sense of the concept, original."[10] This, then, calls into question the idea of canonic originality and the authority of the author, who becomes a "kind of Magellanic cloud of interactive and changing energies, partial introspections, moments of compacted consciousness, mobile, unstable, as it were, around an even more indeterminate central region or black hole of the subconscious, of the unconscious or the pre-conscious."[11]

The result of this Derridean strategy, for its supporters, is an emancipatory anti-authoritarianism, but for Steiner its threat is anti-humanistic. Not only does Deconstruction abandon the "institutional consensus" of Western humanistic civilization, "a syllabus of agreed reference and exemplariness, across the ages," it also, like Heideggerian philosophy, divorces ethics from aesthetics. Steiner argues that Deconstruction uses the vulnerabilities of human language, which Steiner fully accepts and has acknowledged in *After Babel,* to promote spurious ideas that have the potential to further corrode Western culture, and even the act of creation itself. To equate Beethoven's composition of a sonata with a violinist's performance of that same sonata is to "confound *poiesis,* the act of creation, of bringing into autonomous being, with the derivative, secondary *ratio* of interpretation or adaptation."[12] The Derridean view of language, as an unfixed maze of signifiers that does not correspond to any form of reality but only to itself, results in the destruction of humanism and its classical notions of reality, truth, meaning, and knowledge. For Steiner, Deconstruction "coincide[s] with a spell of enervation and profound self-doubt" in Western history and, as such, it represents another instance of the crisis of Western culture in its "reversal [of] the natural order of values."[13]

Deconstruction presents a momentous challenge for Western humanistic culture because there is, according to Steiner, no "adequate logical or epistemological refutation of deconstructive semiotics," largely owing to the fact that there are "no valid procedures of decision between competing and even antithetical ascriptions of meaning."[14] Nevertheless, he feels the "summons of nihilism demand answer."[15] Steiner believes that the question of meaning is also a question of morality, and it is our "abandonment of this high and rigorous ground, in the name of nineteenth-century positivism and twentieth-century secular psychology, which has brought on much of the . . . anarchy in which we now find ourselves."[16] Unsatisfied with the commonsense, liberal (by which Steiner means British) dismissal and unworried circumvention of "French theory,"[17] Steiner suggests that we must instead "meet the challenge of autistic textuality or, more accurately, 'anti-textuality' on grounds as radical as its own, [and to do so] we must bring to bear on the act of meaning, on the understanding of meaning, the full force of moral intuition. The vitally concentrated agencies are those of tact, of courtesy of heart, of good taste, in a sense not decorous or civil, but inward and ethical."[18] Steiner realizes the challenges facing this perspective in contemporary culture, as "such focus and agencies cannot be logically formalized. They are existential modes. Their underwriting is, as we shall be compelled to propose, of a transcendent kind. This makes them utterly vulnerable. But also 'of the essence', this is to say, essential."[19]

So, against the current of Deconstruction, Steiner argues, we must read *as if* the text in front of us is meaningful, and *as if* the historical and cultural setting of the text is significant to its meaning. The poem is the product of *poiesis,* the creative act, upon which the commentary is contingent. Therefore, the primary text comes before the commentary. Sense is a matter of trust for Steiner, who calls this "Cartesian-Kantian wager, our leap into sense."[20] Metaphorically, he grounds this wager on meaning in an explicitly Christian image, that of the Eucharist:

> Where we read truly, where the experience is to be that of meaning, we do so as if the text (the piece of music, the work of art) *incarnates* (the notion is grounded in the sacramental) *a real presence of significant being.* This real presence, as is an icon, as in the enacted metaphor of the sacramental bread and wine, is, finally, irreducible to any other formal articulation, to any analytic deconstruction or paraphrase . . . These are not occult notions. They are of the immensity of the commonplace . . . To be "indwelt" by music, art, literature, to be made responsible, answerable to such habitation as a host is to a guest—perhaps unknown, unexpected—at evening, is to experience the *commonplace mystery of a real presence.*[21]

There is nothing absurd or superstitious about this argument, Steiner tells us. The very foundations of hermeneutics and criticism in Western culture are religious, deriving from the study of Holy Scripture, and he argues that for centuries, "we have borrowed, traded upon, made small change of the reserves of transcendent authority [without having made] any return deposit."[22] Steiner realizes how vulnerable this religious interpretation of culture is to secular critique, even to outright dismissal,[23] but he prefers the "inevitable embarrassment which must accompany any public avowal of mystery . . . to the slippery evasions and conceptual deficits in contemporary hermeneutics and criticism."[24]

Moreover, as first suggested in *Tolstoy or Dostoevsky,* Steiner argues that a culture in which God's presence no longer exerts any pressure will not produce "certain dimensions of thought and creativity."[25] Today, by which Steiner means after the Shoah, it may be "that nothing more is available to us than the absence of God," yet "wholly felt and lived, that absence is an agency and *mysterium tremendum*":[26]

> The density of God's absence, the edge of presence in that absence, is no empty dialectical twist. The phenomenology is elementary: it is like the recession from us of one whom we have loved or sought to love or of one before whom we have dwelt in fear. The distancing is, then, charged with the pressures of a nearness out of reach, of a remembrance torn at the edges. It is this absent "thereness", in the death-camps, in the laying waste of a grimed planet, which is articulate in the master-texts of our age. It lies in Kafka's parables, in the namings of Golgotha in Beckett's *Endgame,* in the Psalms to No-one of Paul Celan.[27]

Steiner believes that God's presence, even as absence, gives our humanity substance, meaning, and inspiration in that it provides a stable foundation and rationale for our existence. Just as we must approach a text with the assumption that it is meaningful and translatable, humanity must "wager on transcendence" and live *as if* God existed, in the hope of God's existence. Without this wager, both ethics and aesthetics are vulnerable to the impulses of nihilism.

Steiner's Shoah

Steiner's ongoing analysis of the Holocaust also reflects this turn toward theology, specifically to what he considers its theological origins. In 1987, Steiner publishes an essay entitled "The Long Life of Metaphor: An Approach to the Shoah,"[28] which begins by asking the question of whether or not the Shoah is like other acts of atrocity in human history. Steiner acknowledges the fact that "quantitatively there have been worse killings," and he is not convinced by the argument that the Nazis innovated ethnically motivated genocide or that the Holocaust is unique for its application of technology or bureaucracy, however modern, to the process of mass murder.[29] While he is no longer absolutely certain the Holocaust is unique, given the human capacity for mass murder, and finds the question itself "deeply unsettling, even repellent,"[30] he maintains that "*if* there are qualitative differences between the Shoah and the innumerable examples of mass-murder which punctuate history both before and since, they must lie very deep: in that symbolic and metaphysical-theological realm which I want to point towards."[31]

Steiner's approach to the Holocaust and antisemitism, he tells us, is stimulated by the failure of empirical techniques and positivist methodologies to explain the sources of the Shoah in European high culture, certain key aspects of Nazi policy, and the postwar phenomenon of "antisemitism without Jews":

> [Historians] have quite markedly, failed to explain—except on the rather trivial level of Hitler's private pathology—the Nazi decision to press on with the "Final Solution" when even a brief suspension of the death transports, roundups, and extermination industry would have freed desperately needed resources for the defense and survival of the Reich. Nor do "rationalistic" and immanently grounded explanations explain the continuation of virulent Jew hatred in countries, in societies where there are virtually *no Jews left* (as in Poland, in Austria, in the Ukraine). The seeds of Auschwitz—the Nazi sense of victory over the Jews as outweighing the ruin of Germany; Jew-hatred where only phantoms are left. These are the questions that demand an attempt at an answer. And it is that attempt which leads me to test a different order or framework of thought and speech.[32]

Before discussing this different framework, however, Steiner addresses the larger meaning of the Holocaust for contemporary world Jewry. He argues that the presumed uniqueness of the Holocaust has "become vital to Judaism now" as it is used by some to underwrite "certain essential aspects of the re-creation of nationhood in Israel, a re-creation whose uniqueness, whose transcendence of normal probability even in secular perceptions, subtly counterbalances that of the world of Auschwitz, of Bergen-Belsen."[33] Steiner suggests that it is understandable that the Holocaust, "the remembrance of Auschwitz, the haunting apprehension that, somewhere, somehow, the massacres could begin anew, is today the cement of Jewish identity."[34] This is largely owing to the fact that the Holocaust and the continuing threat of antisemitism remain the only common bonds between those in a community divided by Orthodoxy, atheism, Zionism, conservatism ("conservative American Jew"), socialism, and communism.[35] In this situation, however, he argues that the Holocaust is often misused to fulfill contemporary needs (which are at odds with Steiner's conception of Judaism): "Israel has too often invoked the Shoah as an apologia, as a justification for the more extreme gestures of its policies, both inside its borders and beyond them. The horror of the Shoah and of its recall, in books, in pictures, in the media, has provided the non-practicing, the largely assimilated Jew in the West, notably in the United States, with a subtly self-flattering, self-dramatising aura of tragic 'belonging'."[36] Even Holocaust survivors now seem to offend Steiner by their cultivation of celebrity: "A disturbingly commercialized pathos of horror has arisen around certain survivors and their all-too-eloquent and sometimes even theatrical witness."[37] Holocaust historians, by contrast, are celebrated for their memorialization of the Shoah: "By simple virtue of their publication of the documentary records of the death camps, of the massacres at large, of Jewish resistance, the historians of the Shoah have performed an absolutely essential act of truthful remembrance, of resurrection. Theirs has been the *kaddish* against lies—and against that greatest lie, which is forgetting."[38] He concludes his critique of the contemporary Jewish world with the following qualification: "We are, in certain respects, a traumatised, a crazed people. How could we not be? Especially where it is that trauma which keeps us from final dispersal."[39]

Steiner then returns to the "different order or framework of thought and speech" to which he first referred. There are two aspects to this framework: his theory of antisemitism, *the blackmail of transcendence,* and the beginnings of a new theory of the relationship between the Jewish denial of Jesus and Christian antisemitism. Before reiterating the dynamic at the heart of *the blackmail of transcendence,* Steiner briefly introduces a discussion of Paul's narrative on the Jewish rejection of Jesus and its implications:

> Embryonic or fully spelt out, several scenarios spring from the Pauline source. Christ was the long-awaited Messiah . . . foretold in their own Torah, prayers, and prophecy, whom the Jewish people handed over to abominable torment and death. In doing so, Judaism eradicated from within itself . . . the act of divine election . . . Israel passed into the limbo of theological sterility and despair . . . A second scenario is no less ominous. By refusing to recognise Jesus of Nazareth as the foretold Messiah, the Jews have postponed the day of man's salvation, the apocalyptic enfranchisement of suffering humanity and the eternal justice and peace which

> are to attend the Second Coming. Israel's refusal of Christ has, literally, condemned mankind to the treadmill of history. The Jews therefore hold the *Ecclesia* in particular, and humanity in general, hostage. There can be no liberation, no salvation from the agonies, bloodshed and injustice of history until Judaism recognises the authentic messianic truth of Jesus's ministry and incarnation.[40]

Here we see the ideas of the reactionary French Catholic philosopher Pierre Boutang, with whom Steiner claims to have shared some of the "stellar hours" of his life.[41] Steiner's memoir, *Errata,* explains their shared love of teaching, "utter passion for Scripture and the classics, for poetry and metaphysics," and while "dialectically divided, [they] are at one in intuiting that the question of the existence, of the conceivability or negation of God, however one approaches it, reinsures seriousness of mind and spirit."[42] It is Boutang's religious reading of the Jewish rejection of Jesus, however, that demonstrates to Steiner the deep connection between Pauline Christianity and Jew hatred:

> As a young *camelôt du roi,* a royalist and absolutist acolyte of Maurras and the *Action française,* Boutang . . . has been a pamphleteer against Jews, whose mystery of survival obsesses him. On a mundane level, Pierre Boutang sees in the Jew the virus of secular, capitalist rationality after the "catastrophe" of the French Revolution. The Jews incarnate and exploit a damnable modernity. On an eschatological level, in the unfathomable scenario of the *mysterium* of revelation, the Jews, by virtue of their rejection of the Messiah-Jesus, hold mankind to ransom. There can be, believes Boutang, no kingdom of love and of pardon on this earth so long as the Jew remains outside the *ecclesia.*[43]

Steiner, then, attempts to connect the Jewish rejection of Jesus and the charge of deicide to the Jewish invention of morality in the image of an almighty, all-seeing, all-demanding God *(the blackmail of transcendence)*, and, in turn, connects these two processes to the waning of formal religion in Western society:

> The force, the obsessive depth of a doctrine become greater as this doctrine passes into the individual and collective unconscious in the guise of symbol

> and metaphor. Such symbolic and metaphoric obsessions with the psyche become virulent when the doctrine which they represent has lost or begun to lose its own plausibility and intellectual coherence.
>
> This is only an apparent paradox. It is when they are exhausted or degenerating that organs and muscle tissue secrete contagious and maleficent substances into the human body. So it was that the original Pauline and Patristic theology of Jew-hatred, together with the more general and even deeper-lying resentment of monotheism and sacrificial morality, took on their terrible, festering virulence precisely as Christianity and a belief in God as such began receding from the spiritual habits and intellectual-political adherence of Western civilization. There is a perfect logic in the anti-Semitism of a Voltaire. There is a clear pattern in the fact that the Auschwitz-world erupts out of the subconscious, collective obsessions of an increasingly agnostic, even anti- or post-Christian society. Long-buried, and freed of doctrinal inhibitions and abstractions, the symbols and metaphors which cluster around the Judaic invention and "killing" of God (the two are, psychologically twinned) turned murderous.[44]

We know that Steiner views Nazism as a return to pre-monotheistic paganism, a world, unlike Christendom, where the Jew was no longer necessary for the realization of God's promise in and through Christ, so it is no surprise to Steiner that Auschwitz erupts out of an increasingly agnostic, post-Christian society. The Nazis were freed from the Christian obligation to protect the Jew (both for humanitarian reasons and to preserve the "remnant" of Jews who would in the end confirm Christ as the Messiah) and proceeded to murder the Jewish people in an unbridled, and unprecedented, frenzy of suppressed resentment and ancient hatred.

Steiner realizes that his hypothesis cannot be proven, as its evidence is not "of an empirical or quantifiable kind."[45] Nevertheless, he argues that only "an acute awareness of the life-force of theological-metaphysical metaphor and symbolism" can illuminate the "causal dynamics of Jew-hatred and of the Auschwitz experience."[46] No other approach, asserts Steiner, can explain the self-destructive nature of Nazi antisemitism (which placed the destruction of the Jews ahead of the survival of Germany), the

European-wide indifference toward Jewish suffering, and the presence of antisemitism in the absence of Jews.

Steiner's essay "The Long Life of Metaphor: An Approach to the Shoah" also discusses the poetry of Paul Celan, a survivor of the Holocaust, whom Steiner celebrates as one of the greatest poets in modern European literature.[47] After Auschwitz, which is for Steiner a horrifying symbol of God's absence, Jews face the challenge of speaking to and about God. They also face the difficulty of using language to try to conceptualize and understand Auschwitz while wondering whether the "limits of language do not fall short of the limits of the Shoah-experience."[48] Paul Celan is central to Steiner's thought on language and Holocaust representation because he alone, in Steiner's opinion, has managed to create a new language of representation and, through it, was able to pierce the heart of the Shoah experience, and this in German. Celan's poetry turned the German language against itself, purifying it by expunging its Nazi residue, and used it to communicate a profoundly Jewish experience. As evidence of his argument in this essay, Steiner cites Celan's poem "Psalm":

> Niemand knetet uns wieder aus Erde und Lehm,
> niemand bespricht unsern Staub.
> Niemand.
>
> Gelobt seist du, Niemand.
> Dir zulieb wollen
> wir blühn.
> Dir
> entgegen.
>
> Ein Nichts
> waren wir, sind wir, werden
> wir bleiben, blühend:
> die Nichts—, die
> Niemandsrose.
>
> Mit
> dem Griffel seelenhell,

dem Staubfaden himmelswüst
der Krone rot
vom Purpurwort, das wir sangen
über, o über
dem Dorn.

No-one kneads us again out of earth and loam,
No-one bespeaks our dust.
No-one.

Praise unto thee, No-one.
For love of you will
we bloom.
Towards/against
You.

A nothing
were we, are we, will
we remain, blooming:
No-one's-rose.

With
the stylus soul-bright
the dust-thread sky-waste,
the crown reddened
by the purple word, which we sang
above, o above
the thorn.[49]

Only Celan has found adequate expression for the "No-oneness" that was God during the Shoah, argues Steiner. Through his poem, Celan confronts the absence, impotence, and indifference of God during the Holocaust. And through the name "Niemand," Celan stresses the "exit of God" from language and from the bounds of human experience. Yet Steiner points out that even after Auschwitz, in the absent face of God, Celan sustains the perennial Jewish tradition of dialogue with God. Steiner reads the poem as an "accusation out of ash, [a] blossoming indictment that, alone, tells against the finality of annihilation."[50] Celan's poetry, according to Steiner, takes readers into a "sphere of lived metaphor, of language *beside itself,* which is one of the (wholly insufficient) images or tropes whereby we can come nearer the question with which I began: that of the very possibilities of human discourse in regard to God and to the Shoah—a duality that has for the Jew, been made an irreparable unison. To ask what, if any, are such possibilities is to ask metaphysically and theologically. It is to recognize the essential inadequacy of pragmatic-positivist levels of argument."[51]

Steiner and Celan share similar concerns: the effects of the Shoah on the form and content of language; the crucial role of German, in both confronting the Shoah and redeeming language generally; and the impossible necessity of communicating between the world of Auschwitz and our own. Yet Steiner most intensely responds to what he sees in Celan's work as a decision to operate within a theological context to find meaning in the Shoah experience. As it concerns the presence and absence of God in the world, Celan's poetry is at once theological and metaphysical. The religious concerns of both Celan and Steiner connect them intellectually and explain Steiner's embrace of Celan as the only poet to have reached the heart of the Shoah experience. According to Steiner, Celan's poetry, through its use of metaphor and symbolism, inhabits the theological-metaphysical levels of language and, as a result, grounds the Shoah experience within the definitions of humanity, history, and human speech: "The necessary and sufficient condition for Celan's poems is the situation of all human saying after the Shoah, a situation that Celan lived and articulated in the absent face of God. In this one supreme witness . . . the fate of the Jew, the night-charged genius of the German language, of the idiom of Auschwitz and Belsen, and a profound intimacy with the Hebraic and the Yiddish legacy coalesced; and they coalesced around the central criteria of the theological and the metaphysical orders of questioning."[52]

Even though Steiner sees Celan's suicide as a symbol of "overwhelming desolation," and wonders whether the Shoah "has eradicated the saving grace, the life-giving mystery of meaningful metaphor in Western speech and, correlatively . . . poetry and philosophic thought," he believes that the "compulsion to articulacy within Judaism, the commandment of dialogue even with, even against, a mute God," must persist. He concludes with the admission that it is his belief "that such persistence, with all that it implies not only for the precarious survival of Judaism, but for that, no less precarious, of our civilization as a whole, depends on the seminal force, on the haunting tenacity of the metaphysical and the theological presences in our psyche."[53]

Confronting Christianity

The intellectual influence of another relationship can be seen on Steiner's work at this particular time, especially upon his thinking about the Holocaust and its relationship to the conflict between Christianity and Judaism. Steiner first met the Scottish theologian Donald MacKinnon when he arrived at Cambridge in 1961 and they remained close friends until MacKinnon's death in 1994.[54] In his 1997 memoir, *Errata,* Steiner acknowledges the profound influence of this friendship and his debt to "MacKinnon's essays, to his letters, to the years of dialogue, much of what is central to my later work. There could, for Donald, be no justifiable future for Christianity so long as Christian theology and practice had not faced up to, had not internalised lucidly, its seminal role in the millennial torments of Judaism and the Holocaust."[55] In *The Borderlands of Theology,* published in 1968, MacKinnon makes this position clear: "If for the Christian it is in the events of the first Good Friday that the sense of the final judgment of the world is to be glimpsed, as well as the foundations of its hope, he must also remember that part of the price paid for the accomplishment of these things in human history was the unmentionable horror of anti-semitism whose beginning can be traced in the New Testament itself and whose last manifestation in our own time was Christian acquiescence in the 'final solution'."[56]

It is possible that MacKinnon's work and friendship provided Steiner with some of the necessary confidence to publicly address the failings of Christianity, not an easy task for a Jewish scholar living and working in a Christian environment. Living in England, with its lack of connection to the Holocaust, may have conditioned Steiner to focus his scholarly attention on the specific role of Christian theology in the formation, and determination, of antisemitism. Regardless, in 1989 Steiner makes the decision to publicly denounce Christian antisemitism and the apathy of the churches in relation to Nazism and subsequent atrocities.

Donald MacKinnon was present in King's College Chapel, Cambridge, on Remembrance Sunday, 1989, when Steiner delivered his memorial lecture "Remembering the Future." Steiner begins this address with an acknowledgment that British perceptions of World War II differ from his own and from those of Europeans in general. He assures his audience that he understands the emphasis given to the First World War in British memorialization as it "dealt more harshly with Britain and most of the Commonwealth than did that of 1939–1945."[57] After years of arguing that England must confront the Holocaust and its relationship to it, an argument that precipitated mutual hostility between Steiner and his English hosts, it seems that Steiner now better appreciates the cultural and experiential divide between England and Europe:

> Britain did not witness, let alone endure the long midnight of humanity which extended during the early 1940s from the ravines of Kiev to the torture-cells in occupied France. The pressures of hauntedness are profoundly different. They continue to divide British from continental and East European sensibility. They distance the climate of British theological-philosophic thought and feeling from that of Europe. It is this difference which makes it difficult for someone like myself, who am in several ways a guest among you, to conjoin modes of remembering, of honouring that are England's with those of the continent and of the unspeakable fate of Judaism on that continent. A requiem (let alone a *te deum*) is not a *kaddish*.[58]

Steiner attempts to bridge this divide by discussing what is "common to a complexly divided legacy of sorrow."[59] But he also addresses another commonality between Europe and England in their relationship to the Jewish people: Christianity. To his discussion of the failure of the humanities and enlightened high culture, illustrated by Germans reading Rilke and listening to Schubert the night before operating the gas chambers, Steiner (for the first and only time) adds the practice of singing "Christmas carols with . . . loved ones in the evening."[60] Indeed, the one aspect of the Holocaust that Great Britain can legitimately be asked to confront is the Christian legacy of Jew hatred. Steiner then challenges his audience with the following words:

> How, in God's name, is it possible to be a Christian after Auschwitz? How is it possible to erase from the monstrous chronicle of European antisemitism as it culminated in the *Shoah,* the teachings of Christianity, that dooming of the Jew inherent, eloquent in Pauline doctrines on the Jewish refusal of Christ? As your guest, it is indecorous of me to ask. But Christianity itself has failed to pose the question with anything even approaching the requisite urgency or depth or terror before itself. And because it has failed to do so, and because it persists in politic omission, so many of its current gestures, so much of its present discourse, be it theological or liturgical, are shrunken, are parochial in the lesser sense of that word.[61]

Instead of focusing on the unique "philosophic intent" of the Shoah, in this memorial lecture Steiner employs universal imagery of the inhuman and moves between a discussion of Christian antisemitism, on the one hand, and a variety of other genocides and human-made disasters, on the other. He discusses the murder of European Jewry alongside Stalinism; the religious wars in the Middle East, Northern Ireland, Lebanon, and India; and the Cambodian genocide, stating that "history has granted us no armistice, no exemption from the inhuman."[62] In fact, his discussion suggests that our condition today may even be worse owing to the fact that few people actually knew the details of the Nazi death camp system of extermination, whereas during "the hour of 'The Killing Fields' in Kampuchea, the world was informed. Radio and television brought reports of the homicidal insanities of the *Khmer Rouge,* of the live burial of perhaps tens of thousands of men, women, and children, of the systematic infliction of unspeakable sadism." He goes on, "No one moved. Did you cry out in audible despair and resolution? Did I? And at this hour, it is western arms which are keeping the *Khmer Rouge* in business."[63]

In the final minutes of his presentation, Steiner returns to organized religion, criticizing the churches for their conservative nature in general and their support for the status quo, be it during the Shoah or the other conflicts and genocides mentioned. He argues that the contemporary impotence of synagogue and church, "the one deafened by catastrophe, the other by some immensity of embarrassment," only serves to strengthen one of the major weaknesses in Western culture: the marginality of religion. Steiner leaves his audience with hope for the future by referring to the uniquely hopeful nature of human grammar:

> To hope is to remember the future. It is to remember that which could yet be. The compulsion to hope is at once imperative and enigmatic within us. It forges an indissoluble link between remembrance, even desolate, and bracing "futurity". This ebb and tide, the play on words which makes mourning, in the sense of lamentation, echo morning in the sense of daybreak, would appear to be unique to humanity. It springs from the far threshold of the coming of language. In each use of the past tense we re-enact something of the riddle of the fall; in each use of the future of the verb "to be" something of the wonder of resurrection and the messianic.[64]

Thinking Golgotha and Auschwitz

The troubled relationship between Judaism and Christianity is revisited in 1991, when Steiner delivers a lecture entitled "Through That Glass Darkly" in honor of the esteemed Holocaust historian Raul Hilberg at the University of Vermont. Steiner argues that Jew hatred is a "persistent psychosis of Christianity," and is the result of "unhealed scars left by the Jew's 'No' to the crucified Messiah."[65] Again, the influence of Donald MacKinnon is apparent, and acknowledged by Steiner: "When trying, haltingly, to find a symmetry of the inhuman between the Jewish refusal of the 'man/god' Jesus and the deliberate bestialisation of man, both as butcher and as victim, in the camps, when trying to 'think' Auschwitz and Golgotha as implicated in some interrelated finality, I am carrying forward from the hours with Donald MacKinnon."[66]

In this essay we glimpse a new theme, emanating from Steiner's meditations on the Jewish refusal of Jesus. Steiner argues, "If we sense in the Shoah a singularity, a quantum jump in our long chronicles of inhumanity, it is because mass slaughter and planned elimination, both of which have manifold precedent, were accompanied by, were explicitly designed as the *dehumanization* of the victim."[67] Here, Steiner sees in the Shoah a "symbolic symmetry" with the Jewish denial of Jesus:

> In the fantastications of Nazism, those starved, beaten, gassed to extinction were not men and women and children but vermin, members of a

> species other than that of man. Now observe the symbolic symmetry. In the eye of the believer, God had, through the incarnation of Christ, through the descent of the divine into human form, affirmed, attested to the literal godliness of man. Man had, in Christ, been of the nature of God. This modulation had been scorned by the Jew. Was it not inevitable that the Jew, who had refused transcendence for man, should bear the final, logical consequence, which is to be made less than human?[68]

Steiner now perceives the Shoah as an exercise in cosmic dehumanization, a universal process brought about by Christian theology and its obsessive focus on the Jewish denial of Jesus:

> The Shoah, the death-camps have lowered the fragile threshold of humaneness. If the victims were "un-manned", so were the butchers whose intent and acts diminished them to bestiality. The Jew on his way to the gas-chambers was more than a scapegoat. He was, in a sickness unto death of logic, or reciprocity, the provocation to, the occasion of, his persecutors' descent into animality. It is, in both his agony and in the sadistic beastliness which brought on that agony—the two being rigorously inseparable—the Jew who put in question the belief that our own kind, that *homo sapiens* has, in some manner, been created in God's image. Without the Jew, there would not, there could not have been the cancellation of man that is Auschwitz—a cancellation so symmetrical with that, embodied in Judaism's remembrance of the rejection, of the claims to the divine in Jesus. Erasure for erasure. The eclipse of light over Golgotha and the black hole in history of the Shoah. Darkness calling to darkness and the Jew centrally implicated in both.[69]

This interpretation is predicated on a view of the Holocaust as a descent into barbarism that is wholly unique in its cosmic significance, which forever connects Jews to Christians and vice versa. Auschwitz is conceived as a cosmic act of Christian vengeance against the Jews who, in the Christian imagination, both invented and killed God. After Auschwitz, "Jew and gentile go lamed, as if the wrestling-bout of Jacob had been well and truly lost,"[70] and contemporary Christianity:

> is lamed, possibly terminally, by the paradox of revelation and of doctrine which generated not only the Shoah but the millennia of anti-Jewish violence,

> humiliation and quarantine which are its obvious background. It stands, or should stand, appalled by its own image, by its fundamental failings, whether by omission or commission, in the season of barbarism, increasingly conscious of the fact that the death-camps were modelled on the long habituation of Christian Europe to blueprints of hell (a concept antithetical to Judaism); Catholicism and Protestantism hardly know themselves.[71]

Judaism, by comparison, argues Steiner, suffers from both stasis and trauma-induced aggression:

> Jewish orthodoxy continues in its often jejune formalism, in its feverish atrophy in ritualistic minutiae. Worse: in Israel it has fuelled state savagery and corruption—for let us not forget that each time a Jew humiliates, tortures or makes homeless another human being, there is a posthumous victory for Hitler. In liberal Judaism, in Judaism at large, the winds of spiritual development, of metaphysical exploration, blow faint. Where, now, is there "a guide for the perplexed", or a voice out of the register which produced a Spinoza, a Bergson or a Wittgenstein? With the breakdown of messianic radicalism throughout the Marxist domain, the fertile stress of critical questioning, of utopian immanence, withers away. How Jewish was the Scribe of Revelation when he spoke in bitter contempt of those who "blow neither hot nor cold."[72]

Steiner admits that ecumenical programs may help reconcile individual Jews and Christians but argues that these attempts are not based in theological fact. Christianity and Judaism suffer irreconcilable differences: "the Jew cannot negotiate his rejection of a messianic Jesus" and the Christian cannot accept this rejection as legitimate.[73]

This explanation of the Shoah allows us to better understand Steiner's commitment to theological metaphysical modes of thought in place of those of a strictly positivist historical nature. It also reinforces Steiner's ongoing attempts to sustain our sense of horror and outrage over the murder of European Jewry for the last five decades: "The notion of 'coming to terms' with the Holocaust is a vulgar and profound indecency. Man cannot, he must not ever 'come to terms', *historicize pragmatically or incorporate into the comforts of reason* his derogation from the human within himself. He must not blur the possibility that the death-camps and the world's indifference to them marked the failure of a crucial experiment: man's effort to become fully human" (italics mine).[74] The broader implications of this failure for the condition of Western culture, and the future of humanity, are taken up in Steiner's last major work.

Grammars of Creation

Steiner's Gifford Lectures were delivered in 1990 at the University of Glasgow and published eleven years later as *Grammars of Creation*.[75] This text assembles the major themes of Steinerian cultural criticism into an extremely dense commentary on the crisis at the center of Western civilization. Far more involved than the "exploration of the idea of creation in Western thought, literature, and history" touted by the publisher, *Grammars of Creation* is a 338-page synthesis of Steiner's oeuvre that places Auschwitz and the God question at its center. Steiner begins the discussion with his sense that Western culture suffers from a "core-tiredness," a lethargy at its center, which he believes results from the uninterrupted violence of the twentieth century and the concomitant erosion of idealism in Western hearts and minds. The problem with the twentieth century is not that it is the first century to be characterized by mass murder or enormous violence, it is that the period beginning in 1914 followed a century of growing optimism, in which human beings were believed to be capable of peaceful coexistence, rational problem solving, and improving human living conditions through the technological application of science. This dream, reflected so clearly in Stefan Zweig's memoir *Die Welt von Gestern* (The World of Yesterday),[76] is first betrayed by the hecatomb of World War I, but is eviscerated by the crimes of Nazism. It is because German fascism springs "from within the context, the locale, the administrative-social instruments of the high places of civilization, of education, of scientific progress and humanizing deployment, be it Christian or Enlightened" that the Shoah undoes "previous advances" and calls into question the progressive faith of nineteenth-century liberalism and scientific positivism.[77] In fact, the Shoah provides evidence of the fact that "refined intellectuality, artistic virtuosity and appreciation, scientific eminence will collaborate actively with totalitarian demands or, at best, remain indifferent to surrounding sadism."[78]

Into the "dustbin of history," the West can sweep the following failed vehicles of human progress: religion, education, high culture, science, and the now defunct Marxist experiment of human emancipation. At the end of the twentieth century, exhausted by its failed attempts to emancipate humanity, Steiner wonders how Western culture will orient itself toward the future? After the failure of religion, culture, science, and politics, into what exactly shall Western culture invest its hope for the future? Steiner tells us that "hope is a transcendental inference. It is underwritten by theological-metaphysical presumptions."[79] However, presumptions about the existence of God and His ability to intervene on our behalf have been waning in the West since the seventeenth century. The twentieth century, Steiner argues, "has [not only] put in doubt the theological, the philosophical, and the political-material insurance for hope"[80] but has inaugurated something even more ominous: the eclipse of the messianic. Messianism, according to Steiner, is the source of idealism in Western culture, and while it is rooted in religion it can also be "independent of any postulate of God: it stands for man's access to perfectibility, to a higher and, presumably, enduring condition of reason and of justice."[81]

Steiner relates this crisis of idealism to language, and attempts to gauge its effects on grammar, which he defines as "the articulate organization of perception, reflection and experience, the nerve structure of consciousness when it communicates with itself and others."[82] Here he expands on a theme first mentioned in his Remembrance Day sermon:[83] "Future tenses [of the verb "to be"] are an idiom of the messianic. Take away energizing anticipation, the luminous imperative of waiting, and these tenses will be end-stopped . . . just as the almost imperceptible tectonic movements in the deeps of the earth sever and re-shape continents, so the forces emanating from the eclipse of the messianic will find manifest expression. Grammars of nihilism flicker, as it were, on the horizon."[84] Just as Steiner believes the humanist "walks with his head twisted backward,"[85] he suggests the "utopian, messianic, positivist-meliorist 'futures' presumed, blueprinted in the Western legacy from Plato to Lenin, from the Prophets to Leibniz, may no longer be available to our syntax. We now look back at them."[86] Continuing the argument of *Real Presences,* Steiner argues that without the presence of God, or even the memory of Him in the form of the messianic impulse, it is unlikely that Western culture will continue to produce philosophy, literature, music, and art of the first rank. More than ever, he is convinced that the "armature of *poiesis*" is theological.[87] In our century, however, scientific invention has displaced theologically conditioned understandings of creation, in which the artist mimics or challenges God, the master Creator. The relentless "forward motion" of the sciences, combined with the continued recession of traditional modes of creation, guarantees that technological invention and its idiom will dominate the human future instead. What this means for the ongoing development of Western culture, as we have known it, is uncertain.

As we know, George Steiner is not a religious Jew, and as a result his theological concerns have led to his being accused by critics of wanting "to enjoy a supernatural aesthetic without the obligation of supernatural belief."[88] James Wood is representative of Steiner's critics, who either neglect or simply do not understand his concern with the Holocaust (and by extension the crises of the twentieth century), when he writes, "Secularists believe everything Steiner does, without having to invoke God. A 'leap into sense,' which Steiner promises, is not the same as a leap into God, and does not have to be. A leap into sense is how the secular day begins for most of us. The sun rises, the birds begin their quarrels, the day takes its habitual creeping shape, we rise from bed—and we have leaped into sense, whether happily or unhappily. We do not need to 'wager' on this sense because all our life it has seemed a bet that has already been won for us: the sun rises everyday."[89]

This "common-sense" response to what is for Steiner "of the essence" speaks, once again, to the experiential and philosophical divide between Steiner and his Anglo-American critics. It also misunderstands the religious nature of Steiner's work, its Jewish sources, and its post-Holocaust composition. The two theological elements that underlie Steinerian criticism are the dialogic relationship with God (where God may be absent altogether), and the location of human hope in the messianic. Neither aspect requires a traditional belief in God or formal religious practice.

Perhaps even more obtuse is Roger Kimball, who, in his review of *Grammars of Creation,* interprets Steiner's discussion of the Holocaust as a "rhetorical prop" that "not only gives the appearance of establishing one's credentials as a person of great moral gravity; it also stymies criticism. Who wants to risk the charge of insensitivity by objecting that the Holocaust had nothing to do with the 'ideal of man' as 'language animal'?"[90] As I suggested in the introduction, without a proper understanding of Steiner's personal relationship to the Holocaust, and the subsequent development of his thought on its significance, readers of his analysis of Western culture cannot fully appreciate nor comprehend its content and meaning.

Left Naked to Unknowing

It is instructive that the last chapter of Steiner's memoir deals explicitly with the theological themes of his later works and with his own religious questions. Steiner's religious beliefs, as one might expect, are not easy to characterize. He argues that the attempts by religious Judaism to explain the absence of God during the Shoah offend "intelligence and morality,"[91] while Christianity can really only "convince the convinced."[92] There is no question that the Shoah, a powerful symbol of God's absence, has made any kind of confident religious belief or practice impossible for Steiner. As he writes at the end of *Grammars of Creation,* atheism does not "mock the God-hypothesis [but bears] witness to sombre deprivation. 'He doesn't exist, the bastard' (Samuel Beckett)."[93]

Steiner knows that there is no historical example of a religion that is not the obvious "product of the human imagination and of human discourse."[94] He respects atheism in principle and recognizes that decency and morality are also secular values, all the more so given the bloody history of organized religion. However, the presence of so many great thinkers and artists in the believing camp of Western history convinces Steiner that "to assign to [their] perceptions a merely rhetorical or antiquarian force, is to leave the greater part of our civilization vacant."[95] He suggests we try to "imagine our landscapes without their places of worship; our arts and music without their address to matters of faith; our philosophy and metaphysics, from the pre-Socratics to Heidegger, if they lacked the motion towards, the investigation of, the debate on religious experience, on the first principle or the prime mover."[96]

Music has become an intense love for Steiner and, in its ability to "enact the prayer of the unbeliever or non-practising"[97] among us, it acts as the perfect metaphor for his understanding of meaning:

> Music is meaningful to the utmost; it signifies totally. But neither its meanings nor its significations can be verbalised, adequately paraphrased or translated conceptually into any domain except repeated performance. Logic has no purchase on musical sense. I doubt very much whether neurophysiological hypotheses as to consciousness will ever explicate either the creation of music or its impact upon us. Both of these existential facts . . . are as empirically manifest, as transformative of being as any known to human experience. Yet they seem to lie outside analytical-experimental understanding. The very same intractabilities of the self-evident characterise the signifying "non-sense" of theological and liturgical propositions.[98]

Steiner is not surprised, nor is he bothered, by the fact that God cannot be proven rationally to exist. He asks, "What would God be if His being could be circumscribed, let alone demonstrated by human dialectics and ratiocination?"[99] For Steiner, a "specific agnosticism in respect of reason or 'proof' lies at the base of [his] fragmentary and dishevelled convictions. [He] feel[s] assured that if 'God' exists, He/She—as current courtesies demand—can have nothing whatever in common with the conceptions of Him/Her advanced by human minds, however acute . . . 'God' can be addressed inwardly only as *the totally Other*."[100] So then what is the nature and meaning of a relationship between humanity and God, when God is so totally unlike and apart from human beings? The connection between God and humanity, and the significance of this relationship is, for Steiner, an intuitive sense of the messianic, based upon an understanding of morality, of how things should be on this earth. He believes that our sense that "something . . . has gone hideously wrong" is evidence of a broken contract: "in the presence of the beaten, raped child, of the horse or mule flogged across its eyes, I am possessed, as by a midnight clarity, by the intuition of the Fall. Only some such happening, irretrievable to reason, can make intelligible, though always near to unbearable, the actualities of our history on this wasted earth. We are condemned to be our cruel, greedy, egotistical, mendacious selves. When it was, when it must have been meant to be *otherwise*."[101]

Steiner is not alone in his attempt to find hope and meaning outside human history, in the messianic.[102] His conception conforms to that of another critic who struggled to understand the Holocaust, Theodor Adorno:

> The only philosophy which can be responsibly practiced in the face of despair is the attempt to contemplate all things as they would present themselves from the standpoint of redemption. Knowledge has no light but that shed on the world by redemption: all else is reconstruction, mere technique. Perspectives must be fashioned that displace and estrange the world, reveal it to be, with its rifts and crevices, as indigent and distorted as it will appear one day in the Messianic light. To gain such perspectives without velleity or violence, entirely from felt contact with its objects—this alone is the task of thought.[103]

Steiner's work takes a more explicit theological turn in the early 1980s, stimulated by the threat of Derridean Deconstruction and his continued study of the Holocaust and antisemitism. His theological approach to meaning in *Real Presences* (the lecture is delivered in 1985; the book is published in 1989) can be interpreted as a strategy by which he attempts to protect humanistic culture from what he views as the nihilistic assault of Deconstruction. Similarly, Steiner's work on the Shoah (he no longer uses the anglicized Greek word "Holocaust" to describe the destruction of European Jewry), from this period forward, is engaged with what he considers to be its theological origins. Specifically, Steiner focuses on the troubled relationship between Christianity and Judaism, particularly upon the Christian obsession with the Jewish rejection of Jesus.

Two intellectual friendships influence Steiner's thought during this time. Pierre Boutang, whose belief that the Jewish rejection of Jesus holds humanity captive in a kind of limbo that separates the world from final redemption, demonstrates for Steiner the deep connection between the teachings of Pauline Christianity and Jew hatred. By contrast, Donald MacKinnon, the Anglican philosopher who diagnoses a void at the center of Christianity for its failure to take responsibility for its antisemitic heritage, provides Steiner with intellectual support for his public confrontation with post-Holocaust Christianity. Through conversations with both men, Steiner glimpses what he believes is another level of explanation for the Shoah. The Shoah, now thought to share a symbolic symmetry with the Jewish rejection of Jesus, is the enactment of Christian vengeance for the Jewish denial of Jesus. The rejection of Jesus signified for Christians the Jewish rejection of the transcendent in man, and the result was the vengeful dehumanization of the Jewish people by the Christian world. This theory is connected to Steiner's understanding of antisemitism, *the blackmail of transcendence,* which identifies the Jews as the inventors of God. So, then, for Steiner, the origins of the Shoah lie deep within the religious imagination of Western culture, in which the Jews are responsible for both the creation and the destruction of God.

The last major work composed by Steiner thus far, *Grammars of Creation,* diagnoses the crisis at the center of contemporary Western culture as one of exhaustion and frustration. Steiner's descriptive terminology for Western culture after the Holocaust has consistently signified these feelings: postculture, epilogue, twilight, afternoon. The tools of emancipation in Western history, religion, education, high culture, science, Marxism have all failed to produce their promised results, and there is no clear indication of where the future will lead as a result.

Hope, Steiner tells us, is a religious force, and Western culture has been in retreat from religion for over three centuries. But it is still possible to look toward the human future with hope for its redemption without a formal belief in God. Although the Shoah, and the historical record of human immorality in general, convinces Steiner of the truth of atheism, he refuses, "even at the worst hours, to abdicate from the belief that the two validating wonders of mortal existence are love and the invention of the future tense. Their conjunction, if it will ever come to pass, is the Messianic."[104]

Conclusion

Yosef Hayim Yerushalmi tells us that the verb *zakhar,* to remember, appears in various forms in the Hebrew Bible "no less than one hundred and sixty-nine times, usually with either God or Israel as the subject, for memory is incumbent upon both."[1] The work of George Steiner fulfills this function in two ways. Steiner memorializes the Holocaust and the central European Jewish culture it destroyed, and his later work also reminds us not to forget the human relationship with God. This is the primary purpose of *Zakhor,* the commandment to remember, so as not to forget our relationship to God.

Steiner chooses an old English word, *remembrancer,* by which to define himself as a thinker, writer, and teacher in the period after the Holocaust. The word has several meanings, all of which correspond to Steiner's chosen vocation. The word *remembrancer* signifies a collector of debts due to the sovereign; one who reminds another, or seeks to remember; and, a memento, record, or souvenir.[2] Steiner is all of these things. His confrontation with Christianity is certainly an attempt to remind Christians of the role their "teachings of contempt" have played in the history of antisemitism and the destruction of European Jewry. And this act of reminding can be interpreted as a settling of accounts between Christianity, Judaism, and the Jewish people. Steiner himself can be seen as a kind of human souvenir, or symbol, of the central European Jewish culture that contributed so much to modern European history before its destruction in the Shoah. His entire project on post-Holocaust Western culture is a record of the period of aftermath as it unfolds and evolves throughout Europe, England, and America.

Steiner's role as remembrancer begins as an act of memorialization, on the part of a surviving son, for the lost world of "Central European

Judaism." First introduced to this highly assimilated Jewish culture by his beloved father, Steiner's identification with it is not only intellectual and cultural, but also deeply personal. As mentioned earlier, Steiner is not simply engaged in memorializing this European Jewish world; his work is also an act of *resuscitation*. In opposition to postwar criticism, which dismissed the German Jewish symbiosis out of hand, Steiner's conception of "Central European Judaism" reinvests this influential culture with meaning and respect by modeling his conceptions of Judaism and humanism entirely upon its example. It seems that however difficult it is for Steiner to meditate on the dark subjects of antisemitism and the Holocaust, they force him at the same time to refine his own Jewish identity. Over the years, the result is a deepening love and appreciation for Judaism, as he comes to understand it.

As the facts of the Holocaust begin to emerge from survivor memoirs, historical studies, and court proceedings, Steiner's work is transformed into an act of solidarity with all Jewish victims of the Shoah. Between 1964 and 1969, Steiner rejects his former understanding of the Holocaust as another example of human evil, and comes to recognize the importance of studying the Holocaust in its own unique specificity. This shift leads to Steiner's investigation into the phenomenon of antisemitism and its relationship to the Holocaust. In 1970 Steiner first presents his theory of antisemitism, *the blackmail of transcendence,* which he continues to argue in support of for the remainder of his career. Twenty years later, Steiner integrates this theory with the Christian theology of the Jewish refusal and murder of Jesus. The Holocaust is interpreted as the joint result of the antisemitism produced by these dynamics at work inside Western culture for millennia, and by a secularized Christian culture that no longer needs the Jews for theological reasons and no longer protects them for moral ones. Steiner argues that Auschwitz is a cosmic act of Christian vengeance against the Jews who, in the Christian imagination, both invented and killed God.

One of the central problems in Steiner's work, the humanism-barbarism nexus in Western culture, results from his study of the Holocaust and the discovery that those who executed the Final Solution and managed the death camps were highly cultured, well-educated Germans. In an attempt to understand this paradox, Steiner first suggests that our cultivation of the literary imagination may result in the erosion of moral response to actual human suffering. Fifteen years later, Steiner wades into the controversies over Martin Heidegger and Anthony Blunt in an attempt to further understand the collusion of supreme intellect, aesthetic cultivation, and political corruption. The case of Heidegger convinces Steiner that intellectuals are particularly vulnerable to political corruption and Blunt further exemplifies this susceptibility. Both men betray their vocation by serving political ideologies instead, which Steiner believes attract cloistered intellectuals who can become compelled to take direct action in the "real world." These attempts to answer the question "why the humanities do not humanize" have not, however, convinced Steiner. He claims to be "going to the end of [his] life haunted more and more by [this] question" and admits, "I don't have an answer."[3]

Steiner's celebration of the humanities is, certainly, in honor of the learning they reflect, but more important, that learning itself is the repository of values Steiner believes are invulnerable to time and indispensable to humanity, in spite of the fact that they do not always humanize. Steiner is the proponent of a kind of cosmopolitan humanism, which he believes has been best exemplified by the Jews of central Europe. He is clear in his view that human intelligence and creativity are native to cultures that both embrace cosmopolitan humanism and have some sense of the transcendent. While his celebration of the Jews of central Europe strikes some as chauvinistic, it actually reflects this exact equation between cosmopolitanism and intelligence (as does Steiner's criticism and rejection of Jewish nationalism). He admits to suffering from "the devouring addiction to thinking we can always do better,"[4] and believes that as human beings we have, by definition, an obligation to obey a higher law of humaneness. He eschews boundaries that separate us from one another, be they academic disciplines or national borders, and believes that we are each other's guests on this crowded planet. If we are to survive as civilized human beings we must abandon the vicious and deceitful cause of nationalism and develop more complex, provisional loyalties and solidarities.

Steiner is considered a "religious" critic by some, who see in his cultural criticism an attempt to "reveal or disclose or uncover that fundamental oneness of human identity that underlies the otherwise superficial differences that separate human selves and societies."[5] As we have seen, Steiner's later critical discourse increasingly defers, morally and rhetorically, to a transcendent authority. For Steiner, culture and religion are intricately linked where they contribute to our image of the human, and to our notion of humanity itself. Steiner is inspired by our human creativity, our capacity for language, and our ability for insightful thought and creative invention, all of which result from our relationship to the transcendent. While Steiner's "inner territory" houses this depth of feeling for humanity and a faith in our potential as a future-speaking species, his fear is that modern Western culture, shaken by the failure of its own ideals, will be destroyed through its abandonment of transcendence and the font of human idealism, which is the messianic.

Steiner's humanism, compounded by his own personal history as "a kind of survivor," produces a ceaseless sense of horror and disgust when faced with the Shoah and the interminable inhumanity that it unleashed not only upon the Jewish people, but also on humanity itself. Steiner's outrage, however, is not limited to the crime of the Shoah. He is painfully aware that "history has granted us no armistice, no exemption from the inhuman."[6] Speaking of the Cambodian "Killing Fields," a scenario of what could, and should, have happened obsesses Steiner:

> A number of nations, say Britain, France, the Soviet Union, the United States, but also Israel, would have taken note. They would have declared jointly that they would intervene to halt the massacres. Intervene immediately, massively. They would do so not because of any geopolitical motive or potential gain, not because right and wrong were clear to see in this south-east Asian imbroglio. No. They would intervene simply because no man or woman, getting up in the morning, should have to look in his or her mirror when other men and women are being buried alive, when the very visage of humanity is being defaced. Because, after Auschwitz and the Gulag, the status of humanity is too precarious to suffer blood-lust which can be halted, to bear with Pol Pot (or the genocides in Sri Lanka, or the methodical enslavement and genocide of the native peoples of Amazonia).[7]

Steiner argues that we must, as human beings, create, sustain, and protect our own humane reality because there is No-one to intervene on our behalf. It is up to us, collectively and as individuals, to lower our toleration for acts of inhumanity and for the words that enact them.

Since his days at The University of Chicago, George Steiner has manifested a divided loyalty toward literature and philosophy, unable to choose between them. Later, as an academic, he refused to make the choice and has managed to create a body of work that is respected for its integration of both disciplines, among several others. Another scholar who refused to abandon philosophy for literature is Iris Murdoch, who spoke at length about the differences between these two forms of writing: "Most philosophy, as compared with literature, seems rambling and formless, even when the philosopher is explaining something of great formal complexity. Philosophy is a matter of getting hold of a problem and holding on to it and being prepared to go on repeating oneself as one tries different formulations and solutions. This patient relentless ability to stay with a problem is a mark of the philosopher; whereas a certain desire for novelty usually marks the artist."[8] Indeed, Steiner is a philosopher who has spent his career attempting to understand the nature and meaning of Western culture after Auschwitz. And like those of Iris Murdoch, Steiner's regular forays into fiction are literary extensions of his philosophical concerns. Even some of Steiner's intellectual opponents, like Edward Said, recognize and appreciate the thoughtful, nonideological quality of Steinerian criticism:

> Steiner is that rare thing, a critic propelled by diverse enthusiasms, a man able to understand the implications of trends in different fields, an autodidact for whom no subject is too arcane. Yet Steiner is to be read for his quirks, rather than in spite of them. He does not peddle a system nor a set of norms by which all things can be managed, every text decoded. He writes to be understood by non-specialists, and his terms of reference come from his experience—which is trilingual, eccentric, and highly urbane—not from something as stable as doctrine or authority. This is the other side of his egotism: that he, George Steiner, conscientiously tries to register every response accurately, work through every difficulty, test every feeling, authenticate each experience of the best that is known and thought. As such, then, the critic functions as a real if very unusual person, not an academic abstraction.[9]

Steiner has never wanted to fit into any school of thought or be identified with any particular academic discipline or political program. As someone who believes that "truth is always extraterritorial,"[10] he consciously remains an outsider. The hostility directed toward him for this choice, and for the many other reasons discussed, must have been, at times, exasperating. Regardless of whether or not one is convinced by his arguments, Steiner deserves respect for maintaining, against the grain, his own autonomous ideals and perspectives, whether at Cambridge, in the United States, in academia in general, or within the Jewish communities of Israel and the diaspora. It is Steiner's stubborn dedication to his own intellectual concerns and ways of thinking that allowed for the production of the pioneering studies on the relationship between antisemitism, the Holocaust, and Western culture discussed in this book.

In conclusion, and against the grain of his critics, I suggest that it is very likely that future scholars will recognize George Steiner as an important international interlocutor of the postwar period, especially for his principled interrogation of post-Holocaust Western culture and its Christian heritage.

Notes

The Works of George Steiner

Bibliography

Index

Notes

Introduction

1. In the last two decades Steiner has received official recognition from a variety of learned institutions and governments: Gifford Lecturer, Univ. of Glasgow, 1990; Lecturer, Collège du France, 1992; First Occupant of the Lord Weidenfeld Chair of Comparative Literature, Univ. of Oxford, 1994; Fellow, The British Academy, 1998; Portrait on display at The National Portrait Gallery, London, 2000; Charles Eliot Norton Lecturer, Harvard Univ., 2001; Prince of Asturias Award for Communications and Humanities, Spain, 2001; Commandeur dans l'Ordre des Arts et des Lettres, France, 2001; Jan Patocka Lecturer, Institut für die Wissenschaften vom Menschen, Vienna, 2003; and the Ludwig Börne Prize, Frankfurt, 2003.

2. Bryan Cheyette has made this same argument: Steiner was "the first telling those who would listen in Britain about Heidegger, Benjamin, and Paul Celan—the great German philosophers and poets. Now work on those figures is an industry, but he was a lone voice in the 60s." See Maya Jaggi, "George and His Dragons," the *Guardian,* 17 Mar. 2001, 6.

3. See "The Works of George Steiner" before the bibliography for a complete list of George Steiner's works.

4. George Steiner, introduction to *George Steiner: A Reader* (New York: Oxford Univ. Press, 1984), 10–11.

5. For a discussion of this group of European Jews, see George L. Mosse, *German Jews Beyond Judaism* (Cincinnati: Hebrew Union College Press, 1985).

6. There are critics who reject Western culture as imperialistic and colonialist by nature, aside from, or in addition to, the Holocaust. While Steiner acknowledges the specific crimes of Nazism and European imperialism, especially the destruction of aboriginal populations, this acknowledgment does not force him to reject Western culture in its entirety.

7. Jaggi, "George and His Dragons," 6.

8. Peter Gay, *Savage Reprisals: "Bleak House," "Madame Bovary," "Buddenbrooks"* (New York: W. W. Norton & Company, 2002), 156.

9. Steiner, introduction to *George Steiner: A Reader,* 11–12.

10. George Steiner, "Humane Literacy," in *Language and Silence: Essays on Language, Literature, and the Inhuman* (New Haven: Yale Univ. Press, 1998), 3–11.

11. Sheldon Norman Grebstein, *Perspectives in Contemporary Criticism: A Collection of Recent Essays by American, English, and European Literary Critics* (New York: Harper & Row, 1968), 2.

12. John Carroll, "George Steiner and Cambridge English: A Dismal Case of Rancour," *Meanjin Quarterly*, 1973, 319–20. Steiner's intellectual influences, a specific group of émigré intellectuals, are not my focus but are discussed in relation to particular publications and the general trajectory of his oeuvre.

13. The following works are by leading historians who recognize the importance of the Holocaust to our understanding of the structure of twentieth-century European history: Eric Hobsbawm, *Age of Extremes: The Short Twentieth Century, 1914–1991* (London: Abacus, 1995); François Furet, *The Passing of an Illusion: The Idea of Communism in the Twentieth Century* (Chicago: Univ. of Chicago Press, 1999); Dan Diner, *Das Jahrhundert Verstehen: Eine universalhistorische Deutung* (München: Luchterhand, 1999), and "The Destruction of Narrativity: The Holocaust in Historical Discourse," in *Catastrophe and Meaning: The Holocaust and the Twentieth Century*, ed. Moishe Postone and Eric Santner (Chicago: Univ. of Chicago Press, 2003), 67–80; Anson Rabinbach, "'The Abyss That Opened Up Before Us': Thinking about Auschwitz and Modernity," in Postone and Santner, *Catastrophe and Meaning: The Holocaust and the Twentieth Century*, 51–66; Moishe Postone, "The Holocaust and the Trajectory of the Twentieth Century," in Postone and Santner, *Catastrophe and Meaning: The Holocaust and the Twentieth Century*, 81–114; and Mark Mazower, *Dark Continent: Europe's Twentieth Century* (New York: Vintage, 2000).

1. Exile and Edification

1. Else Franzos was the great-niece of novelist Karl Emil Franzos (1848–1904), famous for his depictions of Jewish life in Eastern Europe and for his discovery and publication of Georg Büchner's play *Wozzeck*. This side of Steiner's family came from Galicia.

2. George Steiner, *Errata: An Examined Life* (London: Weidenfeld & Nicolson, 1997), 12.

3. Steiner, *Errata*, 11.

4. Jaggi, "George and His Dragons," 6.

5. Steiner, *Errata*, 10.

6. Steiner, *Errata*, 11.

7. Steiner, *Errata*, 9–10.

8. The German word *Bildung*, somewhat like the word *edification*, combines the meanings of the following words: education, culture, and character formation.

9. Steiner, *Errata*, 13.

10. Steiner, *Errata*, 9.

11. "Ce qui est intéressant, c'est que mes parents m'ont donné le temps et l'histoire comme identité religieuse. Je suis juif jusque dans mes attaches les plus profondes, mais par l'histoire, la souffrance et le destin de mon peuple." (What is interesting is the fact that my parents gave me time and history as a religious identity. I am Jewish, but through the history,

suffering, and fate of my people.) Ramin Jahanbegloo and George Steiner, *Entretiens* (Paris: Éditions du Félin, 1992), 55. (Unless otherwise noted, all translations are my own.)

12. Steiner, *Errata,* 9.

13. "Comme il devait subvenir au besoin de ses parents, il a refusé ce poste mais j'ai compris plus tard qu'il désirait que je sois ce que lui-même n'a pú être et cela est demeuré en moi comme une parole donnée à ne jamais rétracter un pacte sacré." (Since he had to meet the needs of his parents, he refused the position but I later understood that he wanted me to be what he could not be and this has stayed with me like a word given and never to be retracted, a sacred pact.) Jahanbegloo and Steiner, *Entretiens,* 26–27.

14. Steiner, *Errata,* 12.

15. Steiner, *Errata,* 8.

16. "Il a senti la montée de l'hitlérisme dès la fin de la Première Guerre mondiale, saisissant que la survie matérielle de ce pays ainsi que son génie culturel n'avaient plus d'assise réelle. La peur de la guerre allait engendrer de violents bouleversements, les boucs émissaires étaient tout trouvés. La menace laissait entendre que des événements dramatiques surviendraient." (He felt the rise of Hitlerism right after the First World War, understanding that the material well-being and cultural genius of the country no longer had any real foundation. The fear of war would engender violent upheavals where the scapegoats were already determined. The menace made clear that dramatic events were to take place.) Jahanbegloo and Steiner, *Entretiens,* 22.

17. Steiner, *Errata,* 8. In the same context, Steiner has stated, "Pour ma part, je considère que cette décision paternelle a été le premier acte d'une clairvoyance dont la puissance approchait la force profonde du *Unheimliche,* de l'inquiétante étrangeté." (For my part, I consider this paternal decision to be the first act of clairvoyance, the power of which approaches the profound force of the *Unheimliche,* of disquieting strangeness.) Jahanbegloo and Steiner, *Entretiens,* 23.

18. Steiner, *Errata,* 9.

19. Steiner, *Errata,* 10–11. Interestingly, similar criticisms were directed toward George Steiner in postwar England when he labored to stress the importance of the Holocaust to the study of the nature and purpose of the humanities.

20. Jaggi, "George and His Dragons," 6.

21. On 2 March 2002, six months after Al Qaeda attacked the United States, Steiner told an audience of British Jews, "keep your bags packed and make sure your children learn foreign languages, to equip yourselves for permanent displacement." See Melanie Phillips, "A Jewish Sense of Foreboding," *Daily Mail,* 6 Mar. 2002, http://pws.prserv.net/mpjr/mp/dm060302.htm (accessed 9 Dec. 9, 2002).

22. Simon Schama remembers hearing "someone in a Cambridge common room pestering the self-designated 'non-Jewish Jew' and Marxist historian Isaac Deutscher, himself a native of [Lithuania], about his roots. 'Trees have roots,' he shot back, scornfully, 'Jews have legs.'" Simon Schama, *Landscape and Memory* (Toronto: Vintage, 1996), 29. George Steiner

does not attribute the phrase to Deutscher, whom he knew as a contributor to the *Economist,* but uses it to convey his own perception of the Jewish mission in the world. Jews are "to show that whereas trees have roots, men have legs and are each other's guests." See George Steiner, "A Kind of Survivor," in *George Steiner: A Reader* (New York: Oxford Univ. Press, 1984), 232.

23. "Si je répète dans chacun de mes livres—bien que cela mette en colère un bon nombre de lecteurs—que l'arbre a des racines, l'homme des jambes, et que c'est là un progrès immense, je suis ainsi le droit chemin que m'a tracé mon père. Jamais il ne se contentait de dire: 'N'est-ce pas que ce que l'on a est magnifique,' sans ajouter immédiatement 'Tu vas voir, ce qui se passe ailleurs est aussi passionnant.' C'est aussi mon credo." (If I repeat in each of my books, even though it makes many readers angry, that trees have roots, men have legs, and that is immensely progressive, I am following the path my father set for me. Never would he say contentedly: "Don't you think what we have is magnificent," without immediately adding, "You'll see, what goes on elsewhere is as fascinating." That is also my credo.) See Jahanbegloo and Steiner, *Entretiens,* 28–29.

24. Tredell, Nicolas, "George Steiner," in *Conversations with Critics* (Manchester: Carcanet, 1994), 75.

25. George Steiner, "The Art of Criticism II," interview by Ronald A. Sharp, *Paris Review,* no. 137 (1995): 62.

26. Steiner, "Art of Criticism II," 62–64.

27. "Ce fut un choc pour ma mère mais son effondrement ne fut que temporaire. Mon père voyait ce deuxième exil du même oeil que le premier: cela appartenait à l'Histoire et n'avait rien d'inattendu pour lui. Malgré toutes ses souf-frances, il le considérait comme une expérience enrichissante" (It was a shock for my mother but her collapse was only temporary. My father saw this second exile the same way he saw the first: it belonged to history and was not a surprise. Despite the difficulties, he considered it an enriching experience). Jahanbegloo and Steiner, *Entretiens,* 31.

28. Steiner, *Errata,* 27.

29. For a discussion of Steiner's years at the Manhattan Lycée and their influence on the formation of his literary sensibility, see Jeffrey Mehlman, "George Steiner at the *Lycée Français,*" in *Émigré New York: French Intellectuals in Wartime Manhattan, 1940–1944* (Baltimore: Johns Hopkins Univ. Press, 2000), 104–16.

30. "Ruth Lilian Steiner," letter of introduction, 10 Sept. 1940, 1–2, Schlesinger Library, Radcliffe Institute for Advanced Study, Harvard University.

31. "Ruth Lilian Steiner," letter of introduction, 2.

32. Jahanbegloo and Steiner, *Entretiens,* 29.

33. In her remarks in a Radcliffe yearbook, Ruth Lilian Steiner recalled that as of 1940 the family "expected to return to Paris 'shortly'" so no thought was given to which American college she would attend in the fall term. See Lilian Hertzberg Steiner, *Class of 1942,* 1982 Yearbook, 1–2, Schlesinger Library, Radcliffe Institute for Advanced Study, Harvard University.

34. "J'assume la grave responsabilité de te coûter l'Académie française." Antoine Spire and George Steiner, *Barbarie de l'Ignorance* (Latresne [Bordeaux]: Éditions du Bord de l'Eau, 1998), 20.

35. Steiner, *Errata,* 40.

36. The Manhattan Project was a secret program created by President Roosevelt in 1941 to develop the atomic bomb. News that the Germans had split the atom in 1939 forced the American government to take action. Research stations were established at Columbia University, at The University of Chicago, in Oak Ridge, Tennessee, and at Los Alamos, New Mexico.

37. Irving Kaplansky was the mathematics professor who rejected Steiner as a graduate student. Years later, when Steiner sent him a copy of an article he had just published in *Nature* on the history of a mathematical problem, Kaplansky responded, "Thank you for your very interesting paper. I have no regrets for contributing to the history of literature." Steiner loved the answer. See Steiner, "Art of Criticism II," 66.

38. Steiner, *Errata,* 44–45.

39. Steiner, *Errata,* 46–47.

40. George Steiner, "Intellectual Passions," in *An Unsentimental Education: Writers and Chicago* (Chicago: Univ. of Chicago Press, 1995), 182.

41. Steiner, "Intellectual Passions," 184.

42. Steiner, "Intellectual Passions," 186.

43. George Steiner, "An Examined Life," review of *Unseasonable Truths,* by Harry S. Ashmore, *New Yorker,* 23 Oct. 1989, 142.

44. The nomination for the Rhodes scholarship must come from the nominee's undergraduate institution.

45. Steiner, "Art of Criticism II," 68.

46. "Mais il y avait un tel climat de solidarité que je n'ai jamais rencontré ailleurs cette fierté et cette décence qui règnaient alors. Je suis tombé profondément amoureux de l'Angleterre." Jahanbegloo and Steiner, *Entretiens,* 40–41.

47. In 1888 Ludwik Bernsztajn vel Niemirowski (Lewis Namier) was born into a Polonized Jewish family living in Wola Okrzejska (in Russian Poland). The family soon moved to a town called Koszylowce, just south of Tarnopol (in Austrian Poland), where he grew up. After short stays, as a young man, in Vienna and Lausanne, Lewis arrived in England in 1907 at the age of nineteen. See Julia Namier, *Lewis Namier: A Biography* (Oxford: Oxford Univ. Press, 1971). According to Steiner, Namier and Steiner's father were boyhood friends in Galicia. Steiner recalls a family story in which the boys shared the cost of Monypenny and Buckle's six-volume biography of their hero, Benjamin Disraeli. See Peter Scott, "Survivor and Outsider," *Times Higher Education Supplement,* 15 Feb. 1985, 11.

48. Scott, "Survivor and Outsider."

49. George Steiner, *The Death of Tragedy* (New York: Knopf, 1961).

50. Steiner discusses his doctoral defense in an interview with Ramin Jahanbegloo. See Jahanbegloo and Steiner, *Entretiens,* 41–48.

51. George Steiner (as F. George Steiner), *The Fantasy Poets: Number Eight.* (Swinford, UK: O. Mellor & R. Smith, 1952).

52. George Steiner (as F. George Steiner), *Malice: Chancellor's English Essay Prize* (Oxford: Basil Blackwell, 1952).

53. Steiner, *Errata,* 129. For additional discussion of Humphry House, see Jahanbegloo and Steiner, *Entretiens,* 42–45.

54. Zara Shakow Steiner, born in New York to Lithuanian Jewish parents, took her BA and MA at Oxford University and her PhD at Harvard. A highly respected scholar of European strategy and diplomacy, Shakow is Fellow Emeritus of New Hall, University of Cambridge, where she served as College Lecturer and Director of Studies in History from 1967 to 1998.

55. During the early 1940s, J. Robert Oppenheimer directed the Manhattan Project from Los Alamos National Laboratory in New Mexico. From 1946 to 1952 he chaired the civilian advisory committee to the Atomic Energy Commission, a government agency charged with the development and control of the US atomic energy program following World War II. In 1953, during the height of McCarthyism, Dr. Oppenheimer was accused of holding Communist sympathies and had his security clearance revoked.

56. Oppenheimer began the interview by telling Steiner, who had traveled overseas for the meeting, that he would give him only five minutes, as he did not think much of journalists. For Steiner's recollection of this encounter, see Jahanbegloo and Steiner, *Entretiens,* 45–48.

57. George F. Kennan developed the postwar American foreign policy of Soviet containment.

58. Ed Regis, *Who Got Einstein's Office? Eccentricity and Genius at the Institute for Advanced Study* (New York: Addison-Wesley, 1987), 4–5.

59. For the particular details of this exchange, see Steiner, "Art of Criticism II," 68–69; and Jahanbegloo and Steiner, *Entretiens,* 45–48.

60. George Steiner, *Tolstoy or Dostoevsky: An Essay in the Old Criticism* (New York: Knopf, 1959).

61. Scott, "Survivor and Outsider," 11.

62. Steiner, "Art of Criticism II," 70.

63. Today the Steiners' children are academics teaching at American universities. David Steiner is dean of the School of Education at Hunter College, CUNY. His primary areas of research are the philosophy of education and American K–12 education reform. Deborah Tarn Steiner is professor of classics at Columbia University. Archaic and Classical Greek literature, Greek religion and mythology, and Epinician poetry are her areas of research.

64. Interestingly, Frederick, Else, and Lilian (Hertzberg) Steiner never returned to Europe to live but chose to reside in New York City. It was obviously very important to Frederick Steiner that his son should study at Anglo-American universities but also that, afterward, he live and work as a scholar in Europe.

65. Steiner, "Art of Criticism II," 71.

66. Steiner, "Art of Criticism II," 71–72.

67. Mark Krupnick, "Steiner's Literary Journalism: 'The Heart of the Maze,'" in *Reading George Steiner,* ed. Nathan Scott, Jr. and Ronald A. Sharp (Baltimore: Johns Hopkins Univ. Press, 1994), 45.

68. In addition to his father's wishes, Steiner remained in England largely because of the fact that his wife, Zara Shakow, had her own well-established career to maintain at Cambridge. Steiner's compromise began in 1974 when he began teaching at Geneva during the academic year, returning to England for the summer.

69. Steiner, *Errata,* 11.

70. Steiner, *Errata,* 156.

71. Steiner, *Errata.*

72. Steiner, *Errata,* 157.

73. Steiner, *Errata,* 156.

74. Steiner, *Errata,* 9.

75. As a result, it is difficult to evaluate the effects of these divergent attitudes toward Zionism upon their larger views of Jewish identity. Steiner's view of Jewish identity, first nurtured by his father, has indeed developed independently since Frederick's death in 1968.

2. Early Writings, 1952–1961

1. See the following early works on antisemitism and the Holocaust: *Dialektik der Aufklärung* (1947), *The Authoritarian Personality* (1950), *Minima Moralia: Reflexionen aus dem beschädigten Leben* (1951), *Prismen: Kulturkritik und Gesellschaft* (1955), *Noten zur Literatur* (1958), and "Was bedeutet: Aufarbeitung der Vergangenheit," in *Erziehung zur Mündigkeit* (1959); Hannah Arendt, *The Origins of Totalitarianism* (New York: Harcourt Brace, 1951) and *Eichmann in Jerusalem* (New York: Viking, 1963); Léon Poliakov, *Bréviaire de la haine. Le IIIe Reich et les Juifs* (Paris: Calmann Lévy, 1951); Viktor Frankl, *Ein Psycholog erlebt das Konzentrationslager* (1946); Bruno Bettelheim, *The Informed Heart: Autonomy in a Mass Age* (1960); Paul Celan, *Der Sand aus den Urnen* (1948), *Mohn und Gedächtnis* (1952), *Von Schwelle zu Schwelle* (1955), and *Sprachgitter* (1959); Elie Wiesel, *Un di velt hot geshvign* (Buenos Aires: Tsentral-Farband fun Poylische Yidn in Argentine, 1955) and *La Nuit* (Paris: Éditions de Minuit, 1958); Primo Levi, *Se questo è un uomo* (Turin: Einaudi, 1958).

2. Nothing human is alien to me.

3. George Steiner, *Malice* (Oxford: Basil Blackwell, 1952), 13.

4. Steiner, *Malice,* 15.

5. Steiner, *Malice,* 14.

6. Steiner, *Malice,* 15.

7. Steiner, *Malice,* 16–17.

8. George Steiner, "A Kind of Survivor," in *George Steiner: A Reader,* 230.

9. Steiner, *Malice,* 22.

10. Steiner, *Malice,* 23.

11. Steiner, *Malice.*

12. A similar, yet more complex, dynamic propels Steiner's theory of antisemitism, first discussed in 1970, in which Gentiles resent Jews for creating and imposing upon them an ethical universe that continually reveals their moral inadequacies.

13. Steiner, *Malice,* 16–17.

14. Steiner, *Malice,* 23.

15. Steiner, *Malice,* 24.

16. George Steiner, "Marxism and the Literary Critic," in *Language and Silence,* 306.

17. Steiner, "Marxism and the Literary Critic," 311.

18. Steiner, "Marxism and the Literary Critic," 319.

19. Steiner, "Marxism and the Literary Critic," 310.

20. Steiner, "Marxism and the Literary Critic," 323.

21. Steiner, "Marxism and the Literary Critic."

22. Steiner, "Marxism and the Literary Critic," 329.

23. Steiner, "Marxism and the Literary Critic," 338. See Georg Lukács, *Der Historische Roman* (Berlin: Aufbau Verlag, 1955).

24. Steiner, "Marxism and the Literary Critic," 334.

25. Steiner, "Marxism and the Literary Critic," 336.

26. See George Steiner, "Why English? The English Association Presidential Address" (Oxford: Oxford Univ. Press, 1975), and "The Archives of Eden," *Salmagundi* (Fall 1980–Winter 1981): 57–89.

27. George Steiner, "The Hollow Miracle," in *Language and Silence,* 95.

28. Steiner, "The Hollow Miracle," 108.

29. Steiner, "The Hollow Miracle."

30. Steiner, "The Hollow Miracle," 96.

31. Steiner, "The Hollow Miracle."

32. Steiner, "The Hollow Miracle," 97.

33. This is also the case during and after the Nazi period. According to Steiner, the best German writers and playwrights are those living in exile: Thomas and Heinrich Mann, Werfel, Feuchtwanger, Zweig, Hermann Broch, Brecht, and Zuckmayer. Steiner, "The Hollow Miracle," 102.

34. Steiner, "The Hollow Miracle," 97.

35. Steiner, "The Hollow Miracle," 98. In this essay, Steiner uses the (uncapitalized) word *holocaust* to refer to the First World War instead of the mass murder of European Jewry.

36. Steiner, "The Hollow Miracle."

37. Steiner, "The Hollow Miracle," 99.

38. Steiner argues that this process is continuing under Soviet influence: "In these past ten years [1957–1967], a new chapter has begun in the complex history of the German language and of its articulations of political reality. East Germany is once again developing much of the grammar of lies, of totalitarian simplifications, which was brought to such a high degree

of efficiency in the Nazi era. Walls can be built between two halves of a city, but also between words and humane content." Steiner, "The Hollow Miracle," 95.

39. Steiner, "The Hollow Miracle," 101.

40. Steiner, "The Hollow Miracle," 109.

41. In a concluding footnote, added eight years later in a reissued version of this essay, Steiner admits that "it is precisely by turning to face the past that German drama and fiction have resumed a violent, often journalistic, but undeniable force of life." Steiner, "The Hollow Miracle."

42. Steiner, *Tolstoy or Dostoevsky*.

43. New Criticism is an Anglo-American movement in literary criticism dating from the 1920s, which takes its name from John Crowe Ransom's book *The New Criticism*, published in 1941. New Critics emphasized close textual analysis and reading literature for its own sake, against the traditional biographical and historical approach to literature, which interprets poetry and prose as forms of sociology, philosophy, or ethics. See Karl Beckson and Arthur Ganz, *Literary Terms: A Dictionary* (New York: Noonday Press, 1989), 175–76. The para-Marxist critics, whom Steiner celebrates, were engaged in work that valued both approaches to literature and attempted to bridge the divide between them.

44. Steiner, *Tolstoy or Dostoevsky*, 3.

45. Steiner, *Tolstoy or Dostoevsky*, 4–5.

46. Steiner, *Tolstoy or Dostoevsky*, 5. Steiner maintains this perspective on criticism throughout his career, although he does not retain the same certainty that people want to preserve the Western cultural legacy, or that culture is able to protect civilization from evil.

47. Steiner, *Tolstoy or Dostoevsky*, 28.

48. Steiner, *Tolstoy or Dostoevsky*, 6–7. This last point is precisely the argument Steiner develops thirty years later in *Real Presences* (Chicago: Univ. of Chicago Press, 1991). And the accompanying idea that the "artist both imitates and rivals the shaping powers of the Deity" is the opening theme of Steiner's Gifford Lectures, published in 2001 as *Grammars of Creation* (New Haven: Yale Univ. Press, 2001). *Grammars of Creation*, 7.

49. Norman Cohn, *The Pursuit of the Millennium* (New York: Essential Books, 1957).

50. Steiner, *Tolstoy or Dostoevsky*, 258.

51. George Steiner, *The Death of Tragedy* (London: Faber & Faber, 1961).

52. In 1959, Steiner was invited to participate in the Gauss Seminar in Criticism at Princeton, chaired by R. P. Blackmur. A Ford Foundation Grant, awarded through the Council of the Humanities at Princeton, to further work in comparative literature, funded the writing of *The Death of Tragedy*.

53. Steiner, *Death of Tragedy*, viii.

54. Steiner, *Death of Tragedy* [1961], 8–9.

55. Steiner, *Death of Tragedy* [1961], 4.

56. Steiner, *Death of Tragedy* [1961].

57. Steiner, *Death of Tragedy* [1961], 6–7.

58. In 1979, Steiner wrote a new foreword for the book in which he limited his definition of absolute tragedy even further: "What I identify as 'tragedy' in the radical sense is . . . a view of reality in which man is taken to be an unwelcome guest in the world. . . . The plays which communicate this metaphysic of desperation would include *The Seven Against Thebes, King Oedipus, Antigone,* the *Hippolytus* and, supremely, the *Bacchae.*" See Steiner, foreword to *The Death of Tragedy* (New York: Oxford Univ. Press, 1980), xi.

59. Steiner, *Death of Tragedy* [1980], 20–21.

60. Steiner, *Death of Tragedy* [1980], 343.

61. Steiner, *Death of Tragedy* [1980], 315–16.

62. Steiner, *Death of Tragedy* [1980], 351–52.

63. It is unclear whether this journey through Poland was for this purpose specifically. In 1957, Steiner was a visiting scholar in Austria, during which time he traveled east to Hungary to visit Georg Lukács and to deliver letters from Lucien Goldmann. Lukács had just returned from banishment in Romania and was living under house arrest in Budapest. It is possible that this journey through Poland occurred during this period. See Eva L. Corredor, *Lukács after Communism: Interviews with Contemporary Intellectuals* (Durham, NC: Duke Univ. Press, 1997), 61–74.

64. Steiner, *Death of Tragedy* [1980], 352.

65. Steiner, *Death of Tragedy* [1980], 352–53.

66. Steiner, *Death of Tragedy* [1980]. Steiner does not elaborate on the relationship between tragedy and theology in this work. He does, however, place this theme at the center of an essay, published forty-three years later, in which he reconsiders the genre of tragedy. Here, the key aspect to authentic tragedy is the "logic of estrangement from life, of man's ontological fall from grace," something he inferred in *The Death of Tragedy* but "had not underlined . . . adequately." See George Steiner, "'Tragedy,' Reconsidered," *New Literary History* 35 (2004): 4.

67. In 1963, Steiner met a second time with Lukács, where they discussed *The Death of Tragedy.* Lukács did not like the work, found it too idealistic, and criticized what he saw as the enormous influence of Walter Benjamin on Steiner's thought. He warned Steiner, "This is where you are going and *das ist mystisch*" (it is mystical). See Corredor, *Lukács after Communism,* 62.

68. Steiner, "Marxism and the Literary Critic," 323.

69. Steiner, "Georg Lukács," in *Language and Silence,* 328.

3. Surviving in Cambridge, 1961–1974

1. See Mark Krupnick, "Why Are English Departments Still Fighting the Culture Wars?" *Chronicle of Higher Education* 49, no. 4 (20 Sept. 2002): B16.

2. Nathan A. Scott Jr. and Ronald A. Sharp, eds., *Reading George Steiner* (Baltimore: Johns Hopkins Univ. Press, 1994), ix.

3. Steiner, *Errata,* 155.

4. John Carroll, "George Steiner and Cambridge English: A Dismal Case of Rancour," *Meanjin Quarterly,* 1973, 318–22.

5. See James Mountford, *British Universities* (London: Oxford Univ. Press, 1966), 9.

6. Carroll, "George Steiner and Cambridge English," 319.

7. George Steiner, "F. R. Leavis," in *Language and Silence,* 221.

8. Steiner, "F. R. Leavis," 221–22.

9. See Geoffrey Grigson, "Noaks Is No Fool," *New Statesman,* 22 Oct. 1971, 545–46; James Wood, "George Steiner's Unreal Presence," in *The Broken Estate: Essays on Literature and Belief* (New York: Random House, 1999), 143–58; and Edward Skidelsky, "Beware the False Prophet," *New Statesman,* 19 Mar. 2001, 52.

10. See James Fenton, "The Cloud of Knowing," *New Statesman,* 1 Dec. 1978, 743–44; and Jay Parini, "The Question of George Steiner," *Hudson Review,* Autumn 1985, 496–502.

11. See Bernard Bergonzi, "George Steiner: On Culture and on Hitler," in *The Myth of Modernism* (New York: St. Martin's Press, 1986), 161–71; Nicholas Krasso, "Words, Words, Words," *New Statesman,* 20 Oct. 1967, 513; and "The Poetics of Cultural Criticism," *Times Literary Supplement,* 17 Dec. 1971, 1565. For American criticism of Steiner, in the same vein, see the following: Eliseo Vivas, "Too Clever by Half," *National Review,* 31 Dec. 1971, 1477–78; Sven Birkerts, "George Steiner," in *An Artificial Wilderness: Essays on 20th-Century Literature* (New York: William Morrow, 1987), 317–22; John Simon, "Made of Steiner Stuff," *New Criterion,* Oct. 1989, 64–70; and John Simon, "The Theatre Critic and His Double," in *Acid Test* (New York: Stein and Day, 1964), 257–64. And for the suggestion that Steiner's celebrated ancestral connection to the giants of central European thought is a figment of his own imagination, see Theodore Solotaroff, "A Kind of Survival," in *New Republic,* 13 May 1967, 21–22.

12. See George Steiner, "The Unfinished," *New Yorker,* 17 Apr. 1995.

13. See George Steiner, *Why English?* (London: Oxford Univ. Press, 1975), and George Steiner, "New Movements in European Culture," *Times Literary Supplement,* 7 Jan. 1988, 10, 22.

14. See George Steiner, "The State of Europe," *Granta* 30 (Winter 1990): 129–32.

15. Today, Steiner admits this was a mistake on his part as the lecture series was most likely a peace offering on the part of many dons. "J'ai commis de graves erreurs plus encore lorsque j'ai écrit *La Culture contre l'homme.* Il est possible que l'établissement anglais m'ait tendu une branche d'olivier en me demandant de faire des conférences à la mémoire de T. S. Eliot" (I committed even greater mistakes when I wrote *Culture Against Man* [published in English as *In Bluebeard's Castle*]. It is possible that the English establishment was holding out an olive branch by asking me to present lectures in memory of T. S. Eliot). See Jahanbegloo and Steiner, *Entretiens,* 52.

16. T. S. Eliot, *Notes Towards the Definition of Culture* (London: Faber & Faber, 1948).

17. See George Steiner, "A Reading Against Shakespeare," in *No Passion Spent: Essays, 1978–1995* (New Haven: Yale Univ. Press, 1996), 108–28.

18. George Steiner, "Hitler's Vienna," *Salmagundi,* Summer/Fall 2003, 64.

19. Carroll, "George Steiner and Cambridge English," 318.

20. Carroll, "George Steiner and Cambridge English," 319.

21. Carroll, "George Steiner and Cambridge English," 322.

22. Jaggi, "George and His Dragons," 7.

23. "Philosopher and Political Thinker Sir Isaiah Berlin Dies," *BBC News,* 8 Nov. 1997, http://news.bbc.co.uk/1/hi/uk/24540.stm (accessed 21 Dec. 2005).

24. "Philosopher and Political Thinker Sir Isaiah Berlin Dies." Isaiah Berlin died on Wednesday, 5 November 1997, in Oxford.

25. For a discussion of Isaiah Berlin's life and work, see Ramin Jahanbegloo, *Conversations with Isaiah Berlin* (London: Phoenix Press, 1993).

26. Michael Ignatieff, *Isaiah Berlin: A Life* (New York: Metropolitan Books, 1998), 35.

27. Ignatieff, *Isaiah Berlin,* 36.

28. See the introduction and the previous chapter for a discussion of this type of criticism.

29. Clive James has suggested that in addition to being traumatized by the murder of his own relatives in Riga (and perhaps guilty for the role he had played in representing the British government against Zionist interests during the war), Isaiah Berlin did not feel that he had anything of value to contribute to the work of Holocaust scholars, given the fact that Hitler had few ideas for Berlin to actually critique. See Clive James, "On Isaiah Berlin," http//www.clivejames.com (accessed 21 Dec. 2005).

In an interview with Ramin Jahanbegloo, Isaiah Berlin discusses the extent of his knowledge about the murder of European Jewry during the war, but does not offer any explanation for his neglect of the subject in his work. See Isaiah Berlin and Ramin Jahanbegloo, *Conversations with Isaiah Berlin* (London: Phoenix Press, 2000), 19–23.

30. Ian MacKillop, *F. R. Leavis: A Life in Criticism* (London: Penguin, 1995), 51.

31. Anne Samson, *F. R. Leavis* (Toronto: Univ. of Toronto Press, 1992), 10–11. F. R. Leavis, who returned from World War I and began studying English at Cambridge, is generally celebrated as one of the greatest literary critics of the twentieth century. Like George Steiner, Leavis was for years a director of English Studies, part-time lecturer, and finally a fellow at Downing College. Passed over for decades by the English Faculty, Leavis was appointed University Reader in English only in 1959, three years prior to retirement. See John Ferns, *F. R. Leavis* (New York: Twayne Publishers, 2000).

32. See Samson, *Leavis,* 10–14.

33. Brian Doyle, *English and Englishness* (London: Routledge, 1989), 83.

34. Samson, *Leavis,* 13.

35. Under the tripartite system of English education, first introduced by the Butler Education Act in 1944, secondary schools were divided into three classes: Grammar Schools (for the academically oriented), Secondary Modern Schools (for those not suited to academic schooling), and Secondary Technical Schools (for scientific and mechanical education). Based on the results of the "11 plus" exam, an I.Q. test taken at the age of eleven, students were

enrolled in one of the three types of schools. The 1976 Education Act did abolish all but 164 Grammar Schools (which are today fully independent) to form neighborhood comprehensive schools. Three years later, a new Education Act allowed these schools to select up to 10 percent of the student body based upon academic ability.

36. The *Times Literary Supplement* ran a series entitled "The State of English" from 25 February to 14 April 1972, in which a variety of contemporary concerns are discussed. The letters of response to this series reflect the ongoing hostility between Steiner and Cambridge English.

37. George Steiner, *Language and Silence: Essays on Language, Literature, and the Inhuman* (New Haven: Atheneum, 1967).

38. George Steiner, "Humane Literacy," in *Language and Silence: Essays on Language, Literature, and the Inhuman* (New Haven: Yale Univ. Press, 1998), 4–5.

39. Steiner, "Humane Literacy," 5.

40. Steiner, "Humane Literacy."

41. Steiner, "Humane Literacy," 11.

42. Steiner, "Retreat from the Word," *Language and Silence,* 26.

43. Steiner, "Retreat from the Word." Steiner also attempts to explain the malaise in English literature as the consequence of a failure of nerve on the part of the humanities in the face of growing mathematical and scientific certainty. And he criticizes the attempts to make literature, history, and philosophy more scientific in what he terms their new "fallacy of imitative form." Steiner, "Humane Literacy," *Language and Silence,* 11.

44. Steiner, "To Civilize Our Gentlemen," *Language and Silence,* 61.

45. Steiner, "To Civilize Our Gentlemen," 61.

46. Steiner, "To Civilize Our Gentlemen," 66.

47. Jaggi, "George and His Dragons," 6.

48. George Steiner was ahead of his time in many ways. The discipline he practiced so early at Cambridge is now recognized as comparative literature. Oxford, the alma mater that rejected his first doctoral dissertation in 1950 for its comparative nature, finally acknowledged its debt to Steiner in 1994 when the university invited him to be the first occupant of the Lord Weidenfeld Chair of Comparative Literature, which he gratefully accepted.

49. In 1959, Adorno published an essay on the need for Germany to come to terms with its past: "Was bedeutet: Aufarbeitung der Vergangenheit," in *Erziehung zur Mündigkeit* (1959). He also delivered a version of his essay entitled "Commitment" on Radio Bremen on 28 March 1962. In April 1966, Adorno presented *Erziehung nach Auschwitz* (Education after Auschwitz) in a radio address, arguing, "the call for Auschwitz never to happen again is the most important in all of education." See Theodor Adorno, "Erziehung nach Auschwitz," in *Erziehung zur Mündigkeit* (Frankfurt: Suhrkampf, 1971), 88–104.

50. Hannah Arendt, *Eichmann in Jerusalem* (New York: Viking, 1963). The Eichmann Trial was held in Jerusalem from 11 April to 11 August 1961. Eichmann was found guilty on 11 September 1961, sentenced to death, and hanged at midnight on 31 May 1962.

51. See note 1 in chapter 2 for a list of books written by these individuals.

52. Sylvia Plath, *Ariel* (New York: Harper & Row, 1965); Léon Poliakov, *Bréviaire de la haine. Le IIIe Reich et les Juifs* (Paris: Calmann-Lévy, 1951); Gerald Reitlinger, *The Final Solution: The Attempt to Exterminate the Jews of Europe, 1939–1945* (London: Vallentine, Mitchell, 1953); Alan Bullock, *Hitler: A Study in Tyranny* (London: Harper & Row, 1952); Raul Hilberg, *The Destruction of the European Jews* (Chicago: Quadrangle Books, 1961); Fritz Stern, *The Politics of Cultural Despair: A Study in the Rise of the Germanic Ideology* (New York: Anchor Books, 1961); Stanley Milgram, "Behavioral Study of Obedience," *Journal of Abnormal and Social Psychology* 67 (1963): 371–78; George Mosse, *The Crisis of German Ideology: Intellectual Origins of the Third Reich* (New York: Grosset, 1964); and Richard L. Rubenstein, *After Auschwitz: Radical Theology and Contemporary Judaism* (New York: Bobbs Merrill, 1966).

53. The first of many death camp trials held in Germany, the Frankfurt Auschwitz Trial began 20 December 1963 and ended 20 August 1965. The first Treblinka Trial was held in Düsseldorf from October 1964 to August 1965. In Munich, the Belzec Trial began in January 1965. The Sobibor Trial, held in Hagen, took place between September 1965 and December 1966. And the second Treblinka Trial was held in Düsseldorf from September 1969 to December 1970.

54. Against this broad trajectory, Peter Novick, Alan Mintz, and Arnold Jacob Wolf argue that for the first twenty years or so after World War II, the Holocaust was rarely discussed in America. Peter Novick asserts that the Six-Day War, of June 1967, first stimulates the interest of American Jews in the Holocaust. See Peter Novick, *The Holocaust in American Life* (New York: Houghton Mifflin, 1999). For a recent, more nuanced, approach to the subject via the medium of film, see Julian Levinson, "The Maimed Body and the Tortured Soul: Holocaust Survivors in American Film," *Yale Journal of Criticism* 17, no. 1 (2004): 141–60. And for a broader historical perspective, see Moishe Postone and Eric Santner, eds., introduction to *Catastrophe and Meaning: The Holocaust and the Twentieth Century* (Chicago: Univ. of Chicago Press, 2003), 1–14.

55. In the preface to *Language and Silence,* Steiner admits that the essays in this volume, in most cases, are a "response to a specific occasion: the publication of a book, the production of a play or opera, a political event." See Steiner, *Language and Silence,* vii. In this text, Steiner refers specifically to *The Diary of Anne Frank* and to the work of Theodor Adorno, Hannah Arendt, Bruno Bettelheim, Chaim Kaplan, Jean François Steiner, Léon Poliakov, Rolf Hochhuth, and Sylvia Plath, among others.

56. George Steiner, "A Responsion," in *Reading George Steiner,* 279.

57. For a discussion of *Anno Domini,* see Lillian Kremer, *Witness Through the Imagination: Jewish American Holocaust Literature* (Detroit: Wayne State Univ. Press, 1989).

58. George Steiner, *Anno Domini: Three Stories of the War* (Woodstock, NY: Overlook Press, 1964), 73–75.

59. Steiner, "A Responsion," 276.

60. Steiner, "Kind of Survivor," in *Language and Silence,* 140.

61. Steiner, "Kind of Survivor," 141.

62. Steiner, "Kind of Survivor," 145.

63. Steiner, "Kind of Survivor," 146–47. Steiner is a proponent of the view that modern culture, particularly that emanating out of Vienna, is the creation of central European Jewry. For a discussion of this debate, see Steven Beller, *Vienna and the Jews, 1867–1938: A Cultural History* (Cambridge: Cambridge Univ. Press, 1995).

64. Steiner, "Kind of Survivor," 149.

65. Theodore Solotaroff, review of *Language and Silence* by George Steiner, *New Republic,* 13 May 1967, 21–22.

66. Steiner, "Art of Criticism," *Paris Review,* 72–73.

67. The history of the German Jewish encounter is a large field of scholarship. For its reevaluation after the Holocaust, see the work of Gershom Scholem, George L. Mosse, Peter Gay, and Paul Mendes Flohr.

68. Steiner, "Kind of Survivor," 152.

69. Steiner, "Kind of Survivor," 153.

70. Steiner, "Kind of Survivor,"

71. George Steiner, "Postscript," *Language and Silence: Essays on Language, Literature, and the Inhuman* (New Haven: Yale Univ. Press, 1998), 156.

72. Steiner, " Kind of Survivor," 140.

73. Steiner, "Postscript," 156.

74. Steiner, "Postscript," 157.

75. Steiner, "Postscript," 168.

76. Steiner, "Postscript," 165.

77. Steiner, "Postscript," 167.

78. Steiner, *Malice,* 16–17.

79. Steiner, "Postscript," 167.

80. Steiner, "Postscript," 157.

81. Steiner, "Postscript," 163.

82. Steiner, "Postscript," 162–63.

83. Steiner, "Postscript," 157.

84. Steiner, "Postscript."

85. Steiner, "Postscript," 161.

86. Steiner, "Postscript," 162.

87. Steiner, "Dying Is an Art," 301.

88. Steiner, "Dying Is an Art."

89. Steiner, "Dying Is an Art."

90. Steiner, "In Extremis," in *The Cambridge Mind: Ninety Years of the Cambridge Review, 1879–1969,* ed. Eric Homberger, William Janeway, and Simon Schama (London: Jonathan Cape, 1970), 305.

91. Steiner, "In Extremis," 304.

92. William Styron wrote the Holocaust novel *Sophie's Choice,* which deals with the post-war lives of death camp survivors in New York City.

93. George Steiner, *In Bluebeard's Castle: Some Notes Towards the Redefinition of Culture* (New Haven: Yale Univ. Press, 1971), 33.

94. Eliot, *Notes Towards the Definition of Culture.* This text consists of six essays on the subject of culture, which, Eliot argues, requires the following three conditions to flourish: a social class structure to facilitate the hereditary transmission of culture; diverse local cultures; and a balance of unity and diversity in religion. An essay on "The Unity of European Culture," which Eliot delivered over German radio in 1946, is appended to this volume. It was his attempt to remind the peoples of Europe that in spite of World War II they still share a common culture, which they must continue to protect and defend. Eliot's analysis of culture separates it entirely from the world of politics, and for him Nazism is strictly a political phenomenon. These conceptions, of culture and Nazism, preclude the kind of analysis Steiner advocates.

95. Steiner, *In Bluebeard's Castle,* 3.

96. Steiner, *In Bluebeard's Castle,* 33–34.

97. Steiner, *In Bluebeard's Castle.* In fairness to Eliot, although the book was published in 1948, it was written primarily between 1943 and 1946. It is fair to assume that the English public knew little about the systematic murder of Europe's Jews during the war, and very few people had any understanding of what we now term the Holocaust in the immediate years after World War II. Even Steiner, as late as the 1950s, saw the mass murder of European Jewry within a more universal framework of human evil and world war.

98. Steiner, *In Bluebeard's Castle,* 34.

99. Steiner, *In Bluebeard's Castle.*

100. Steiner, *In Bluebeard's Castle.* There is now a well-worn debate on the nature of T. S. Eliot's attitudes toward the Jewish people, as a result of his use of antisemitic imagery in five specific poems ("Burbank," "Gerontion," "Sweeney among the Nightingales," "A Cooking Egg," and "Dirge") and a set of lectures given in 1933 in which Eliot said, "reasons of race and religion combine to make any large number of free-thinking Jews undesirable." Craig Raine, *In Defence of T. S. Eliot* (London: Picador, 2000), 321. The debate essentially revolves around the question of whether or not the antisemitic images in these poems reflect Eliot's actual attitude toward Jews. See Anthony Julius, *T. S. Eliot: Antisemitism and Literary Form* (Cambridge: Cambridge Univ. Press, 1995) for an argument that Eliot is an antisemite and that his work is supportive of the phenomenon itself. For the opposite view, see Raine, *In Defence of T. S. Eliot.*

101. Steiner, *In Bluebeard's Castle.*

102. Steiner, *In Bluebeard's Castle.*

103. Steiner, *In Bluebeard's Castle,* 36.

104. Steiner, *In Bluebeard's Castle.*

105. Steiner, *In Bluebeard's Castle,* 41.

106. Steiner does not explain how the Jewish people actually enact *the blackmail of transcendence* throughout human history, only that it occurs three specific times.

107. Steiner, *In Bluebeard's Castle,* 44.

108. Steiner, *In Bluebeard's Castle,* 37.

109. Steiner, *In Bluebeard's Castle,* 38.

110. Steiner, *In Bluebeard's Castle,* 41.

111. The "claims of the ideal" is Henrik Ibsen's phrase, which Steiner uses interchangeably with *the blackmail of transcendence.* Ibsen's character, Gregers Werle, in the play *The Wild Duck,* is an "impractical idealist who pesters mankind with his 'claims of the ideal' because he has a sick conscience and despises himself." See Henrik Ibsen, *The Wild Duck,* trans. Michael Meyer (London: Methuen, 1968).

112. Steiner, *In Bluebeard's Castle,* 42.

113. Steiner, *In Bluebeard's Castle,* 43.

114. Steiner, *In Bluebeard's Castle.*

115. Steiner, *In Bluebeard's Castle,* 45.

116. Steiner, *In Bluebeard's Castle,* 41.

117. Steiner, *In Bluebeard's Castle,* 46. An obvious, but unmentioned, influence on Steiner's work is Horkheimer and Adorno's essay "Elements of Anti-Semitism," which interprets the phenomenon as nature's revenge for the triumph of civilization, the basis of which results from the Jewish transformation of taboos into civilizing maxims. See Max Horkheimer and Theodor Adorno, *Dialectic of Enlightenment* (New York: Continuum Books, 1997), 168–208. For a brief discussion of Steiner's (mis)interpretation of Adorno's comments on Auschwitz, see Michael Rothberg, "After Adorno: Culture in the Wake of Catastrophe," *New German Critique* 72 (Fall 1997): 45–81.

118. Steiner, *In Bluebeard's Castle,* 55.

119. Asshole of the world.

120. Steiner, *In Bluebeard's Castle,* 54.

121. Steiner, *In Bluebeard's Castle,* 55–56.

122. Steiner, *In Bluebeard's Castle.*

123. Steiner, *In Bluebeard's Castle,* 16.

124. Steiner, *In Bluebeard's Castle,* 14.

125. Steiner defines the term *ennui,* not simply as "boredom" but as "manifold processes of frustration, of cumulative *décoeuvrement,* Energies eroded to routine as entropy increases." Steiner, *In Bluebeard's Castle,* 9.

126. Steiner, *In Bluebeard's Castle,* 16–20.

127. Steiner, *In Bluebeard's Castle,* 23–24.

128. Steiner, *In Bluebeard's Castle,* 11, 23.

129. Steiner, *In Bluebeard's Castle,* 33.

130. George Steiner, *Nostalgia for the Absolute* (Toronto: CBC Enterprises, 1983). Steiner delivered these five Massey Lectures on the CBC program *Ideas* in the fall of 1974.

131. Steiner, *Nostalgia*, 2.

132. Steiner, *Nostalgia*, 3.

133. Steiner, *Nostalgia*, 4.

134. It is possible that Steiner's title is a variation of Iris Murdoch's "Nostalgia for the Particular," a lecture on language and experience, delivered at a meeting of the Aristotelian Society in London on 9 June 1952. See Iris Murdoch, "Nostalgia for the Particular," in *Existentialists and Mystics: Writings on Philosophy and Literature*, ed. Peter Conradi (London: Penguin, 1999). This edition includes a foreword by George Steiner.

135. Steiner, *Nostalgia*, 36–37.

136. Steiner, *Nostalgia*, 10.

137. Steiner, *Nostalgia*, 9.

138. Steiner, *Nostalgia*, 11.

139. Steiner, *Nostalgia*, 21–22.

140. Steiner, *Nostalgia*, 12–13.

141. Steiner, *Nostalgia*, 23.

142. Steiner, *Nostalgia*, 14.

143. Steiner, *Nostalgia*, 27.

144. Steiner, *Nostalgia*, 33.

145. Steiner, *Nostalgia*, 32–33.

146. Steiner, *Nostalgia*, 56–57.

147. Steiner, *Nostalgia*, 60.

148. Steiner, *Nostalgia*, 60–61.

149. Steiner, *Nostalgia*, 46.

150. Steiner, *Nostalgia*.

151. Steiner, *Nostalgia*.

152. Steiner, *Nostalgia*, 48.

4. Translation and Treason, 1974–1985

1. Steiner first met Gershom Scholem, the respected scholar of Jewish mysticism, at the University of Zurich and the two corresponded for years thereafter. Alexis Philonenko, historian and philosopher, was Steiner's colleague at Geneva. They dined together weekly and shared a dedicated correspondence for two decades. Philonenko introduced Steiner to the Catholic philosopher Pierre Boutang, who remained marginalized in France until his death in 1998 for his far right nationalist sensibilities. In spite of Boutang's antisemitism, Steiner claims to have felt close to him, sharing his "utter passion for Scripture and the classics, for poetry and metaphysics." Steiner, *Errata*, 138. See chapter 9 of Steiner's memoir, *Errata: An Examined Life*, for a brief discussion of the impact of these relationships on his life and work.

2. Steiner, "To Civilize Our Gentlemen," in *Language and Silence*, 65.

3. During the 1970s the traditional barrier between Anglo-American and Continental philosophy began to weaken, allowing analytical philosophy to enter German, Italian, and

(post Franco) Spanish circles, and French thought to migrate into British and North American universities, especially into literature departments. For a discussion of this process, see Anthony Kenny, ed., *The Oxford History of Western Philosophy* (Oxford: Oxford Univ. Press, 1997).

4. George Steiner, *Extraterritorial: Papers on Literature and the Language Revolution* (New York: Atheneum, 1971). This text is a collection of ten essays that appeared in the *New Yorker, Encounter,* and the *TLS* between 1968 and 1971.

5. Steiner, "The Language Animal," in *Extraterritorial,* 73.

6. Steiner, "The Language Animal."

7. Steiner, "The Language Animal," 101.

8. Steiner, "The Language Animal," 65.

9. To this end, Steiner argues in support of future cooperation between academic disciplines: "If we allow 'linguistics' to include ancillary disciplines such as 'ethno-linguistics' or linguistic anthropology, 'social-linguistics' and the study of speech lesions and pathologies ('psycho-linguistics'), the extent of relevance to the history and criticism of literature becomes unmistakable." See George Steiner, "Whorf, Chomsky, and the Student of Literature," *New Literary History* 4, no. 1 (Autumn 1972): 31.

10. Steiner, "Cry Havoc," *Extraterritorial,* 36. The three texts by Céline are *Bagatelles pour un Massacre* (1937), *L'Ecole des Cadavres* (1938), and *Le Beaux Draps* (1941).

11. Steiner, "Cry Havoc," 42–43.

12. This essay discusses this same tendency in Erika Ostrovsky's book *Céline and His Vision* (New York: New York Univ. Press, 1968).

13. Steiner, "Cry Havoc," 44. An even greater host to this coexistence is Lucien Rebatet, the author of *Les Deux Etendards,* who collaborated actively with the Nazis and supported their assault on the Jews. Steiner, "Cry Havoc."

14. Steiner, "Cry Havoc," 46.

15. Steiner, "Cry Havoc."

16. George Steiner, *After Babel: Aspects of Language and Translation* (Oxford: Oxford Univ. Press, 1975).

17. George Steiner, "An Exact Art," in *No Passion Spent: Essays 1978–1995* (New Haven: Yale Univ. Press, 1996), 192–93. For an extended discussion of this subject, see Steiner, *After Babel,* 103–14.

18. Steiner, "Whorf," 15.

19. For a discussion of this debate, based on comments that Noam Chomsky made in private correspondence with George Steiner, see Steiner, "Tongues of Men," in *Extraterritorial,* 102–25.

20. Ernst Bloch, *Geist der Utopie* (1918) and *Das Prinzip Hoffnung,* 3 volumes (1954–59).

21. Steiner, *After Babel,* 227.

22. Steiner, *After Babel,* 228.

23. Steiner, *After Babel,* 229.

24. Steiner, *After Babel,* 238.

25. Steiner, *After Babel,* 239–40.

26. Steiner, *After Babel.*

27. Steiner, "Hollow Miracle," in *George Steiner: A Reader,* 213.

28. The Steiner family maxim is Spinoza's insight from *The Ethics:* "All things excellent are as difficult as they are rare."

29. George Steiner, *The Portage to San Cristóbal of A.H.* (London: Faber & Faber, 1981). The story first appeared in *Kenyon Review* (Spring 1979) while a shorter section was published in *Granta* (1980) before the text was published as a novella in 1981. Christopher Hampton adapted the novel for the stage in 1982, and the play was performed in London that same year at the Mermaid Theatre, and at the Hartford Stage, in Connecticut, the following year.

For a discussion of Steiner's fictional treatment of the Holocaust, see Kremer, *Witness Through the Imagination,* 324–55.

30. George Steiner, "The Art of Criticism II," 56.

31. Steiner, *Portage,* 33.

32. Alvin Rosenfeld, "Steiner's Hitler," review of *The Portage to San Cristóbal of A.H.,* by George Steiner, *Salmagundi,* no. 52–53 (Spring–Summer 1981): 170.

33. See Morris Dickstein, "Alive and 90 in the Jungles of Brazil," review of *The Portage to San Cristóbal of A.H.,* by George Steiner, *New York Times Book Review,* 2 May 1982, 13, 21; Martin Gilbert, "Who Do You Think You Are Kidding, Mr. Hitler?" review of *The Portage to San Cristóbal of A.H.,* directed by Christopher Hampton, *Times (London),* 6 Mar. 1982, 9; Lionel Abel, "So Who Is to Have the Last Word?" *Partisan Review* 53, no. 3 (1986): 358–71; Joseph Lowin, "Steiner's Helicopters," *Jewish Book Annual* 41 (1983–1984): 48–56; Hyam Maccoby, "George Steiner's 'Hitler,'" *Encounter* 58, no. 5 (May 1982): 27–34; and Rosenfeld, "Steiner's Hitler," 160–74.

Of the four major points "Hitler" argues in self-defense, three are mentioned in books and essays written by Steiner. The suggestion that National Socialism may be a "vengeful parody" of the Judaic concepts of divine election and promised land is found in the essay "A Kind of Survivor." See Steiner, "A Kind of Survivor," in *Language and Silence,* 153. *The blackmail of transcendence* is first established in Steiner's T. S. Eliot Memorial Lectures, published as *In Bluebeard's Castle: Some Notes Towards the Redefinition of Culture.* See Steiner, *In Bluebeard's Castle,* 29–56. This theory is also reiterated ten years later in Steiner's short story "Proofs." See George Steiner, *Proofs and Three Parables* (London: Faber & Faber, 1992). Finally, Steiner makes the point that Stalin killed more people than Hitler in an essay on the Holocaust written in 1987, and again in 1990: "Quantitatively—and this is, by itself, something of an obscene criterion—there have been worse killings. Responsible historians put at ten or twelve million the number of human beings done to death by the Stalinist regime during the crisis of the *Kulaks* and the subsequent purges and deportations." See George Steiner, "The Long Life of Metaphor: An Approach to 'the Shoah,'" *Encounter,* Feb. 1987, 57; and George Steiner, "Remembering the Future," *Theology* 93 (Nov./Dec. 1990): 437–44.

Alvin Rosenfeld has located the fourth point made by "Hitler," that he is responsible for the foundation of the State of Israel, in an antisemitic tract written by Hennecke Kardel. Kardel's *Adolf Hitler: Begründer Israels* is out of print; however, there is an English version now in its fourth edition. See Hennecke Kardel, *Adolf Hilter—Founder of Israel: Israel in War with Jews* (N.p.: Modjeskis Society, 1996). This book mentions a character named Jacob Grill who was supposedly an ex-Catholic priest and former Jew who befriended Hitler in Vienna and introduced him to Jewish concepts and beliefs. See Alvin Rosenfeld, *Imagining Hitler* (Bloomington: Indiana Univ. Press, 1985), 96–97.

34. Robert Boyers, "Steiner's Holocaust: Politics and Theology," *Salmagundi,* no. 66 (Winter/Summer 1985): 26–49.

35. Hyam Maccoby, "George Steiner's Hitler," review of *The Portage to San Cristóbal of A.H.,* by George Steiner, *Encounter* 58, no. 5 (May 1982): 30. Unfortunately, *The Portage* is misused under the title "George Steiner in Hitler's Defense" on an antisemitic website, maintained by the revisionist *Historical Review Press.* See *Historical Review Press,* 12 Oct. 2003, http://www.ety.com/HRP/jewishstudies/evilsincemoses.htm.

36. Rosenfeld, "Hitler," *Salmagundi,* 173.

37. George Steiner, *The Portage to San Cristóbal of A.H.* (Chicago: Univ. of Chicago Press, 1999), 49.

38. George Steiner, afterword to *The Portage to San Cristóbal of A.H.* (Chicago: Univ. of Chicago Press, 1999), 174.

39. Steiner, "Art of Criticism II," 56.

40. Steiner, "Art of Criticism II," 57–58.

41. Boyers, "Steiner's Holocaust: Politics and Theology," 49.

42. Steiner, *Bluebeard's Castle,* 46.

43. For a general discussion of this text, see Timothy Gould, "On Heidegger's Track: A Response to a Portrayal by George Steiner," *Soundings* 68 (Summer 1985): 229–52.

44. Heidegger was also known for his oratorical gifts. Based upon firsthand accounts by those such as Gadamer, Löwith, and Arendt, Steiner claims Heidegger "acted through the spoken word." Steiner goes so far as to argue that, as a result of the power of his oratory, reading Heidegger may not be conducive to understanding him. See George Steiner, "Heidegger, Again," *Salmagundi,* Spring/Summer 1989, 35–38.

45. George Steiner, *Heidegger* (London: Fontana, 1978), 16–17.

46. Steiner, *Heidegger,* 21.

47. Steiner, *Heidegger,* 19. In an attempt to address the paradox of humanism and barbarism in Western culture, in the third lecture of *In Bluebeard's Castle,* Steiner refers to Heidegger as a profound example of the problem: "One of the principal works that we have in the philosophy of language, in the total reading of Hölderlin's poetry, was composed almost within earshot of a death camp. Heidegger's pen did not stop nor his mind go mute." Steiner, *Bluebeard's Castle,* 78.

48. Steiner, *Heidegger,* 13.

49. George Steiner, "Heidegger's Silence," *George Steiner: A Reader,* 258.

50. Steiner, "Heidegger's Silence," 261.

51. Steiner, "Heidegger's Silence," 262–63.

52. Steiner, "Heidegger's Silence," 263.

53. Steiner, "Heidegger's Silence," 262.

54. Steiner, "Heidegger's Silence."

55. Steiner, "Heidegger's Silence," 263–64.

56. Steiner, "Heidegger's Silence."

57. Steiner, "Heidegger's Silence," 264.

58. Steiner, "Heidegger's Silence," 265.

59. Steiner, "Heidegger, Again," 31.

60. Steiner, "Heidegger, Again," 31–33.

61. Steiner, "Heidegger, Again," 32.

62. Steiner, "Heidegger, Again," 35.

63. Steiner, "Heidegger, Again."

64. Steiner, "Heidegger, Again," 34–35.

65. Victor Farias, *Heidegger et le nazisme* (Paris: Verdier, 1987).

66. The controversy is made more complex, argues Steiner, by the problem of Deconstruction, whose hermeneutic Heidegger influenced directly. Steiner assures readers that "*Sein und Zeit* and Heidegger's theory of a language that speaks man rather than being spoken by him, is utterly seminal in the modern anti-humanistic movement. There is little in Deconstruction or in Foucault's 'abolition of man' . . . which is not voiced in Heidegger's *a*-humanism." Steiner, "Heidegger, Again," 46–48.

67. Steiner, "Heidegger, Again," 47.

68. Steiner, "Heidegger, Again."

69. Steiner, "Heidegger, Again." 45.

70. Paul Antschel (Celan is an anagram he later adopted) lived in Czernowitz, Bukovina [Romania] before World War II. His mother and father were killed somewhere in Transnistria, having refused to go into hiding with their son. Celan spent the war in several Romanian forced labor camps and after 1948 left Bucharest for Vienna to escape Stalinism. Within a year he left Austria for France, and settled in Paris with his new wife and their son, Eric. For many years, and even after his great literary success, Celan suffered serious bouts of depression and hospitalization, finally succumbing to despair in April 1970 by drowning himself in the Seine. For a complete study of Paul Celan and his work, see John Felstiner, *Paul Celan: Poet, Survivor, Jew* (New Haven: Yale Univ. Press, 1996).

71. Steiner, "Heidegger, Again," 53.

72. Steiner, "Heidegger, Again," 54.

73. George Steiner, "The Cleric of Treason," *George Steiner: A Reader,* 191. In a book review published in 2001, Steiner states that "between 1941 and 1945 [Blunt] passed 1,771

documents to Soviet Intelligence . . . [and] who betrayed certain anti-Stalinist refugees in London to Soviet surveillance." See George Steiner, "Ice Cold in Arcadia: Privacy, Hauteur and Deception: Anthony Blunt's Strange Career," review of *Anthony Blunt,* by Miranda Carter, *Times Literary Supplement,* 2 Nov. 2001, 3.

74. Sir Anthony Blunt (he was knighted in 1956) was Slade Professor of Fine Art successively at Oxford and Cambridge, Fellow of the British Academy (1950), Fellow of the Society of Antiquaries (1960), and Surveyor of the Queen's Pictures and Advisor for the Queen's Pictures and Drawings (1952 and 1972, respectively). He published over twenty-five monographs, including studies of Poussin, William Blake, seventeenth- and eighteenth-century Italian painting and French architecture, and on the relations between the baroque and antiquity. See Steiner, "Cleric of Treason," 182.

75. Steiner, "Cleric of Treason," 185–87.

76. Steiner, "Cleric of Treason," 191.

77. Steiner, "Cleric of Treason."

78. Steiner, "Cleric of Treason," 192.

79. Steiner, "Cleric of Treason," 194–95.

80. Steiner, "Cleric of Treason," 197.

81. Steiner, "Cleric of Treason," 198.

82. Steiner, "Cleric of Treason."

83. Steiner, "Cleric of Treason," 200.

84. Steiner, "Heidegger, Again," 47.

85. Steiner, "Cleric of Treason," 200.

86. George Steiner, "Our Homeland, the Text," in *No Passion Spent,* 304–27.

87. Julien Benda, *La Trahison des clercs* (Paris: Bernard Grasset, 1927).

88. Steiner, "Our Homeland," 320.

89. Steiner, "Our Homeland," 310.

90. Ibid., 318. Steiner's short story "A Conversation Piece" attempts to illustrate this contention by depicting a group of Jews engrossed in debating the *akedah* (the Binding of Isaac) on their way into the gas chambers. See George Steiner, "A Conversation Piece," in *Proofs and Three Parables,* 101–14.

91. Steiner, "A Conversation Piece."

92. Steiner, "A Conversation Piece," 319.

93. Steiner, "A Conversation Piece."

94. Steiner, "A Conversation Piece," 322.

95. Steiner, "A Conversation Piece."

96. Steiner, "A Conversation Piece," 326.

97. Steiner, "A Conversation Piece."

98. Steiner, "A Conversation Piece," 324. Zionism and the State of Israel have been topics of significant debate between Steiner and his critics, making him the target of some hostility. See the analyses of Frederick Krantz, "George Steiner's Negative Midrash on Israel and

Zionism: A Critique," *Zionist Ideas* 17 (1988): 27–77; Assaf Sagiv, "George Steiner's Jewish Problem," *Azure*, Summer 5763/2003, 130–54; and Dow Marmur, "The Struggle Between Text and Land in Contemporary Jewry: Reflections on George Steiner's *Our Homeland, The Text*," *History of European Ideas* 20 (1995): 807–13.

99. In this essay, Steiner states, "the noble Greek word, 'holocaust', signifying a solemn burnt offering, has no legitimate place in [his discussion of Jewish prophecy]." From this essay onward Steiner uses the terms "Shoah" (Hebrew for "Catastrophe") or "Whirlwind" when speaking of the Holocaust. See Steiner, "Our Homeland," 313.

100. Steiner, *The Portage to San Cristóbal of A.H.* (Chicago: Univ. of Chicago Press, 1999), 169–70.

101. George Steiner, "Who Do You Think You Are Kidding, Dr. Gilbert?" *Times (London)*, 11 Mar. 1982, 12.

102. George Steiner, "Inscrutable and Tragic: Leo Strauss's Vision of the Jewish Destiny," review of *Jewish Philosophy and the Crisis of Modernity*, by Leo Strauss, *Times Literary Supplement*, 14 Nov. 1997, 5.

103. One could argue that American Jewry, in their allegiance to the United States, also betray the ethics and cosmopolitan intelligence of Judaism. For Steiner's critical characterization of "conservative American Jews," see Steiner, "A Kind of Survivor."

104. George Steiner, *The Dissent from Reason: Contemporary Intellectual Currents in the Western World. The B'nai B'rith Jerusalem Address, 1986* (Washington: B'nai B'rith International, 1986), 22.

105. Steiner, "Our Homeland," 327.

106. Steiner, "Our Homeland," 321.

107. Steiner, *Heidegger*, 20.

108. Why this dynamic is not found within Judaism is not explained by Steiner. It is possible that he sees Jewish nationalism as strictly a post-Holocaust phenomenon disconnected from (pre-Holocaust) religious Judaism and from the cosmopolitan humanism of central European Jewish intellectuals.

109. Steiner has been critical of Zionism since the mid-1960s; however, this work is more directly a response to the ongoing conflict between Israelis and Palestinians. The Palestinian *Intifada* (Uprising) will officially begin the following year, in 1986.

110. It is interesting to note that current discussions of anti-Zionism exclude George Steiner. He is not mentioned in these debates nor has he written on the subject. Anyone familiar with the writings of contemporary anti-Zionists will recognize that Steiner's writings about Israel are fundamentally different. Actually, they are the product of another time and place. While Steiner is not a Zionist, or a nationalist of any kind, he is also not an antisemite. Steiner supports the right of Israel to exist, and while he repudiates Israeli aggression he also recognizes that it has been primarily reactive and defensive. He also does not minimize the problem of antisemitism, including forms emanating from the Arab and Muslim worlds. For current discussions of this important subject, see Alvin Rosenfeld, *"Progressive"*

Jewish Thought and the New Anti-Semitism (New York: American Jewish Committee, 2006); Bernard Harrison, *Israel, Anti-Semitism, and Free Speech* (New York: American Jewish Committee, 2007); Alvin Rosenfeld, "Rhetorical Violence and the Jews," *New Republic,* 27 Feb. 2007; and Benjamin Weinthal and Alex Feuerherdt, "Does Jewish Antisemitism Exist?" (interview with Alvin Rosenfeld), *Jerusalem Post,* 11 Dec. 2008.

5. The Meaning of Meaning, 1985–2007

1. Steiner, "A Responsion," 280–81.

2. "A Responsion."

3. "A Responsion." The ban on graven images is the Second Commandment (Exodus 20:4, and also Deuteronomy 4:15–17) of the Hebrew Bible. While Rabbinic Judaism does not enforce a complete ban on visual art, the Christian tradition does, by comparison, provide abundant discussion of the relationship between religion and aesthetics, and of the transcendent quality of artistic inspiration. For an excellent refutation of the categorical argument that Judaism is aniconic, see Kalman P. Bland, *The Artless Jew: Medieval and Modern Affirmations and Denials of the Visual* (Princeton, NJ: Princeton Univ. Press, 2000).

4. See Mark H. Ellis, "Questioning Conversion: Gillian Rose, George Steiner, and Christianity," in *Revolutionary Forgiveness: Essays on Judaism, Christianity, and the Future of Religious Life* (Waco, TX: Baylor Univ. Press, 2000), 229–58.

5. For critiques of Steiner's use of Christian theology and philosophy, see Krantz, "George Steiner's Negative Midrash"; and Sagiv, "Steiner's Jewish Problem," *Azure,* Summer 5763/2003, 130–54.

6. Krantz, "George Steiner's Negative Midrash," 74.

7. See Norman Finkelstein, "George Steiner's Presences," *Salmagundi* 87 (Summer 1990): 260–67.

8. George Steiner, *Real Presences* (Chicago: Univ. of Chicago Press, 1989). For the 1985 lecture, see George Steiner, "Real Presences," in *No Passion Spent,* 20–39.

9. The English word *author* comes from the Latin *Auctoritas,* for "authority." Deconstruction eliminates the classical humanist presumption of the authority and prestige of the author. See Steiner, *Real Presences,* 126.

10. Steiner, "Real Presences," 28.

11. Steiner, "Real Presences," 29.

12. Steiner, "Real Presences," 32.

13. Steiner, "Real Presences," 33.

14. Steiner, "Real Presences," 29–30.

15. Steiner, "Real Presences," 29–31.

16. Steiner, "Real Presences," 31.

17. In this way of thinking, "The carnival and saturnalia of post-structuralism . . . will pass as have so many other rhetorics of reading. . . . The 'common reader', Virginia Woolf's positive rubric, the serious scholar, editor and critic will get on, as they always have, with the

work at hand. . . . So robust and fertile a pragmatism . . . bids one acknowledge, as out of the corner of a clear eye, that all determinations of textual meaning are probabilistic, that all critical assessments are ultimately uncertain; but . . . draw confident reinsurance from the cumulative . . . weight of historical agreement and practical persuasion." Steiner, "Real Presences," 30–31.

18. Steiner, "Real Presences," 32.

19. Steiner, "Real Presences." Teaching is also related to the transcendent, according to Steiner, who interprets the practice as an *imitatio* (imitation) of divine disclosure. In 2001, Steiner gave the Charles Eliot Norton Lectures at Harvard University, in which he connected the irreverent nature of contemporary culture to the corrosion of teaching as a vocation. See George Steiner, *Lessons of the Masters* (Cambridge: Harvard Univ. Press, 2003).

20. Steiner, "Real Presences," 35.

21. Ibid., 36. Derrida himself argues that "it would be possible to show that all the names related to fundamentals, to principles, or to the center have always designated the constant of a presence—*eidos, arche, telos, energeia, ousia . . . aletheia,* transcendentality, consciousness, or conscience, God, man, and so forth." See Jacques Derrida, "Structure, Sign, and Play in the Discourse of the Human Sciences," in *The Structuralist Controversy,* ed. Richard Macksey and Eugenio Donato, 247–65 (Baltimore: Johns Hopkins Univ. Press, 1970), 249.

22. Steiner, "Real Presences."

23. There are countless reviews of *Real Presences,* many of which focus on the assumption that Steiner is an atheist. See James Wood, "George Steiner's Unreal Presence," in *The Broken Estate: Essays on Literature and Belief* (New York: Random House, 1999), 143–58. For a less hostile response, see Karl-Josef Kuschel, "Presence of God? Towards the Possibility of a Theological Aesthetic in an Analysis of George Steiner," *Literature and Theology* 10, no. 1 (Mar. 1996): 1–19.

24. Steiner, "Real Presences," 38.

25. Steiner, *Real Presences,* 229.

26. Steiner, "Real Presences," 39.

27. Steiner, *Real Presences,* 229–30.

28. George Steiner, "The Long Life of Metaphor: An Approach to the Shoah," *Encounter,* 1987, 55–61. The same essay was published in German in 1987: see George Steiner, "Das Lange Leben der Metaphorik: Ein Versuch über die Shoah," *Akzente* 34, no. 3 (1987): 194–212. And one year later, the same essay was republished in Berel Lang, *Writing and the Holocaust* (New York: Holmes & Meier, 1988).

29. Steiner, "Long Life of Metaphor," 57.

30. Steiner, "Long Life of Metaphor," 56.

31. Steiner, "Long Life of Metaphor," 57.

32. Steiner, "Long Life of Metaphor," 58.

33. Steiner, "Long Life of Metaphor."

34. Steiner, "Long Life of Metaphor."

35. Steiner, "Long Life of Metaphor."

36. Steiner, "Long Life of Metaphor."

37. Steiner, "Long Life of Metaphor."

38. Steiner, "Long Life of Metaphor," 58.

39. Steiner, "Long Life of Metaphor."

40. Steiner, "Long Life of Metaphor," 59.

41. Steiner and Boutang debated the Antigone myth and the biblical story of the Sacrifice of Isaac on French television in 1987. These dialogues were published under the incorrect title *Dialogues: Sur le mythe d'Antigone sur le sacrifice d'Abraham* (Paris: J. C. Lattès, 1994). For a discussion of the dialogues and the relationship between Steiner and Boutang, see Jeffrey Mehlman, "Writing Lives: Speculations of a Biographer-in-Waiting," *Common Knowledge* 4, no. 3 (Winter 1995): 97–112.

42. Steiner, *Errata,* 138.

43. Steiner, *Errata,* 137–38.

44. Steiner, "Long Life of Metaphor," 59. Steiner does not elaborate on how exactly these two are twinned psychologically.

45. Steiner, "Long Life of Metaphor."

46. Steiner, "Long Life of Metaphor."

47. See note 70 in chapter 4 for biographical information on Paul Celan.

48. Steiner, "Long Life of Metaphor," 55.

49. Steiner, "Long Life of Metaphor," 60.

50. Steiner, "Long Life of Metaphor."

51. Steiner, "Long Life of Metaphor," 61.

52. Steiner, "Long Life of Metaphor," 60.

53. Steiner, "Long Life of Metaphor," 61.

54. For the eulogy delivered at MacKinnon's funeral, see George Steiner, "Tribute to Donald MacKinnon," *Theology* 98 (Jan./Feb. 1995): 2–9. For a discussion of the intellectual influence of Donald MacKinnon upon George Steiner, see Graham Ward, "Tragedy as Sub-clause: George Steiner's Dialogue with Donald MacKinnon," *Heythrop Journal* 34, no. 3 (July 1993): 274–87.

55. Steiner, *Errata,* 136.

56. Donald MacKinnon, *The Borderlands of Theology* (London: Lutterworth, 1968), 103.

57. George Steiner, "Remembering the Future," *Theology* 93 (Nov./Dec. 1990), 438.

58. Steiner, "Remembering the Future," 438–39.

59. Steiner, "Remembering the Future," 439.

60. Steiner, "Remembering the Future."

61. Steiner, "Remembering the Future," 440.

62. Steiner, "Remembering the Future."

63. Steiner, "Remembering the Future," 440–41.

64. Steiner, "Remembering the Future," 443–44. This subject will be pursued by Steiner in *Grammars of Creation.*

65. George Steiner, "Through That Glass Darkly," *No Passion Spent* (New Haven: Yale Univ. Press, 1996), 336.

66. Steiner, *Errata,* 136.

67. Steiner, "Through That Glass," 342.

68. Steiner, "Through That Glass," 342–43.

69. Steiner, "Through That Glass," 343.

70. Steiner, "Through That Glass," 345.

71. Steiner, "Through That Glass," 344.

72. Steiner, "Through That Glass," 345.

73. Steiner, "Through That Glass," 343–44.

74. Steiner, "Through That Glass."

75. George Steiner, *Grammars of Creation* (New Haven: Yale Univ. Press, 2001).

76. Stefan Zweig, *The World of Yesterday* (Lincoln: Univ. of Nebraska Press, 1964).

77. Steiner, *Grammars of Creation,* 4–5.

78. Steiner, *Grammars of Creation,* 5.

79. Steiner, *Grammars of Creation,* 7.

80. Steiner, *Grammars of Creation,* 9.

81. Steiner, *Grammars of Creation,* 10. Steiner's definition of secular messianism reveals the Jewish influence on his thinking on the subject. The critics of the Frankfurt School, especially Walter Benjamin, Theodor Adorno, and Erich Fromm, define messianism in similar terms.

82. Steiner, *Grammars of Creation,* 6.

83. See the quotation on page 119 of this chapter.

84. Steiner, *Grammars of Creation,* 10–11.

85. Steiner, "Cleric of Treason," 198.

86. Steiner, *Grammars of Creation,* 15.

87. Steiner, *Grammars of Creation,* 337.

88. Wood, "George Steiner's Unreal Presence," 151.

89. Wood, "George Steiner's Unreal Presence," 150.

90. Roger Kimball, "Is the Future Just a Tense?" review of *Grammars of Creation,* by George Steiner, *New York Times Book Review,* 2 Sept. 2001, 12.

91. For an introduction to the Jewish religious response to the Shoah, see the following work on post-Holocaust Jewish theology: Richard Rubenstein, *After Auschwitz* (Indianapolis: Bobbs-Merrill, 1966) and *The Cunning of History* (New York: Harper & Row, 1975); Emil Fackenheim, *God's Presence in History* (New York: New York Univ. Press, 1970) and *The Jewish Return into History* (New York: Schocken, 1980); Ignaz Maybaum, *The Face of God after Auschwitz* (Amsterdam: Polak & van Gennep, 1965); Eliezer Berkovits, *Faith after the Holocaust* (New York: KTAV, 1973), *Crisis and Faith* (New York: Sanhedrin Press, 1976), and *With God*

in Hell (New York: Hebrew Publishing, 1979). For the second wave of response to these original theological works, see the work of the following scholars: Michael Wyschogrod, Robert Gordis, Arthur Green, Jacob Neusner, Arthur A. Cohen, Michael Meyer, Gerson Greenberg, and Steven Katz. For a recent evaluation of the same subject, see the following essay collection: Steven Katz, ed., *The Impact of the Holocaust on Jewish Theology* (New York: New York Univ. Press, 2005).

92. Steiner, *Errata,* 158–59.

93. Steiner, *Grammars of Creation,* 337.

94. Steiner, *Errata,* 159.

95. Steiner, *Errata,* 163.

96. Steiner, *Errata,* 164.

97. Steiner, *Errata.*

98. Steiner, *Errata,* 164–65.

99. Steiner, *Errata,* 165–66.

100. Steiner, *Errata,* 166–67.

101. Steiner, *Errata,* 169.

102. Walter Benjamin's conception of the messianic is an obvious influence on Steiner, as Georg Lukács had suggested to Steiner in 1963.

103. "Philosophie, wie sie im Angesicht der Verzweiflung einzig noch zu verantworten ist, wäre der Versuch, alle Dinge so zu betrachten, wie sie vom Standpunkt der Erlösung aus sich darstellten. Erkenntnis hat kein Licht, als das von der Erlösung her auf die Welt scheint: alles andere erschöpft sich in der Nachkonstruktion und bleibt ein Stück Technik. Perspektiven müßten hergestellt werden, in denen die Welt ähnlich sich versetzt, verfremdet, ihre Risse und Schründe offenbart, wie sie einmal als bedürftig und entstellt im Messianischen Lichte daliegen wird. Ohne Willkür und Gewalt, ganz aus der Fühlung mit den Gegenständen heraus solche Perspektiven zu gewinnen, darauf allein kommt es dem Denken an." Theodor Adorno, *Minima Moralia: Reflexionen aus dem beschädigten Leben* (Frankfurt a. Main: Suhrkamp, 1969), 281.

104. Steiner, *Errata,* 170–71.

Conclusion

1. Yosef Hayim Yerushalmi, *Zakhor: Jewish History and Jewish Memory* (Seattle: Univ. of Washington Press, 1996), 5.

2. See *The Oxford English Dictionary,* s.v. "Remembrancer."

3. Peter Applebome, "A Humanist and Elitist? Perhaps," *New York Times,* 18 Apr. 1998, B7.

4. See George Steiner, "George Steiner Interviewed by Eleanor Wachtel," interview by Eleanor Wachtel, *Queen's Quarterly* 99, no. 4 (Winter 1992): 846.

5. Giles Gunn, "On New Uses of the 'Secular' and the 'Religious' in Contemporary Criticism: Edward Said, George Steiner, and the Counter-Example of Eric Heller," in *Morphologies*

of Faith: Essays in Religion and Culture in Honor of Nathan A Scott, Jr., ed. Mary Gerhart and Anthony C. Yu (Atlanta: Scholars Press, 1990), 54–55.

6. Steiner, "Remembering the Future," 440.

7. Steiner, "Remembering the Future," 441.

8. Iris Murdoch, "Literature and Philosophy: A Conversation with Bryan Magee," in *Existentialists and Mystics: Writings on Philosophy and Literature,* ed. Peter Conradi (London: Penguin, 1999), 5–6.

9. Edward Said, "Himself Observed," review of *George Steiner: A Reader,* by George Steiner, *Nation,* 2 Mar. 1985, 244.

10. Steiner, "Our Homeland, The Text," 322.

The Works of George Steiner

Books

1952	*The Fantasy Poets: Number Eight.* Swinford, UK: O. Mellor and R. Smith. (As F. George Steiner)
1959	*Tolstoy or Dostoevsky: An Essay in Contrast.* London: Faber & Faber.
1961	*The Death of Tragedy.* London: Faber & Faber.
1964	*Anno Domini: Three Stories of the War.* New York: Atheneum.
1967	*Language and Silence: Essays on Language, Literature, and the Inhuman.* London: Faber & Faber.
1970–73	*Roots of the Right: Readings in Fascist, Racist, and Elitist Ideology.* 5 vols. New York: Harper & Row. (Editor)
1971	*Extraterritorial: Papers on Literature and the Language Revolution.* New York: Atheneum Books.
1971	*In Bluebeard's Castle: Some Notes Toward the Redefinition of Culture.* New Haven: Yale Univ. Press.
1974	*Fields of Force: Fischer and Spassky at Reykjavik.* New York: Viking.
1974	*Nostalgia for the Absolute.* Toronto: CBC Enterprises.
1975	*After Babel: Aspects of Language and Translation.* London: Oxford Univ. Press.
1978	*Heidegger.* London: Fontana.
1978	*On Difficulty and Other Essays.* New York: Oxford Univ. Press.
1981	*The Portage to San Cristóbal of A.H.* London: Faber & Faber.
1984	*Antigones: How the Antigone Legend Has Endured in Western Literature, Art, and Thought.* London: Clarendon Press.
1984	*George Steiner: A Reader.* New York: Oxford Univ. Press.
1989	*Real Presences.* Chicago: The Univ. of Chicago Press.
1992	*Proofs and Three Parables.* London: Faber & Faber.
1994	*Dialogues: Sur le mythe d'Antigone sur le sacrifice d'Abraham* [sic]. Paris: J. C. Lattès, 1994. (With Pierre Boutang)

1996 *The Deeps of the Sea and Other Fiction.* London: Faber & Faber.
1996 *Homer in English.* London: Penguin, 1996. (Editor)
1996 *No Passion Spent: Essays, 1978–1995.* New Haven: Yale Univ. Press.
1997 *Errata: An Examined Life.* London: Weidenfeld & Nicolson.
2001 *Grammars of Creation.* New Haven: Yale Univ. Press.
2003 *The Lessons of the Masters.* Cambridge: Harvard Univ. Press.
2008 *My Unwritten Books.* London: Orion Publishing.

Uncollected Essays

1952 *Malice: Chancellor's English Essay Prize.* Oxford: Basil Blackwell.
1970 "In Extremis." In *The Cambridge Mind: Ninety Years of the Cambridge Review, 1879–1969,* edited by Eric Homberger, William Janeway, and Simon Schama, 303–7. London: Jonathan Cape.
1970 "The Unique and the Universal," letter to the editor. *Commentary* 49 (May): 4–12.
1972 "Whorf, Chomsky, and the Student of Literature." *New Literary History* 4, no. 1 (Autumn): 15–34.
1973 "The City Under Attack." *Salmagundi,* Fall, 3–18.
1974 "Can Literature Compete?—A Radio Discussion Between Andrew Shonfield, George Steiner, and Julian Mitchell." *Listener,* 25 July, 121–22.
1975 "Why English? The English Association Presidential Address." Oxford: Oxford Univ. Press.
1980–1981 "The Archives of Eden." *Salmagundi,* Fall 1980–Winter 1981, 57–89.
1982–1983 "In Lieu of a Preface." *Salmagundi,* Fall 1982–Winter 1983, 4–9.
1982 "Who Do You Think *You* Are Kidding, Dr. Gilbert?" *Times (London),* 11 Mar., 12.
1983 "Literary Theory in the University: A Survey." *New Literary History,* Winter, 411–51.
1986 "The Dissent from Reason: Contemporary Intellectual Currents in the Western World." B'nai B'rith Jerusalem Address. Jerusalem: B'nai B'rith World Centre.
1987 "The Long Life of Metaphor: An Approach to 'the Shoah.'" *Encounter,* Feb., 55–61.
1988 "New Movements in European Culture." *Times Literary Supplement (TLS),* 7 Jan., 10, 22.

1989 “Has Truth a Future?” In *From Creation to Chaos: Classic Writings in Science,* edited by Bernard Dixon, 184–97. London: Basil Blackwell.

1989 “Heidegger, Again.” *Salmagundi,* Spring/Summer, 31–55.

1990 “Remembering the Future.” *Theology* 93 (Nov./Dec.): 437–44.

1990 “The State of Europe.” *Granta* 30 (Winter): 129–32.

1990 “Struck Dumb.” In *Living Philosophies: The Reflections of Some Eminent Men and Women of Our Time,* edited by Clifton Fadiman, 213–22. New York: Doubleday, 1990.

1991 “Levinas.” *Cross Currents* 41 (Summer): 243–48.

1995 “Intellectual Passions.” In *An Unsentimental Education: Writers and Chicago,* edited by Molly McQuade, 181–89. Chicago: Univ. of Chicago Press.

1995 “Tribute to Donald MacKinnon.” *Theology* 98 (Jan./Feb.): 2–9.

1997 Introduction to *The Trial,* by Franz Kafka. New York: Schocken Books, 1997.

1998 Introduction to *The Origin of German Tragic Drama,* by Walter Benjamin. New York: Viking.

2002 “The Muses’ Farewell.” *Salmagundi,* Summer/Fall, 148–56.

2002 “At Five in the Afternoon.” *Kenyon Review* 24 (Winter): 81–113.

2003 “Hitler’s Vienna.” *Salmagundi,* Summer/Fall 2003, 64–71.

2004 “‘Tragedy’ Reconsidered,” *New Literary History* 35: 1–15.

Selected Book Reviews

1984 “Enormities Beyond Measure.” Review of *Hitler, Germans, and the “Jewish Question,”* by Sarah Gordon. *TLS,* 13 July, 793.

1984 “Songs of a Torn Tongue.” Review of *Paul Celan: Gesammelte Werke,* by Paul Celan. *TLS,* 28 Sept., 1093–94.

1987 “Graven Images.” Review of *Aby Warburg,* by E. H. Gombrich. *New Yorker,* 2 Feb., 95–98.

1989 “An Examined Life.” Review of *Unseasonable Truths,* by Harry S. Ashmore. *New Yorker,* 23 Oct., 142–46.

1989 “So Much Darkness Dispelled.” Review of *Paul Celan: Materialien,* edited by Werner Hamacher and Winfried Menninghaus. *TLS,* 10/16 Feb., 135–36.

1993 “Sainte Simone.” Review of *Simone Weil’s Philosophy of Culture: Readings Toward a Divine Humanity,* ed. Richard H. Bell. *TLS,* 4 June, 3–4.

1995 "A Lacerated Destiny." Review of *Paul Celan: Poet, Survivor, Jew,* by John Felstiner, and *Paul Celan and Franz Wurm: Briefwechsel,* by Barbara Wiedemann. *TLS,* 2 June, 3–4.

1995 "The New Nouvelle Héloïse?" Review of *Hannah Arendt/Martin Heidegger,* by Elzbieta Ettinger. *TLS,* 13 Oct., 3–4.

1995 "The Unfinished." Review of *The Man Without Qualities,* by Robert Musil. *New Yorker,* 17 Apr., 101–6.

1997 "Inscrutable and Tragic: Leo Strauss's Vision of the Jewish Destiny." Review of *Jewish Philosophy and the Crisis of Modernity,* by Leo Strauss. *TLS,* 14 Nov., 4–5.

1999 "The Magician in Love." Review of *Hannah Arendt and Martin Heidegger: Briefe, 1925–1975,* edited by Ursula Ludz. *TLS,* 29 Jan., 3–4.

1999 "Work in Progress." Review of *The Arcades Project,* by Walter Benjamin. *TLS,* 3 Dec., 3–4.

2001 "Ice Cold in Arcadia: Privacy, Hauteur and Deception: Anthony Blunt's Strange Career." Review of *Anthony Blunt,* by Miranda Carter. *TLS,* 2 Nov., 3–4.

Bibliography

Abel, Lionel. "So Who Is to Have the Last Word?" *Partisan Review* 53, no. 3 (1986): 358–71.

Adorno, Theodor W. "Commitment." *New Left Review* 87/88 (Dec. 1974): 75–89.

———. *Minima Moralia: Reflexionen aus dem beschädigten Leben.* Frankfurt a. Main: Suhrkamp, 1969.

Almog, Shmuel. "The Racial Motif in Renan's Attitude to Jews and Judaism." In *Antisemitism Through the Ages,* edited by Shmuel Almog, 255–77. New York: Pergamon Press, 1988.

Alter, Robert. "Against Messiness." Review of *No Passion Spent* and *The Deeps of the Sea and Other Fiction,* by George Steiner. *Times Literary Supplement (TLS),* 12 Jan. 1996, 23–24.

———. "The Unique and the Universal." *Commentary,* May 1970, Letters from Readers section, 14

———. "Zionism for the 70's." *Commentary* 49 (Feb. 1970): 47–57.

Améry, Jean. *At the Mind's Limits: Contemplations by a Survivor on Auschwitz and Its Realities.* Bloomington: Indiana Univ. Press, 1980.

Arendt, Hannah. *The Jew as Pariah: Jewish Identity and Politics in the Modern Age.* Edited by Ron H. Feldman. New York: Grove Press, 1978.

———. *The Origins of Totalitarianism.* New York: Harvest, 1973.

"Art and Intellect in America: A Symposium." In *Salmagundi,* no. 50–51 (Fall 1980–Spring 1981): 53–253.

"The Art of Criticism II." Interview by Ronald A. Sharp. *Paris Review,* no. 137 (1995): 42–102.

Aschheim, Steven E. *Culture and Catastrophe: German and Jewish Confrontations with National Socialism and Other Crises.* New York: New York Univ. Press, 1996.

Asensio, Juan. *Essai sur l'oeuvre de George Steiner: La parole soufflé sur notre poussière.* Paris: Harmattan, 2001.

Bailey, Nancy Martin. "George Steiner's Concept of Culture: Its Significance for Education." MA thesis, Univ. of Illinois at Urbana-Champaign, 1981.

Barth, J. Robert. "Coleridge and George Steiner: The Transcendence of Art." *Wordsworth Circle* 28 (Winter 1997): 48–53.

Bauer, Yehuda, and Nathan Rotenstreich, eds. *The Holocaust as Historical Experience.* New York: Holmes & Meier, 1981.

———. *Rethinking The Holocaust.* New Haven: Yale Univ. Press, 2001.

Beckson, Karl, and Arthur Ganz. *Literary Terms: A Dictionary.* New York: Noonday Press, 1989.

Bellebaum, Paul. *Denken über Kunst: Platon, Goethe, Tolstoj, Rudolf Steiner, und George Steiner: Fünf Essays.* Schloss Hamborn: Möllmann, 1998.

Beller, Steven. *Vienna and the Jews, 1867–1938: A Cultural History.* Cambridge: Cambridge Univ. Press, 1995.

Benda, Julien. *Trahison des clercs.* Paris: Bernard Grasset, 1927.

Benjamin, Walter. *Illuminations: Essays and Reflections.* Edited by Hannah Arendt. Translated by Harry Zohn. New York: Random House, 1988.

Berger, Peter. "Rebuilding Economies after External Shocks: The Case of the League of Nations' Aid to Austria and Hungary, 1922–1926." *Development and Finance* 2 (2003): 64–74.

Bergonzi, Bernard. *The Myth of Modernism and Twentieth-Century Literature.* New York: St. Martin's Press, 1986.

Bernstein, Michael André. *Foregone Conclusions: Against Apocalyptic History.* Berkeley: Univ. of California Press, 1994.

Birkerts, Sven. "George Steiner." In *An Artificial Wilderness: Essays on 20th-Century Literature.* New York: William Morrow & Company, 1987.

Bland, Kalman P. *The Artless Jew: Medieval and Modern Affirmations and Denials of the Visual.* Princeton, NJ: Princeton Univ. Press, 2000.

Boyers, Robert. "A Refusal to Mourn the Fate of the Muses." *Salmagundi,* Summer/Fall 2002, 157–66.

———. "Steiner's Holocaust: Politics and Theology." *Salmagundi,* no. 66 (Winter/Spring 1985): 26–49.

———, ed. *The Legacy of the German Refugee Intellectuals.* New York: Schocken, 1972.

Burke, Kenneth. "The Rhetoric of Hitler's 'Battle.'" In *The Philosophy of Literary Form: Studies in Symbolic Action,* 191–220. 2nd ed. Baton Rouge: Louisiana State Univ. Press, 1967.

Carroll, John. "George Steiner and Cambridge English: A Dismal Case of Rancour." *Meanjin Quarterly* 32 (Sept. 1973): 318–22.

Castañón, Adolfo. *Lectura y catarsis: tres papeles sobre George Steiner seguidos de un ensayo bibliográfico y de una hemerografía del autor.* Mexico: Ediciones Sin Nombre: Ediciones Casa Juan Pablos, 2000.

Chatterley, Catherine D. "Steiner's Shoah: A Conversation in Silence." MA thesis, Concordia Univ. (Montreal), 1997.

Cheyette, Bryan. "Between Repulsion and Attraction: George Steiner's Post-Holocaust Fiction." *Jewish Social Studies* 5, no. 3 (1999): 67–81.

Cohn, Norman. *The Pursuit of the Millennium.* New York: Essential Books, 1957.

———. *Warrant for Genocide: The Myth of the Jewish World-Conspiracy and the Protocols of the Elders of Zion.* London: Penguin Books, 1970.

Conradi, Peter, ed. *Existentialists and Mystics: Writings on Philosophy and Literature.* London: Penguin, 1999.

"'The Consciousness Industry': A Symposium." New York, The New School, Apr. 1997. *Salmagundi,* no. 118–19 (Spring/Summer 1998): 106–90.

Contemporary Authors 31 (1990): s.v. "George Steiner."

Contemporary Literary Criticism 24 (1983): s.v. "George Steiner."

Contemporary Literary Critics, 1977, s.v. "George Steiner."

Critical Survey of Literary Theory, 1987, s.v. "George Steiner."

Davie, Donald. "The Clans and Their World-Pictures." Review of *After Babel,* by George Steiner. *TLS,* 31 Jan. 1975, 98–100.

de Cessole, Bruno, and George Steiner. *George Steiner: Entretien avec Bruno de Cessole.* Paris: Éditions du Centre Georges Pompidou, 1994.

Des Pres, Terrence. "Kulturkritiker." Review of *Antigones,* by George Steiner. *Nation,* 2 Mar. 1985, 246–48.

Deutscher, Isaac. *The Non-Jewish Jew and Other Essays.* New York: Oxford Univ. Press, 1968.

Dickstein, Morris. "Alive and 90 in the Jungles of Brazil." Review of *The Portage to San Cristóbal of A.H.,* by George Steiner. *New York Times Book Review,* 2 May 1982: 13, 21.

Dictionary of Literary Biography 67 (1988): s.v. "George Steiner."

Dictionary of Literary Biography: Holocaust Novelists, 2004, s.v. "George Steiner."

Diner, Dan. *Das Jahrhundert Verstehen: Eine universalhistorische Deutung.* Munich: Luchterhand, 1999.

Doyle, Brian. *English & Englishness.* London: Routledge, 1989.

Dresden, Sem. *Persecution, Extermination, Literature.* Toronto: Univ. of Toronto Press, 1995.

Eiland, Howard. "Nietzsche's Jew." *Salmagundi* 66 (Winter–Spring 1985): 104–17.

Eliot, T. S. *Notes Towards the Definition of Culture*. London: Faber & Faber, 1948.

Ellis, Mark H. "Questioning Conversion: Gillian Rose, George Steiner, and Christianity." In *Revolutionary Forgiveness: Essays on Judaism, Christianity, and the Future of Religious Life*. Waco, TX: Baylor Univ. Press, 2000.

Ezrahi, Sidra DeKoven. *Booking Passage: Exile and Homecoming in the Modern Jewish Imagination*. Berkeley: Univ. of California Press, 2000.

———. *By Words Alone: The Holocaust in Literature*. Chicago: Univ. of Chicago Press, 1982.

Fackenheim, Emil L. *The Jewish Return into History: Reflections in the Age of Auschwitz and a New Jerusalem*. New York: Schocken, 1978.

Felstiner, John. *Paul Celan: Poet, Survivor, Jew*. New Haven: Yale Univ. Press, 1995.

Fenton, James. "The Cloud of Knowing." *New Statesman* (1 Dec. 1978): 743–44.

Ferns, John. *F. R. Leavis*. New York: Twayne Publishers, 2000.

Finch, Roy. "Abel and Steiner." *Partisan Review* 54, no. 2 (1987): 289–98.

Finkelstein, Norman. "George Steiner's Presences." *Salmagundi* 87 (Summer 1990): 260–67.

———. *The Ritual of New Creation: Jewish Tradition and Contemporary Literature*. Albany: State Univ. of New York Press, 1992.

Foucault, Michel. "Monstrosities in Criticism" and George Steiner, "Steiner Responds to Foucault." *Diacritics* 1 (1971): 57–60.

Freud, Sigmund. *Civilization, Society, and Religion: Group Psychology, Civilization and Its Discontents and Other Works*. Vol. 12. Edited by Albert Dickson. Translated by Angela Richards. London: Penguin, 1985.

———. *The Origins of Religion: Totem and Taboo, Moses and Monotheism and Other Works*. Vol. 13. Edited by Albert Dickson. Translated by Angela Richards. London: Penguin, 1990.

Friedländer, Saul. *Nazi Germany and the Jews*. New York: Harper Collins, 1997.

———, ed. *Probing the Limits of Representation: Nazism and the Final Solution*. Cambridge, MA: Harvard Univ. Press, 1992.

———. *Reflections of Nazism: An Essay on Kitsch and Death*. New York: Harper & Row, 1984.

Fulford, Robert. "Erasmus in Toronto." *Queen's Quarterly* 102, no. 2 (Summer 1995): 421–24.

Gay, Peter. *Freud, Jews, and Other Germans: Masters and Victims in Modernist Culture*. New York: Oxford Univ. Press, 1978.

———. *Savage Reprisals: "Bleak House," "Madame Bovary," "Buddenbrooks."* New York: W. W. Norton & Company, 2002.

"George Steiner." Interview by Nicolas Tredell. In *Conversations with Critics,* 75–93. Manchester, UK: Carcanet, 1994.

"George Steiner Interviewed by Eleanor Wachtel." Interview by Eleanor Wachtel. *Queen's Quarterly* 99, no. 4 (Winter 1992): 837–48.

"George Steiner on Literature, Language, and Culture." Television Interview by Bill Moyers. *Bill Moyer's Journal,* produced at WNET, New York, May 22, 1981.

"Gespräch mit George Steiner." Interview by Michael Jakob. *Sinn und Form: Beitrage zur Literatur* 45, no. 4 (1993): 545–55.

Geyer, Michael. "War, Genocide, Extermination: The War Against the Jews in an Era of World Wars." In *Shattered Past: Reconstructing German Histories,* by Konrad H. Jarausch and Michael Geyer, 111–48. Princeton, NJ: Princeton Univ. Press, 2003.

Gilbert, Martin. "Who Do You Think You Are Kidding, Mr. Hitler?" Review of *The Portage to San Cristóbal of A.H.,* directed by Christopher Hampton. *Times (London),* 6 Mar. 1982, 9.

Gilman, Sander. *Smart Jews: The Construction of the Image of Jewish Superior Intelligence.* Lincoln: Univ. of Nebraska Press, 1997.

Gould, Timothy. "On Heidegger's Track: A Response to a Portrayal by George Steiner." *Soundings* 68, no. 2 (Summer 1985): 229–52.

Grebstein, Sheldon Norman, ed. *Perspectives in Contemporary Criticism: A Collection of Recent Essays by American, English, and European Literary Critics.* New York: Harper & Row, 1968.

Grigson, Geoffrey. "Noaks Is No Fool." *New Statesman,* 22 Oct. 1971, 545–46.

Gunn, Giles. "On New Uses of the 'Secular' and the 'Religious' in Contemporary Criticism: Edward Said, George Steiner, and the Counter-Example of Eric Heller." In *Morphologies of Faith: Essays in Religion and Culture in Honor of Nathan A Scott, Jr.,* edited by Mary Gerhart and Anthony C. Yu, 51–68. Atlanta: Scholars Press, 1990.

Hamann, Brigitte. *Hitler's Vienna: A Dictator's Apprenticeship.* Translated by Thomas Thornton. New York: Oxford Univ. Press, 1999.

Hampton, Christopher. "Adaptation of *The Portage to San Cristóbal of A.H.*" In *The Theatre of the Holocaust.* Vol. 2, edited by Robert Skloot, 263–329. Madison: Univ. of Wisconsin Press, 1999.

Heidegger, Hermann, George Steiner, Hugo Ott, and Hans-Georg Gadamer. *Martin Heidegger: Design for Living.* Produced and Directed by Jeff Morgan. 60 min. Films for the Humanities & Sciences, 2000. Videocassette.

Helfant, Sidney, and Gabriel Schoenfeld. "Hitler and the Germans," letter to the editor. *Commentary,* Nov. 1998, 10–11.

Herbert, Ulrich, ed. *National Socialist Extermination Policies: Contemporary German Perspectives and Controversies.* New York: Berghahn Books, 2000.

Hobsbawm, Eric. *The Age of Extremes: The Short Twentieth Century, 1914–1991.* London: Abacus, 1999.

Holocaust Literature: An Encyclopedia of Writers and Their Texts, 2003, s.v. "George Steiner."

Hook, Sidney. "On Being a Jew." *Commentary* 88 (Oct. 1989): 28–36.

Horkheimer, Max, and Theodor W. Adorno. *Dialektik der Aufklärung.* Frankfurt a. Main: S. Fischer, 1969. Translated as *Dialectic of Enlightenment* by John Cumming. New York: Continuum, 1997.

Horowitz, Sara. *Voicing the Void: Muteness and Memory in Holocaust Fiction.* New York: State Univ. of New York Press, 1997.

Howe, Irving. "High Mandarin." Review of *In Bluebeard's Castle,* by George Steiner. *Commentary,* Feb. 1972, 96–99.

Hyde, John Keith. "Two-Story Building: Narrative Transformation in Erich Auerbach, Stephen Crites, and George Steiner." MA thesis, Regent College (Vancouver), 1998.

Ibsen, Henrik. *The Wild Duck.* Translated by Michael Meyer. London: Methuen, 1968.

Idel, Moshe. "George Steiner: A Prophet of Abstraction." *Modern Judaism* 25, no. 2 (2005): 109–40.

Ignatieff, Michael. *Isaiah Berlin: A Life.* New York: Metropolitan Books, 1998.

"Interview with George Steiner." Interview by Eva L. Corredor. In *Lukács after Communism: Interviews with Contemporary Intellectuals,* 61–74. Durham, NC: Duke Univ. Press, 1997.

"Interview with George Steiner." Interview by Frank Levy, Joel Schechter, Carolyn Seeley, Jon Marks, and John McCaffrey. *Yale Theatre* 3, no. 1 (1971): 4–13.

Isser, Edward R. *Stages of Annihilation: Theatrical Representations of the Holocaust.* London: Associated Univ. Presses, 1997.

Jäckel, Eberhard. *Hitler's World View: A Blueprint for Power.* Cambridge, MA: Harvard Univ. Press, 1981.

Jaggi, Maya. "George and His Dragons." *Guardian,* 17 Mar. 2001, 6–7.

Jahanbegloo, Ramin. *Conversations with Isaiah Berlin.* London: Phoenix Press, 1993.

Jahanbegloo, Ramin, and George Steiner. *Entretiens.* Paris: Éditions du Félin, 1992.

Janik, Allan, and Stephen Toulmin. *Wittgenstein's Vienna.* Chicago: Ivan R. Dee, 1996.

Jay, Martin. *Adorno.* Cambridge, MA: Harvard Univ. Press, 1984.

———. *Permanent Exiles: Essays on the Intellectual Migration from Germany to America*. New York: Columbia Univ. Press, 1986.

"Jewish Values in the Post-Holocaust Future: A Symposium." New York, 26 Mar. 1967. *Judaism* 16, no. 3 (Summer 1967): 266–99.

Jordan, Peter, George Steiner, Robert Lifton, Donald Knight, and Vivian Sobchack. *The Sleep of Reason*. Produced by Sue Mathews and Peter Jordan. 48 min. Ronin Films, 1992. Videocassette.

Kafka, Franz and George Steiner. *Franz Kafka: The Trial*. Produced and Directed by David Thomas. 59 min. Films for the Humanities & Sciences, 1999. Videocassette.

Karier, Clarence J. "Humanizing the Humanities: Some Reflections on George Steiner's 'Brutal Paradox.'" *Journal of Aesthetic Education* 24, no. 2 (Summer 1990): 49–63.

Katz, Jacob. "Misreadings of Anti-Semitism." *Commentary* 76 (July 1983): 39–44.

Katz, Steven T. *The Holocaust in Historical Context*. New York: Oxford Univ. Press, 1994.

———, ed. *The Impact of the Holocaust on Jewish Theology*. New York: New York Univ. Press, 2005.

Keren, Michael. "Intellectual Discourse in Israel: George Steiner's 'Our Homeland, The Text' Revisited." *Israel Affairs* 3, no. 2 (Winter 1996): 1–11.

Kimball, Roger. "Is the Future Just a Tense?" Review of *Grammars of Creation*, by George Steiner. *New York Times Book Review*, 2 Sept. 2001, 12.

Knight, Christopher J. "George Steiner's Religion of Abstraction." *Religion and Literature* 28, no. 1 (1996): 49–84.

———. *Uncommon Readers: Denis Donoghue, Frank Kermode, George Steiner, and the Tradition of the Common Reader*. Toronto: Univ. of Toronto Press, 2003.

Koonz, Claudia. *The Nazi Conscience*. Cambridge, MA: Harvard Univ. Press, 2003.

Krantz, Frederick. "George Steiner's Negative Midrash on Israel and Zionism: A Critique." *Zionist Ideas* 17 (1988): 27–77.

Kremer, Lillian. *Witness Through the Imagination: Jewish American Holocaust Literature*. Detroit: Wayne State Univ. Press, 1989.

Krupnick, Mark. "Why Are English Departments Still Fighting the Culture Wars?" *Chronicle of Higher Education* 49, no. 4 (20 Sept. 2002): B16.

Kuschel, Karl-Josef. "Presence of God? Towards the Possibility of a Theological Aesthetic in an Analysis of George Steiner." *Literature and Theology* 10, no. 1 (Mar. 1996): 1–19.

LaCapra, Dominick. *Representing the Holocaust: History, Theory, Trauma*. Ithaca, NY: Cornell Univ. Press, 1994.

———. *Writing History, Writing Trauma.* Baltimore: Johns Hopkins Univ. Press, 2001.

Lang, Berel. *Heidegger's Silence.* Ithaca, NY: Cornell Univ. Press, 1996.

———. *Writing and the Holocaust.* New York: Holmes & Meier, 1988.

———. *Writing and the Moral Self.* New York: Routledge, 1991.

Langer, Lawrence. *Admitting the Holocaust: Collected Essays.* New York: Oxford Univ. Press, 1995.

———. *The Holocaust and the Literary Imagination.* New Haven: Yale Univ. Press, 1975.

Lichtenstein, Leonie. "Rushdie, Steiner, Sobol and Others." *Encounter* 73 (Sept.–Oct. 1989): 34–42.

Lilla, Mark. *The Reckless Mind: Intellectuals in Politics.* New York: New York Review of Books, 2001.

———. "What Heidegger Wrought." *Commentary,* Jan. 1990, 41–51.

"Literature and the Contemporary Jewish Experience: A Colloquium on Jewish Writing, March 1984." *Jewish Quarterly* 31 (1984): 6–19.

Lowin, Joseph. "Steiner's Helicopters." *Jewish Book Annual* 41 (1983–84): 48–56.

Lukács, Georg. *Realism in Our Time: Literature and the Class Struggle.* New York: Harper, 1964.

Maccoby, Hyam. *A Pariah People: The Anthropology of Antisemitism.* London: Constable, 1996.

———. "George Steiner's 'Hitler.'" *Encounter* 58, no. 5 (May 1982): 27–34.

———. *Judas Iscariot and the Myth of Jewish Evil.* New York: Maxwell Macmillan, 1992.

MacKillop, Ian. *F. R. Leavis: A Life in Criticism.* London: Penguin, 1995.

MacKinnon, Donald. *The Borderlands of Theology.* London: Lutterworth, 1968.

Maritain, Jacques. *Antisemitism.* London: Centenary Press, 1939.

Marmur, Dow. "The Struggle Between Text and Land in Contemporary Jewry: Reflections on George Steiner's 'Our Homeland, The Text.'" *History of European Ideas* 20, no. 4–6 (Feb. 1995): 807–13.

Mazower, Mark. *Dark Continent: Europe's Twentieth Century.* New York: Vintage, 2000.

McDowell, John C. "Silenus' Wisdom and the 'Crime of Being': The Problem of Hope in George Steiner's Tragic Vision." *Literature and Theology* 14, no. 4 (Dec. 2000): 385–98.

Mehlman, Jeffrey. "George Steiner at the *Lycée Français.*" In *Émigré New York: French Intellectuals in Wartime Manhattan, 1940–1944.* Baltimore: Johns Hopkins Univ. Press, 2000.

———. "Writing Lives: Speculations of a Biographer-in-Waiting." *Common Knowledge* 4, no. 3 (Winter 1995): 97–112.

Mendes-Flohr, Paul. *Divided Passions: Jewish Intellectuals and the Experience of Modernity.* Detroit: Wayne State Univ. Press, 1991.

———. *German Jews: A Dual Identity.* New Haven: Yale Univ. Press, 1999.

———. "Secular Forms of Jewishness." In *The Blackwell Companion to Judaism,* edited by Jacob Neusner and Alan J. Avery-Peck, 461–75. Oxford: Blackwell, 2000.

Miller, James. "Heidegger's Guilt." *Salmagundi,* no. 109–10 (Winter–Spring 1996): 178–243.

Mosse, George L. *German Jews Beyond Judaism.* Cincinnati, OH: Hebrew Union College Press, 1985.

Mountford, James. *British Universities.* London: Oxford Univ. Press, 1966.

Myers, David. *Resisting History: Historicism and Its Discontents in German-Jewish Thought.* Princeton, NJ: Princeton Univ. Press, 2003.

Namier, Julia. *Lewis Namier: A Biography.* Oxford: Oxford Univ. Press, 1971.

Nietzsche, Friedrich. *The Gay Science.* New York: Random House, 1974.

———. *On the Genealogy of Morals.* Translated by Douglas Smith. Oxford: Oxford Univ. Press, 1998.

Ozick, Cynthia. "George Steiner's Either/Or: A Response." *Salmagundi,* no. 50–51 (Fall 1980–Winter 1981): 90–95.

Pachter, Henry. "In Response to George Steiner." *Salmagundi,* no. 50–51 (Fall 1980–Winter 1981): 96–101.

Parini, Jay. "The Question of George Steiner." Review of *George Steiner: A Reader,* by George Steiner. *Hudson Review,* Aug. 1985, 496–502.

Phillips, Melanie. "A Jewish Sense of Foreboding." *Daily Mail,* 6 Mar. 2002. http://pws.prserv.net/mpjr/mp/dm060302.htm (accessed 9 Dec. 2002].

"A Philosopher's Steiner." Interview by Shiri Lev-Ari. *Ha'aretz,* 10 Nov. 1999.

Plath, Sylvia. *Ariel.* New York: Harper & Row, 1965.

"The Poetics of Cultural Criticism." Review of *In Bluebeard's Castle,* by George Steiner. *Times Literary Supplement,* 17 Dec. 1971, 1565–66.

Postone, Moishe. "Anti-Semitism and National Socialism: Notes on the German Reaction to 'Holocaust.'" *New German Critique* 19 (Winter 1980): 97–115.

———. "Anti-Semitism and National Socialism." In *Germans and Jews since the Holocaust,* edited by Anson Rabinbach and Jack Zipes, 302–14. New York: Holmes & Meier, 1986.

Postone, Moishe, and Eric Santner, eds. *Catastrophe and Meaning: The Holocaust and the Twentieth Century.* Chicago: Univ. of Chicago Press, 2003.

Poteat, William H. "The Extra-Territorial Critic." In *The Primacy of Persons and the Language of Culture: Essays.* Columbia: Univ. of Missouri Press, 1993.

Rabinbach, Anson. *In the Shadow of Catastrophe: German Intellectuals Between Apocalypse and Enlightenment.* Berkeley: Univ. of California Press, 1997.

Regis, Ed. *Who Got Einstein's Office? Eccentricity and Genius at the Institute for Advanced Study.* New York: Addison-Wesley, 1987.

Renan, Ernest. *Etudes d'histoire religieuse.* Paris: M. Levy frères, 1862.

———. *Histoire du peuple d'Israël.* 5 vols. Paris: Calmann Levy, 1887–93.

"The Responsibility of Intellectuals." Saratoga Springs, New York, Skidmore College, 11 Apr. 1985. *Salmagundi,* no. 70–71 (Spring/Summer 1986): 164–95.

Rose, Gillian. *Judaism and Modernity: Philosophical Essays.* Oxford: Blackwell, 1993.

Rosenbaum, Ron. "George Steiner: Singling Out the Jewish 'Invention of Conscience.'" In *Explaining Hitler: The Search for the Origins of His Evil.* New York: Harper, 1999.

Rosenbaum, Ron. *Those Who Forget the Past: The Question of Anti-Semitism.* New York: Random House, 2004.

Rosenfeld, Alvin. *A Double Dying: Reflections on Holocaust Literature.* Bloomington: Indiana Univ. Press, 1980.

———. *Imagining Hitler.* Bloomington: Indiana Univ. Press, 1985.

———. "Steiner's Hitler." *Salmagundi,* no. 52–53 (Spring/Summer 1981): 160–74.

Rothberg, Michael. "After Adorno: Culture in the Wake of Catastrophe." *New German Critique* 72 (Fall 1997): 45–81.

Ryan, Joseph L. "Debate on Israel." *Journal of Palestine Studies,* Winter 1972, 70–79.

Sagiv, Assaf. "George Steiner's Jewish Problem." *Azure,* Summer 5763/2003, 130–54.

Said, Edward. "A Deft Jumble of Cultural Correlatives." Review of *Extraterritorial: Papers on Literature and the Language Revolution,* by George Steiner. *New York Times Book Review,* 1 Aug. 1971, 7.

———. "Himself Observed." Review of *George Steiner: A Reader,* by George Steiner. *Nation,* 2 Mar. 1985, 244–46.

Samson, Anne. *F. R. Leavis.* Toronto: Univ. of Toronto Press, 1992.

Schama, Simon. *Landscape and Memory.* Toronto: Vintage, 1996.

Schoenfeld, Gabriel. "The Great Dictator." Review of *Explaining Hitler,* by Ron Rosenbaum. *Commentary,* Sept. 1998, 52–56.

Scholem, Gershom. *On Jews and Judaism in Crisis: Selected Essays.* Edited by Werner J. Dannhauser. New York: Schocken, 1976.

Schorske, Carl E. *Fin-de-Siècle Vienna: Politics and Culture.* New York: Knopf, 1980.

Scott, Nathan, Jr., and Ronald A. Sharp. *Reading George Steiner.* Baltimore: Johns Hopkins Univ. Press, 1994.

Scott, Peter. "Survivor and Outsider." *Times Higher Education Supplement (THES),* 15 Feb. 1985, 11.

Sharp, Ronald A. "Interrogation at the Borders: George Steiner and the Trope of Translation." *New Literary History* 21, no. 1 (Autumn 1989/1990): 133–62.

Sicher, Efraim, ed. *Breaking Crystal: Writing and Memory after Auschwitz.* Chicago: Univ. of Illinois Press, 1998.

Simon, John. "Made of Steiner Stuff." Review of *Real Presences,* by George Steiner. *The New Criterion,* Oct. 1989, 64–70.

———. "The Theatre Critic and His Double." In *Acid Test,* 257–64. New York: Stein & Day, 1964.

Skidelsky, Edward. "Beware the False Prophet." *New Statesman,* 19 Mar. 2001, 52.

Skloot, Robert. "Holocaust Theatre and the Problem of Justice." In *Staging the Holocaust: The Shoah in Drama and Performance,* edited by Claude Schumacher, 10–26. Cambridge: Cambridge Univ. Press, 1998.

Snow, C. P. *The Two Cultures.* Cambridge: Cambridge Univ. Press, 1993.

Snow, Jon, David Grossman, Natan Sharansky, Elie Wiesel, and George Steiner. *The State of Israel.* Produced by Israel Goldvicht. 79 min. Ergo Media, 1999. Videocassette.

Snowman, Daniel. *The Hitler Emigrés: The Cultural Impact on Britain of Refugees from Nazism.* London: Chatto & Windus, 2002.

"Solitude et Communication: Textes des Conférences et des Entretiens." *Rencontres Internationales de Genève,* 3 Sept. 1975. Neuchâtel: Éditions de la Baconniére, 1975.

Solotaroff, Theodore. "A Kind of Survivor." Review of *Language and Silence,* by George Steiner. *New Republic,* 13 May 1967, 21–24.

Sontag, Susan, Michael Harrington, and Robert Nesbitt. *Marxism Today.* Hollywood: Center for Cassette Studies, 1975. Sound Cassette.

Spire, Antoine, and George Steiner. *Barbarie de l'Ignorance.* Latresne (Bordeaux): Éditions du Bord de l'Eau, 1998.

Steiman, Lionel. *Franz Werfel, The Faith of an Exile: From Prague to Beverly Hills.* Waterloo, ON: Wilfred Laurier Univ. Press, 1985.

———. *Paths to Genocide: Antisemitism in Western History.* New York: St. Martin's Press, 1998.

Steiner, George. "From Without: A Presentation." In *The Future of a Relationship: American Jewry and the People of Israel.* Proceedings of the Sixth Annual

American-Israel Dialogue in Rehovoth, Israel, 30 July–1 Aug. 1968. *Congress Bi-Weekly* 36, no. 3 (24 Feb. 1969): 13–21.

———. *The Pornography Debate.* Hollywood: Center for Cassette Studies, 1979. Sound Cassette.

———. *Vienna 1900.* New York: Films for the Humanities & Sciences, 2000. Videocassette.

Vivas, Eliseo. "Too Clever by Half." *National Review,* 31 Dec. 1971, 1477–78.

Ward, Graham. "In the Daylight Forever? Language and Silence." In *Silence and the Word: Negative Theology and Incarnation,* edited by Oliver Davies and Denys Turner, 159–84. Cambridge: Cambridge Univ. Press, 2002.

———. "Tragedy as Subclause: George Steiner's Dialogue with Donald MacKinnon." *Heythrop Journal* 34, no. 3 (July 1993): 274–87.

Watt, Roderick H. "Hermann Broch's *Adolf Hitler's Farwell Address* and George Steiner's *The Portage to San Cristobal of A.H.*" In *Hermann Broch: Modernismus, Kulturkrise and Hitlerzeit,* edited by Adrian Stevens, Fred Wagner, and Sigurd Paul Scheichl, 173–86. London: Univ. of London Press, 1994.

Wattis, Nigel, David Thomas, Melvyn Bragg, Anthony Burgess, George Steiner, Hermione Lee, and Malcolm Bradbury. *Ten Great Writers: The Seminar.* Produced by David Thomas and Nigel Wattis. 52 min. New York: Films for the Humanities & Sciences, 1999. Videocassette.

White, Harry. "American Musicology and 'The Archives of Eden.'" *Journal of American Studies* 32 (1998): 1–18.

White, Nick. "The Ventriloquial Paradox: George Steiner's 'The Portage to San Cristobal of A.H.'" *New Theatre Quarterly* 18 (1 Feb. 2002): 66–90.

Wood, James. "George Steiner's Unreal Presence." In *The Broken Estate: Essays on Literature and Belief.* New York: Random House, 1999.

———. "Real Absences." Review of *No Passion Spent,* by George Steiner. *New Republic,* 30 Sept. 1996, 32–38.

Young, Michael. "Real Presence and the Conscience of Words: Language and Repetition in George Steiner's *Portage to San Cristóbal of A.H.*" *Style* 26 (Spring 1992): 114–28.

Ziolkowski, Theodore. Review of *George Steiner: A Reader,* by George Steiner. *World Literature Today,* Spring 1985, 323–24.

Index